BARKER PLAYS ONE

Howard Barker

PLAYS ONE

VICTORY
THE EUROPEANS
THE POSSIBILITIES
SCENES FROM AN EXECUTION

OBERON BOOKS
LONDON

First published in this collection in 2006
by Oberon Books Ltd
521 Caledonian Road, London N7 9RH
Tel: 020 7607 3637 / Fax: 020 7607 3629
e-mail: info@oberonbooks.com
www.oberonbooks.com

The Possibilities first published in Great Britain by John Calder
(Publishers) Limited in 1987

Victory and *Scenes from an Execution* first published in Great Britain
by John Calder (Publishers) Limited in 1990

The Europeans first published in Great Britain by John Calder
(Publishers) Limited in 1996

A catalogue record for this book is available from the British
Library.

ISBN: 1 84002 612 X

Cover image and design: Dan Steward

Printed in Great Britain by Antony Rowe Ltd, Chippenham.

Contents

VICTORY
Choices in Reaction

Characters

BRADSHAW, the Widow of a Polemicist

SCROPE, a Secretary

CHARLES STUART, a Monarch

NODD, his Intimate Friend

DEVONSHIRE, a Mistress

BALL, a Cavalier

McCONOCHIE, a Surgeon

CROPPER, Daughter of Bradshaw

BOOT, a Soldier

SHADE, a Soldier

WICKER, a Soldier

DARLING, a Soldier

GAUKROGER, a Captain

ROAST, a Civil Servant

CLEGG, the Poet Laureate

SOUTHWARK, a Male Landowner

CLEVELAND, a Female Landowner

PONTING, a Court Official

HAMPSHIRE, a Male Landowner

BRIGHTON, a Female Landowner

SOMERSET, a Male Landowner

DERBYSHIRE, a Male Landowner

GLOUCESTERSHIRE, a Male Landowner

FEAK, a Republican

PYLE, a Republican Woman

EDGBASTON, a Radical Preacher

HAMBRO, a Banker

MOBBERLEY, a Builder

PARRY, a Stockbroker

UNDY, an Exporter

STREET, a Lawyer

MONCRIEFF, a Minister

GWYNN, a Prostitute

FOOTMAN, to Devonshire

MILTON, a Genius

BEGGARS

ACT ONE

SCENE ONE

A field. A man enters.

SCROPE: I know I swore. I know I promised. On the Bible.
And because I can take or leave the Bible, got your child in
and told me put my two hands on her cheeks and looking
in her eyes say I would not disclose this place. No matter
what the madness, what the torture, leave you underneath
the nettles, safe. I did. I know I did.
(He points to a place. SOLDIERS enter with spades.)

BOOT: A scythe, John!

SHADE: Oh, the cunning of 'im, oh, the artfulness, sneakin'
'is bits under the lush at night...

BOOT: Mind the thistles.

WICKER: Now tell us 'e is twelve foot deep.

SCROPE: Twelve feet at least...

WICKER: Twelve foot, Michael! And the sun like the bald
baker's bollocks!

BOOT: *(To DARLING.)* No, a scythe, you know a scythe, do
you?
(DARLING goes out.)

WICKER: Ow! Thistle got me!

SHADE: This is nothin' to what we 'ave 'ad, is it? Draycott
was under fifteen ton a rock.

BOOT: At low water.

SHADE: At low water. We was in and out like the mad vicar's
dick.

BOOT: *(To DARLING.)* Thank you. That is a scythe.

SHADE: An' Rouse, who 'ad 'imself stuck in the street, 'alf in
the pavement, 'alf in a shop –

BOOT: *(Scything.)* Mind yer legs!

GAUKROGER: I wonder if one of you cunts would
condescend to fetch my stool? In your own time, of course,
at your very own cunt leisure?

BOOT: Captain's stool, John!

(*DARLING hurries out.*)

GAUKROGER: I hate to trouble you cunts, I honestly do.

SHADE: This draper says, 'What! The corpse of a rebel under my shop! Well, I never! 'ow did that come about!' So we go through 'is bedrooms, an' 'is trunks, an' 'is girls. And there it is. Milton. Latin dirt.

GAUKROGER: (*As DARLING brings in a stool.*) Thank you. I have commanded some cunts, but you take the cunt biscuit.

SHADE: So we slit it, this draper's long nose. For misuse of the highway. 'Well I never! Well, I never!' 'e says…

BOOT: (*Scything.*) Mind yer legs.

GAUKROGER: A stool, Mr Scrope? These cunts will be at it all day.

(*SCROPE shakes his head.*)

Who had my sunshade?

(*They are digging.*)

My sunshade?

(*The clash of shovels.*)

I do love the way they pretend to be deaf. They really are such extraordinary cunts.

BOOT: Captain's sunshade!

(*DARLING goes out.*)

GAUKROGER: We never had one out of a field. Under the whispering cow shit and adulterous hips. Gob open to clay and the milkmaid's hot little puddle. But in sight of church steeple, I notice. How picturesque he was and diligent. Was he, Mr Scrope? Cunt picturesque your master?

(*SCROPE bursts into tears.*)

The files are such cunts here. Would one of you run for a whisk?

SCENE TWO

A room. A WOMAN and two OFFICERS of the crown.

BRADSHAW: I am not asking you to sit. If I ask you to sit you will think at least she has good manners, at least she

does things properly, she keeps things clean. I do not wish
to do things properly or keep them clean. What do you
want?

ROAST: I have to inform you –

BALL: Oh, the pontificating shitbag –

ROAST: I am instructed by His Majesty's –

BALL: Oh, the pontificating shitbag –

ROAST: May I just get this –

BALL: No, she is though, isn't she, a most pontificating bag of
shit, Brian –

ROAST: If I could just –

BALL: Laying aside the instructing and informing for a
minute, you have to marvel at her poopy aspect. I do. I
have to marvel at it, all her straight back and white linen,
her simple dignity and so on, it makes me want to kick the
table through the window –

ROAST: I cannot see the point of making this –

BALL: I haven't finished yet!

(*He goes to her.*)

Brian is for being nice. Brian is ice cold and happy. But
Brian never swagged his hours with the bints of Calais.
I will be rude because I have lost fifteen years! Oh, my
breath smells, my breath smells and she winces! Yours does
not, does it, breathe on me, breathe on me –

ROAST: Andrew –

BALL: Oh, breathe on me your English breath, sweeter than
roses, but then you have had English gardens to wipe
your rump against, I have not but I am not angry, no, I'm
not, I have licked Frenchmen's bums for nourishment
and Spaniards' crotches! Breathe on me, breathe on me,
do, when you stand there icy in your purity I could really
dagger you with my old cavalier dick, that or murder, carry
on informing, Billy.

(*He walks away.*)

Carry on!

ROAST: Mrs Bradshaw, the Government is in possession of
your husband's body.

BALL: Oh, Brian is so poop official! We have the rat-gnawed,
stinking thing you clutched in bed once. That is what we

have. What stuck up you when the cold mood took him, when God commanded fuck thy spouse or what you Bible-suckers term it, him who made you buck or whimper, is a nest of worms now and in our possession. Did you see the bollocks, Brian? I did, I thought them very mean and shrivelled little blobs, no parasite would touch them I WISH I COULD BE MORE OFFENSIVE I REALLY DO.

(*She is rigid.*)

Oh, don't stand there like a mask of honour, I shall slap you. Did you swallow him or is that against the scriptures? I shall slap her if she looks like that!

BRADSHAW: How would you have me look?

BALL: Not like that!

ROAST: His body is to be hung in London. His head spiked and exhibited.

BRADSHAW: Why?

ROAST: It was in the King's conditions. He would not return without his father's murderers be on display.

BALL: There is a hole in your stocking, you slag.

BRADSHAW: How long before I can collect and bury him?

ROAST: There is no possibility of burial.

BRADSHAW: What?

ROAST: The pieces must be left to freely disintegrate.

BRADSHAW: What!

BALL: There is a hole in your stocking, I said.

BRADSHAW: That is so disgusting! What?

BALL: No, it is the hole that is disgusting, with its sixpence of white flesh –

ROAST: I THINK WE OUGHT TO CUT THIS OUT.

(*He stares at BALL. BALL shrugs.*)

BALL: All right.

BRADSHAW: Let me bury him. When the public's done with him.

ROAST: I can't.

BRADSHAW: Come on, when they have spat their mouths dry, surely?

ROAST: The orders are the pieces be –

BRADSHAW: Yes, but when they drop, the limbs, they can –

ROAST: I only repeat –

BRADSHAW: I know, but then, when they are in the gutter, then I –

ROAST: You would need to petition –

BRADSHAW: Oh, come on, can I pick his bits or not!
(*Pause.*)
They knew this. Which is why they laid in such strange places. On the seashore and so on. Knew their bits would be hunted…

ROAST: This is a new world, Mrs. I was at Worcester for the Parliament. But in the end it had to stop.

BRADSHAW: Why?

ROAST: Why, because –

BRADSHAW: Yes, why!

ROAST: Because what was needed had been done. And all the rest was chaos.

BRADSHAW: I disagree.

ROAST: You disagree, but people cannot swallow all the change you and your husband wanted –

BRADSHAW: I disagree.

ROAST: (*Going to leave.*) Thank you for your hospitality.

BRADSHAW: What hospitality! There was none!

BALL: One night, I shan't say when, someone, I shan't say who, may toss a flaming haybale through your glass, and up will go your smart, dark privilege, the spotless boards and so discreet few flowers in the oh-so-very-unostentatious bowl…there has been burning up and down the country, singeing rebels' widows in their empty beds, the odour of the stale old crutch and knicker…

BRADSHAW: There is a sort of cleanliness in you. A sort of honour in your vileness I can understand. But you –
(*She looks to ROAST.*)

BALL: Ugh, she flatters me! Ugh! Off, flattery!
(*He pretends to wipe himself. ROAST goes out.*)
I will fuck you, shall I? Say and I will.
(*She looks away.*)
They say you killed old love in England. You never!
(*He goes to the door.*)
I shall come back. And give you a poem.

(He leaves. A young man enters, warily.)

McCONOCHIE: I would have come down, but what help
would I have been? It might have made them worse. I
don't like foul language. Nor do you, of course. Are you
crying? So I listened with the door half open, and my book
on my knees. It was about blood. I would have come down
in the event of violence. Blood has coloured pieces in it. It
is actually not red beneath a microscope. I DON'T SEE HOW
I CAN BE EDUCATED IF THERE IS NO PEACE AND QUIET!

BRADSHAW: I'm sorry.

McCONOCHIE: I have wished – if only you knew how I
wished – my father had been a grocer. You cannot know
how I envy the children of grocers.

BRADSHAW: Yes.

McCONOCHIE: There is no prospect of progress in science
or art without complete and utter stability. The universities
are utterly disorganized! I may not get a place!

BRADSHAW: I know.

McCONOCHIE: I am not a political person and it is most
unjust! *(Pause.)* Did they frighten you? I would have come
down but I hate bad language and anyway you are so very
strong. I do admire you. The things you can take and cry
hardly ever. When I am blown haywire by interruptions.
You are so resilient.

BRADSHAW: They are sticking his head on a spike.

McCONOCHIE: Does that hurt you?

BRADSHAW: No, no it's only a head, it's only my husband's
rotten old head, I often wanted to put it on a spike myself,
what does it matter if your father is hung on a gate?

McCONOCHIE: You are getting emotional, aren't you? I can
tell.

BRADSHAW: What's a gate? What's a spike?

McCONOCHIE: You are.

BRADSHAW: IT'S HIS HEAD.

McCONOCHIE: Yes. Yes. But when you love someone – I
don't know this – I have not actually loved – but when you
love – it is not the flesh, is it, that one loves? Am I being
indelicate?

BRADSHAW: I LOVED HIS HEAD.

McCONOCHIE: Yes, but I think one needs to examine what we mean by –

BRADSHAW: I DO NOT –

McCONOCHIE: All right, you do not, but –

BRADSHAW: YOUR DAD'S HEAD.

(*Pause.*)

McCONOCHIE: Please, you mustn't be angry with me.

BRADSHAW: No.

McCONOCHIE: Or shout. I do not see the point of shouting. Things are difficult enough without recourse to shouting.

BRADSHAW: Yes, I'm sorry.

McCONOCHIE: I could shout as well. There are plenty of things I would like to shout about. I could lie down on the floor and cry. But I don't, do I?

BRADSHAW: No. You don't.

McCONOCHIE: I have my problems too. I want to be a doctor. How am I going to be a doctor? You must help me, please. I am only eighteen. I do think you might give me some advice.

(*Pause.*)

BRADSHAW: We knew this would happen one day. We knew, while we argued in his little room, the ground was going from under our feet, on late summer evenings crossing the lawn, felt the threat in the shadows under the trees, and the mockery of the placid fountain. So he made me swear to bury him in an unmarked spot, in a field where he'd sat, very deep where nothing would come to abuse him. And you, I created like this, to spare you pain. What more can a mother do for her child? No ardour to be bruised, no passion to be beaten for. A cold armouring of the eyes, the slowest of heart beats, and a tongue whose habit is to lie low in the mouth, dark as a bottomfish, not red or roaring and at the end, ripped out. I think you will survive, my dear little blue-eyed boy…

(*He turns away. Pause.*)

McCONOCHIE: I am thinking of changing my name.

BRADSHAW: Good.

McCONOCHIE: And leaving.

(*Pause.*)

I am sorry to bring this up now –

BRADSHAW: No, bring it up now –

McCONOCHIE: I think it would be hypocritical if I spared your feelings today only to wound them tomorrow. I do think that would be hypocritical, don't you?

BRADSHAW: I hate tact and wariness…

McCONOCHIE: I do, too.

BRADSHAW: Idiot kindliness.

McCONOCHIE: Yes, yes!

BRADSHAW: Off with that now. Ditch pity! Ditch fuss.

McCONOCHIE: I do like you.

(*Pause.*)

I am going to Scotland and calling myself McConochie.

BRADSHAW: A very good name. Ideal for a surgeon.

McCONOCHIE: That's what I thought.

BRADSHAW: I am very proud of you. I mean that. Now pack your bag and go.

McCONOCHIE: Now?

BRADSHAW: Yes now. I have done my best by you. Please go.

McCONOCHIE: What – just –

BRADSHAW: Go.

(*Pause. Then he turns and leaves. He passes CROPPER, who enters.*)

They have found him. And stuck his head on a pole.

(*CROPPER goes to her, embraces her.*)

Through his brain. His poor brain. An old spike.

(*She parts from her.*)

Or not, do you think? I say brain, but that's silly, that really is silly, the brain I'd have thought, being soft –

CROPPER: Shh –

BRADSHAW: The very first thing to rot, I imagine –

CROPPER: Don't imagine –

BRADSHAW: I want to imagine! Would go liquid or possibly – I have not seen a brain – dry up like a nut – a rattling nut –

CROPPER: Shh!

BRADSHAW: …in the skull – a pebble – or imagine –

CROPPER: Don't imagine –

BRADSHAW: I will imagine! Stop telling me not to imagine! Alternatively, a skull full of muck, which if tipped, or tilted, would drip through the eyes, would weep its own brains out, cry muck down your skirt, splash dirty intellect on stockings and shoes –

CROPPER: We want you to move in with us.

BRADSHAW: His scrotum, though shrivelled, evidently was intact –

CROPPER: The spare room –

BRADSHAW: ...His scrotum –

CROPPER: Please –

BRADSHAW: ...After how many years? Did you see it? I saw it occasionally, though not in the light, his ardour was strictly nocturnal and grew rare with the strain, they will see it more clearly than I did, see it in hot sun and white light, his thing on some gate, his thing there for pelting and pecking, no, I shan't move in with you, your piety really makes me sick. But thank you. Thank you, and thank you again.

CROPPER: Mother –

BRADSHAW: Oh, didn't I say thank you enough? My manners are in disarray –

CROPPER: I only want to help.

BRADSHAW: Yes... (*Pause.*) He would have had you study Latin. Was all for giving you a tutor. I stopped that. Leave her dark, I said, bovine, religious and clean. Then she will survive and fuck with a farmer. I cannot tell you how glad I am so many of my children died. I should have had to do this six times. Six times indeed!

CROPPER: That is very hurtful. But I shall always love you.

BRADSHAW: Yes, you would do. The more hurtful I am the more you love me. It is all part of being bovine, religious and clean.

CROPPER: I am not bovine!

BRADSHAW: You are bovine. You are breasts and milk and belly, moist and passionate as stables and wet fields. No Latin, but red, oh red inside!

CROPPER: I think you have gone mad.

19

BRADSHAW: Yes. Now blot me out with pigs and children. And when the boots come up the pathway, give them your own bread and beer and jam, and they will see in your eyes your harmlessness. They will!

CROPPER: (*Bitterly.*) I will visit you tomorrow.

BRADSHAW: HE HAD SUCH A HORROR OF BEING DUG!

(*CROPPER turns away, in tears, goes out.*)

Oh, sob, run away and sob! The one will never cry and the other never stops! I SHOULD NOT HAVE BEEN GIVEN CHILDREN!

(*Pause.*)

I will bring you back. I will get your bits, your chops and scrag, your offal and your lean cuts, I will collect them. I will bring your poor bald head away that hurt me so much with its arguments…

SCENE THREE

The KING OF ENGLAND enters a room.

CLEGG: Oh, see the shadows flee the land!
    The dark hour gone, and the dread hand,
    The envy of the world our situation,
    Ecstasy and coronation!

SOUTHWARK: I'm pissed on pomp, look at me, I'm pig hot in this ponce stuff! It's all right for you, your knockers hang out in the breezes…

CLEGG: Our star, our moon, our radiant sun
    Like orbs of wisdom, lo, he comes!
    And through our joyous, ringing city
    Rides his chariot of divinity!

CLEVELAND: I never saw more dug, more boob out, like a market of fresh tit, I thought, the Abbey was a tit market, pew after pew, I never felt more like a nibble at the fruit, blew my eyes hither and thither, screwed in squint I was…

HAMBRO: His father hovered, saw him hovering, I thought, behind the altar, Charles the martyr, noble Stuart…

CLEGG: With fountain and with firework write his name,
    In flower scented of his honour do the same,

Bird chants, the infant gurgles and bee hums
Oh, Charles in all his glory comes!

CHARLES: I did not actually like my dad. My dad who kept
his cock dry for my mother, my mother who was a bint in
essence but would shag monsignors only with her eyes, all
the silliness of confession-boxes and monsignors' knobs.
I adore my mother, I revere my mother, but she was an
unfulfilled bint actually. And my father was in any case a
sod. So there. You cannot wonder at the revolution. I never
wondered at it. I think any nation governed by a bint and a
sod will rise in protest, I said so at the time.

CLEGG: Rejoice, rejoice, this is our day,
Leave labour, toil, depart, the fray,
Both God and Reason annointeth us
Carolingus noble, Carolingus just!

CHARLES: But my father would complicate matters by being
a saint as well as a sod. A most peculiar combination.
Peculiar and incomprehensible. I am neither peculiar nor
incomprehensible. I am a male bint pure and simple. I
assure you, there is no better stimulus to loyalty than for an
apprentice to be molly shagging only minutes after I have
left her off. He grasps your flesh, he shares your monarchy.
(*He turns to HAMBRO.*)
Is that the head?

HAMBRO: (*Looking out the window.*) It's Bradshaw, yes.

CHARLES: There is shagall left of it.

PONTING: He is three years dead and the field was wet.

CHARLES: I will chuck skittles at it. Lower the window. I will
head shy.

PONTING: (*Calling.*) SKITTLES!

CLEVELAND: Oh, what's Charlie up to, and with the
annointment still damp on his forehead! Shall we come?

CLEGG: Now grows my voice thin –

HAMPSHIRE: Good, I have a skinful of yer poetry –

CLEGG: ...Imagination sheer amaze,
My lyre expires from excess of praise,
The hours tarry, drag their feet for fun,
Delay your journey they plead of the sun!

SOMERSET: Shall we come there?

CHARLES: I head shy! I head shy!

CLEVELAND: Oh, look, a bonze all rotten underneath the window…

BRIGHTON: Where?

(*They crowd at the window.*)

CLEVELAND: You are leaning on me.

BRIGHTON: Ugh!

(*They peer in silence.*)

CHARLES: Is it true he wore an iron hat at my father's trial, for fear of murder?

DERBYSHIRE: And a chain vest, certainly.

GLOUCESTERSHIRE: I think you have in that one picture all the vanity and squirming terror of a man who dares to kill his master. Probably a puddle of his poop lay on the usurper's bench at the adjournment.

HAMBRO: Yet we should not resent him.

CHARLES: How's that, Hambro? How not resent him?

HAMBRO: To kill the king is no bad thing provided there follows restoration. It honours monarchy. Is proof of indispensibility.

CHARLES: (*Coldly.*) Where is my duchess? I must grasp her arse.

NODD: Oh, Pam, dear, hither and bring your bum!

PONTING: Lady Devonshire!

NODD: Charlie, what is Hambro?

CHARLES: Billy? Billy is the banker.

NODD: I'd not go chase the clap with him, would you, love?

CHARLES: Not on your belly.

PONTING: The skittles come! The skittles!

CLEGG: The evening falls, by obligation,
Spoils the humour of our situation –

HAMPSHIRE: Oh, fuck this chanting!

CLEGG: Come night or storm we shall not move
Out of the sunlight of our monarch's love!

DEVONSHIRE: I'm here.

CHARLES: Oh, Nodd, am I not a poor male bint, wiping my knob on swan and cockatoo, draping the silk over my rump?

NODD: Now, now, this is the time of your life, silly!

CHARLES: Bradshaw cropped his hair and wore no wig, and
  when he pissed did not wince, I dare say, no tart came
  near his thing –

PONTING: (*Offering a tray.*) Skittles?

CHARLES: ...Did it –
  (*He takes one.*)
  – near – your – thing?
  (*He chucks one.*)

DEVONSHIRE: I'm here.

CHARLES: You may all chuck now, and my hag, let her fling
  at the regicide's bonze! –
  (*They begin throwing in earnest.*)

DEVONSHIRE: (*To SOUTHWARK.*) What are we doing?

SOUTHWARK: Pelting.

CHARLES: The trunk's on Blackfriars, the legs on the Strand.
  Come on, chuck!

NODD: Oh, I 'it 'im!

GLOUCESTERSHIRE: He spun! I touched him, he spun!

CLEVELAND: The eyeballs! The eyeballs are watching us,
  ugh!

HAMPSHIRE: Knock him round, then, knock him round!

DEVONSHIRE: What are we doing, exactly?

NODD: Jaw dropped! Did yer see it?

DEVONSHIRE: I think I'll lie down.

CHARLES: Oh, no, my duchess, my duchess will chuck like
  a man –

DEVONSHIRE: Oh, must I?

CHARLES: (*Propelling her forward to the window.*) Must I, must
  I, she says...

PONTING: MORE SKITTLES!
  (*The SERVANT runs out.*)

DERBYSHIRE: Oh, Teddy –

NODD: Oh, bad chucking, Ted –

HAMPSHIRE: My arm is rheumatic –

DERBYSHIRE: His arm is rheumatic –

NODD: Terrible chucking –

CLEGG: Genius lay down thy arrogance here,
  Martial ardour undo thy mask of fear,

Virgins, youths, pale from celebration
Mock thy stern countenance across the nation!
DEVONSHIRE: Charlie, you are hurting my arse…
CHARLES: Get me then, get me in your hand –
HAMPSHIRE: I struck! I did, see! Shook on its spike!
DEVONSHIRE: Look, do you want me to throw or not?
GLOUCESTERSHIRE: Clipped him! Clipped him on the
   ear!
BRIGHTON: Oh, the ear drops off!
DEVONSHIRE: Because I cannot if –
CHARLES: Oh, tight in your hand!
DEVONSHIRE: I am –
CHARLES: Tighter!
NODD: Oh, poor little ear! 'is little ear, look!
CHARLES: Tighter yet!
DEVONSHIRE: Ouch!
GLOUCESTERSHIRE: Cracked him! He's down!
NODD: 'e's down!
CLEGG: Come nymphs, come satyrs to our court,
   Old Thames thy hoary locks disport,
   And Time delay thy pouring glass,
   This gilded hour wastes too fast!
CLEVELAND: Horrible dust stuff flew away…
BRIGHTON: Dust stuff, Harry –
PONTING: (*Hanging out the window.*) It's down in the yard…
HAMSPHIRE: Down, Charlie…
NODD: Bob done it.
CHARLES: I done too, quicker than I wanted…
PONTING: (*Peering.*) Still in one bit, I'll be buggered…!
CHARLES: Out now, all of you…
CLEGG: Monarchy, our ancient treasure,
   Restores our joy in lavish measure –
BRIGHTON: Did you see that, Harry, grey stuff fly out the
   head?
SOUTHWARK: I been listening to Sam's bum-ache, ain't I?
CLEGG: And spreading dazzling luminosity,
   Irradiates our curiosity!
CHARLES: Out now! Did you hear me?

NODD: Out?

CHARLES: Yes, even you, Nodd –

CLEVELAND: Out?

CHARLES: Yes, you know the word, madam, meaning the contrary of in –

PONTING: We are due on the river in fifteen –

CHARLES: Oh, listen, who is the monarch here? Who wears the ermine bum-fluff, me! I have been down, ain't I, in sight of the tit of England, got the oil of Christ on me, out then when I say it. Out!

(*They depart.*)

Not you!

(*He grabs DEVONSHIRE's wrist. They are alone.*)

DEVONSHIRE: Charlie, I must wash my hand –

CHARLES: No.

DEVONSHIRE: I am sticky –

CHARLES: Lick it, then, cats do –

(*She turns away.*)

I AM A CLOWN!

DEVONSHIRE: Oh, dear…

CHARLES: A CLOWN, MADAM!

(*He walks up and down.*)

Why do I? My little sprig, my little green shoot, poor little flower of my dignity, piss on it, why? It will wither, won't it? Go a monkey to my grave!

DEVONSHIRE: I hope you aren't going to be deep…

CHARLES: This prancing wig and whatnot, garters and the royal etcetera, why!

DEVONSHIRE: Do up your fly.

CHARLES: No, let it out!

DEVONSHIRE: Oh, God he is going to tear his raiment…

CHARLES: Garments down! Out bum! Out all the old flesh, grey and bedroom stale the human meat!

(*He flings off his wig and trousers.*)

DEVONSHIRE: I am not looking.

(*She turns resolutely away.*)

CHARLES: Hear me, please!

DEVONSHIRE: You are always like this when you've come.

CHARLES: Yes, it is the only time I see things.

Thank you, Rob. Now go down to the yard and fetch me
Mr Bradshaw's head.

NODD: Do wha' –

CHARLES: Oh, now, don't quarrel! And see it washed,
and the sparse hairs parted, as he would have wished, no
mockery.

(*NODD shrugs, starts to go.*)

Rob.

(*He stops.*)

We shall go drinking, soon. In dirty jerkins over Brixton.

NODD: Yup.

(*He goes out. HAMBRO enters.*)

CHARLES: And Rob!

(*He reappears.*)

I think, ask Lady Devonshire postpone her coach. I do
not now, but a time will come I'll want her. I guarantee no
sooner will she pass the toll than my knob will be up and
barking for her.

(*NODD goes out. CHARLES walks a little, adjusts his sash.*)

What, Billy?

HAMBRO: It's time.

CHARLES: Oh, it is, is it?

HAMBRO: Time, yes, and such a shame to spoil the day. The
people line the river.

CHARLES: Oh, let 'em wait. I'm king, ain't I?

HAMBRO: Indeed, but –

CHARLES: No, no, I'm the bloody monarch –

HAMBRO: Quite, but –

CHARLES: MONARCH, MONARCH!

(*HAMBRO is silent, looks at the floor. CHARLES beckons him
with a finger.*)

Billy, what if I am barmy? I think the dad had it, you see,
suppose I'm barmy?

HAMBRO: What if you're –

CHARLES: Sister-fucking – up nieces – down nephews – bad
blood and funny bones – Stuart eggs all broken in the
saucepan – what then, Billy? Would yer have me quietly
butchered?

HAMBRO: I prefer not to imagine –

CHARLES: Billy won't imagine! Billy won't!

(*He goes close to him.*)

Or don't it really matter any more?

(*Pause.*)

Billy, I do not like you awfully. You have such cold grey eyes and never fuck nobody. I wish I was cleverer, I would follow your tricks like the dog to the bitch's arse. I think you entertain some sort of treason.

HAMBRO: Treason?

CHARLES (*Mocking.*) What! Treason! What!

(*He smiles.*)

No, Billy, darling, I mean I don't think you love me, do you, my flesh, the bone and blood of Charlie? Do you? Really love me?

HAMBRO: I was prime mover in your –

CHARLES: Prime mover, oh, prime mover, yes, you would be, I never saw a man more purely prime moving, a prince among prime movers, it clings like shit to the instep the prime mobility of you. Billy, did you not get this day for me, you did and thank you, I am well primed though not exactly moved, but never mind, you primed the day, oh, thank you, Billy, but –

(*He looks closely at him.*)

I wish you fucked more…

(*Pause.*)

Off now. I come.

SCENE FOUR

BRADSHAW's house at dusk. SCROPE enters.

SCROPE: I sinned.

BRADSHAW: I was afraid you would appear.

SCROPE: (*Flinging himself down.*) I sinned! I sinned!

BRADSHAW: Just at the moment I wanted to be alone, at the very moment I most needed to collect my thoughts, I knew you would appear –

SCROPE: I sinned!

BRADSHAW: And be very abject.

SCROPE: One blow!

BRADSHAW: Will you not shout, please?

SCROPE: One blow and I gave away the place! One blow
and I led them to his grave!

BRADSHAW: How many blows did you want?
(*Pause.*)

SCROPE: It wasn't a blow…

BRADSHAW: What was it, then?

SCROPE: A flick.

BRADSHAW: A flick?

SCROPE: A flick of a glove…

BRADSHAW: What sort of glove? A mailed glove?

SCROPE: A CALF GLOVE.

BRADSHAW: Well, flicks can be painful.

SCROPE: You mock me! You mock my cowardice!

BRADSHAW: Mr Scrope, I have pain, too –

SCROPE: MY COWARDICE!

BRADSHAW: What of my pain, Mr Scrope!
(*He looks at her, sobs.*)

SCROPE: I have no courage… I have no dignity…

BRADSHAW: No, but you have your teeth. After the glove
comes the fist, and after the fist comes the boot, and after
the boot –

SCROPE: What I would not give for courage!

BRADSHAW: No. Let us chuck courage and hang on to our
teeth.

SCROPE: I betrayed him!

BRADSHAW: Mr Scope, I am beginning to think you overdo
the abject rather –

SCROPE: I BETRAYED HIM!

BRADSHAW: You did not, then! He betrayed himself.
(*Pause.*)

SCROPE: How?

BRADSHAW: By sharing his secret with a man who, in the
last resort, preferred to keep his teeth.

SCROPE: There! You mock me!

BRADSHAW: Not at all. He was an appalling judge of
 character.

SCROPE: Well, you accuse me, then!

BRADSHAW: I accuse no one. I am done with accusing. I am
 done with shame, and conscience, duty, guilt, and power,
 all of it! All of your words, chuck out!
 (*Pause.*)
 Now, shake hands with me, I'm leaving.

SCROPE: (*Amazed out of crying.*) Leaving?

BRADSHAW: Yes. Now. In the dead of night. In what I stand
 up in.
 (*Pause.*)
 Scrope, your lip is quivering. Do stop, you look an old man
 suddenly…
 (*She turns away.*)

SCROPE: Where? Where to?

BRADSHAW: London, to collect his pieces. And nowhere
 after that.

SCROPE: Why?

BRADSHAW: Why? Because we must crawl now, go down
 on all fours, be a dog or rabbit, no more standing up
 now, standing is over, standing up's for men with sin and
 dignity. No, got to be a dog now, and keep our teeth. I am
 crawling and barking, stalking, fawning, stealing breakfast,
 running when I see a stick, taken when I'm taken, pupping
 under hedges, being a proper four-legged bitch.
 (*Pause. He stares at her.*)
 Well, of course I shall have to learn it! Can't be be a dog
 overnight!

SCROPE: (*As she turns to go.*) I think my master's wife is ill…

BRADSHAW: Ill, me? I am weller than I ever was!

SCROPE: How can I see you, who was wife to the President
 of the Council, and walked with him in honour and in –

BRADSHAW: Oh, down I go! See!
 (*She goes down on all fours.*)
 Bow! Ow! Ow!

SCROPE: Oh, you shame him!

BRADSHAW: I shame him? What about him shaming me? Getting his ugly reason out, his great moral purpose, showing it in public, and his wisdom! Could not walk with him five minutes but he had his wisdom out, forever exhibiting his mind, was ever a mind hung out so much in public, dirty thing it was, great monster of a mind so flashed and brazenly dangled? Ugh! No, I was shamed if anybody was!

SCROPE: I think you should see a doctor.

BRADSHAW: A doctor? Don't you mean a vet?

SCROPE: You have gone mad with grief!

BRADSHAW: No, sane with it. Now, stand away from the window, I am leaving by it. There is a spy watches the door –

SCROPE: I refuse –

BRADSHAW: Now, be a good secretary and –

SCROPE: I must refuse –

BRADSHAW: Don't be silly, Scrope –

SCROPE: I WILL BE HONOURABLE IN THIS AT LEAST.

BRADSHAW: Scrope, I will push you over...

(*Pause. Then he stands aside, bitterly. She goes to climb through the window.*)

SCROPE: I must come, then, mustn't I?

(*She looks at him.*)

It is my duty.

BRADSHAW: I really do not want –

SCROPE: I MUST.

(*Pause.*)

BRADSHAW: Then throw away your satchel. You won't need pen and paper on four legs.

SCROPE: (*Taking out a book.*) Mr Bradshaw's 'Harmonia' I will not part with. Read it every night beneath the hedge.

BRADSHAW: Idiot.

SCROPE: Bring comfort to us in our –

BRADSHAW: Chew it, suck the moisture out the ink –

SCROPE: (*Stuffing the book in a pocket.*) It's gaol to have in your possession –

BRADSHAW: Quick! Someone's coming! Quick!

(*They climb out of the window. McCONOCHIE comes in holding a book.*)

McCONOCHIE: (*Rehearsing.*) Guid morning to ye...is it noo a fine sky o'er the Firth of Forth...
(*He stops.*)
The capital of Scotland is Edinburgh. The Highlands are high. The Lowlands are low...
(*He walks a little, stops.*)
The sheep are in the heather...the coos are in the burn...
(*He goes as if to shake hands.*)
I am McConochie, surgeon of Leith...
(*And again.*)
McConochie at your service, Bachelor of Medicine, Physician of Dundee...
(*He ruminates.*)
Dun-dee... Dun-dee...no, Leith.
(*He proceeds to a rocking chair, sits and reads. BALL appears at the window, climbs in.*)

BALL: Across the lawn I come, left off my boots, and sockless like a cavalier. But you will dry my poor wet feet in your lap, in your hot place, oh, excuse the cavalier in me, I know it offends but I have thought a lot of you in your cold puritan shift and come to master you, like taking England back. I looked at England through a telescope from Calais thinking of your starched under-things and uncoloured face, and the smell of you, a little musty, I expect, the musty hair of a sad-eyed puritan, oh, I shall have you shuddering with love, do reply, but very sweetly, and with dignity, no cock and cunt talk, you are not a cavalier tart, are you? Oh, the modesty of a real woman it does wonders to me, I am hard as rock...

McCONOCHIE: (*In terror.*) I think you have come to the wrong house, sir...

BALL: What.

McCONOCHIE: I think you have, sir –

BALL: WHAT!

McCONOCHIE: (*Jumping up.*) Don't hit me, please, I am only a surgeon!

BALL: (*Drawing a dagger.*) Oh, I stab you, I kill the rebel filth!

McCONOCHIE: (*On the ground.*) Mercy!

BALL: What do you do in this stinking house? In this disgusting cleanliness? I burn it! I burn it! What do you do?

McCONOCHIE: Surgeon, sir!

BALL: (*Releasing him.*) I shall burn it, I shall! All this polish and this timber, I was a pig in Calais while they lorded it. Lorded it, I say lorded it, whatever they do in their stiff-gobbed manner! Who do you examine? In her starchy knicker with your prod? Where is the woman? Where is the widow of the king's assassin, the murdered saint's accuser, where's his pale wife? I did not prattle all my knob talk for your dirty doctor's ear.

McCONOCHIE: Ow!

BALL: Where is she?

McCONOCHIE: Don't know sir!

BALL: Get her, then, and quick about it, in her shift or naked off her pot, for all I care!
(*McCONOCHIE hurtles out the room.*)
Oh, after I shall write a sonnet, when the fire has gone, a melancholy piece on how her sad face was like a pearl, and her hair like silvered weed flowing o'er the pillow...
(*McCONOCHIE enters with a sheet of paper.*)

McCONOCHIE: She's gone...

BALL: Gone! Oh, shit and piss! Then I have lost the cunt I wanted!
(*He snatches the paper from McCONOCHIE. Reads.*)
'Have gone to be an animal' – what is this – 'in time of animals' – what's this!

McCONOCHIE: Don't know sir.

BALL: Oh, yes, I think you do –

McCONOCHIE: No –

BALL: In time of animals! You have had her!

McCONOCHIE: Never!

BRADSHAW: (*Grabbing him.*) Oh, I'll stick my dagger in your crack if you dirty doctor got in there before me!

McCONOCHIE: Never! Never!

BALL: Dog-wise, yes, you did, I know it from your simper!

(*McCONOCHIE sobs.*)

I never knew a doctor not share the sickbed of his patient
had she got half a tit was healthy…

McCONOCHIE: No…no…

BALL: (*His dagger out.*) Deny once more, I'll slit your carotids
– there – I know a surgeon's patter – and see your gore
across the shiny boards, I swear it!

(*McCONOCHIE freezes.*)

So, was she hot for you? You being animal? Oh, was she,
hot and clinging?

McCONOCHIE: Yes…

BALL: And whispered you were wonder to her, being animal,
sheer wonder, did she?

McCONOCHIE: Yes…

BALL: (*Throwing him down.*) Oh, God and Christ, I do want a
puritan woman! They know what they do with their eyes
cast down and starchy collars! They do know it! 'Gone to
be an animal!' Well, mistress, I shall find you in your den!
(*He turns to go, stops.*)

Can you cure me of what I've got? It stings me something
awful.

McCONOCHIE: I don't know what you –

BALL: I'll sit and unbutton. And if it rises thinking of the
Bradshaw woman, tap it with some cold instrument. And
blunt, mind you…

(*He sits, unbuttons. McCONOCHIE looks.*)

Why are you snivelling? Am I so ill you cannot keep your
tears back?

McCONOCHIE: No, I…

BALL: Touch it, then, it won't bite you…

(*McCONOCHIE feigns an examination.*)

I have been on my own soil for six months now, hounding
communists and antichrists, doing the midnight knock on
the doors of old republicans. It is my treat. I have been on
an eight-year holiday. How is it?

McCONOCHIE: Mild, mild, I think…

BALL: Eight years, watching the cliffs of England from a
whore's back on the continent, jostling Louis le this and
Monsignor that, purple vicars and slag duchesses. I did not

think I should get back, let alone rip down the lanes and
burn the manors of this lot. How mild? No other quack
could shift it.

McCONOCHIE: Mild…and yet…tenacious…

BALL: Where's the sense in History? I came here to a feast
of bonfire and applauding. Who would have flung shit in
my eye once were all bow and scraping, and me with not a
clean whole garment! I don't pretend to know no history.
How is the knob, then? Can you cure him?

McCONOCHIE: (*Bluffing.*) It is a somewhat rare infection…

BALL: Rare, is it? It would be.

McCONOCHIE: Rare, definitely, rare, yes…

BALL: What became of all the roundhead troopers? Is their
armour up behind the door? Or rusting in the cabbages? I
seen none since I came here, prance in their cottages and
get only silence, muddy silence, and they used to yell so
much, chivvied the world's guts once – ow! Don't pluck it,
quack, examine it!

McCONOCHIE: I am very sorry… I am not a pox
specialist…

BALL: What are you, then!

McCONOCHIE: (*Shaking.*) It is not my speciality…

BALL: Listen quack, I get no fuck here, very well, but I shall
have a cure for my trouble!

McCONOCHIE: Yes –

BALL: Get down your pox book –

McCONOCHIE: Yes –

BALL: And study it –

McCONOCHIE: Yes –

BALL: Fast! In Jesus' name, I shall leave here healthy!
(*McCONOCHIE rises and hurries to the door.*)
Quack!
(*He stops.*)
Listen. Now the puritans are done for you will make a
living as a cock specialist, if you're so minded. We bring
from Europe every boil and sore now, it's the restoration
of old lewdness and the reign of fucking. Specialize in

troubles of the mucus and you will live in posh, if posh you fancy.

(*McCONOCHIE perceives.*)

Christ knows why I favour you like this. Do you angle after posh? I never knew a doctor didn't.

McCONOCHIE: Yes.

BALL: Start here, then. On my ailing foreskin.

(*Pause. Then filled with inspiration, McCONOCHIE turns to leave. He stops at the door.*)

McCONOCHIE: Perhaps a little essence of saltpetre?

BALL: Why not? Fling the contents of the pharmacy at it.

McCONOCHIE: (*His mind racing.*) Or sulphur in suspension of boracic…

BALL: You mix, I'll do the swallowing.

(*McCONOCHIE leaves.*)

And I spend the night here! Among her things, run my fingers through her garments, slip her knicker on my haunches and dream in her bed. Tomorrow I'll pursue her.

SCENE FIVE

A field. A man digging, a woman watching, and a preacher.

FEAK: I done enough. Bring out the dead, Mrs.

EDGBASTON: In certain knowledge of thy resurrection, in confidence thy mouth will speak again, sleeping only till the call come, we plant thee like a seed to rise when anger warms the ground!

PYLE: (*Taking a rifle from a cloth.*) Anybody looking?

FEAK: Give us it.

EDGBASTON: Oh, Lord of Battles, bless thy son, and keep his silence brief!

FEAK: (*Handling it fondly, offering the muzzle.*) Give 'im a kiss, eh?

(*PYLE kisses the muzzle.*)

And you, Bob…

(*EDGBASTON kisses it.*)

Bye bye, pal…

EDGBASTON: Oh, death and mutilation to thy enemies! He shall return to us in blood and smoke, I vow!

37

FEAK: Where ain't I carted that bloody gun…

PYLE: Where ain't I cleaned it…

EDGBASTON: A crop of armour and a field of bullets from thy temper shall be harvested!

PYLE: Scotland, Ireland, Flanders, Jamaica…

FEAK: All for nothing.

PYLE: Good times…

FEAK: Ta ta, pal, it won't be Sue's fault you get dirt up yer spout now…

PYLE: Good times…

EDGBASTON: Oh, let his sleep be brief before our wrath return to boil, in blood and terror drive the stinking Stuart from our soil!

FEAK: (*To EDGBASTON.*) All right. Bob, you done?
 (*He nods.*)
 Cover it up, ducks.
 (*PYLE begins filling the grave.*)
 We was the champions. Now look at us. Time's a cunt.

PYLE: So's God.

EDGBASTON: Now, sister, you are letting your grief run away with you…

PYLE: Am I? I said He's a cunt, didn't I? He is a cunt.

EDGBASTON: And did He not guide the parliament to raise the standards of revolt? Did He not steer the Lord Protector in his –

PYLE: Oh, fuck the Protector, Bob…

EDGBASTON: I will not hear this scandal of Almighty God!

FEAK: Yer can't tell Sue, Bob, she's defaced too many monuments. Always first up cathedral aisles, our Sue, 'ammer flyin', trail a' broken glass an' angels' 'eads…

PYLE: Good times…

FEAK: Must end…

EDGBASTON: It is one thing to wreck the graven image, but another to attack His dwelling place inside our hearts.

PYLE: (*Patting down the earth with the flat of the shovel.*) Show a bloke a good thing…
 (*She notices BRADSHAW and SCROPE are watching them. Pause.*)

BRADSHAW: I must say I have some trouble following the Lord myself. His ways and so on. I expect we got too proud, don't you? He really has a passion about proudness. One day you're prancing and the next day you are in the trough. And vice versa, I expect, well, look at Charles Stuart, have you got a bun or something, we are starving. (*They look at her.*)

Well, if not a bun, a –

FEAK: We are fuckin' ragbags as it is –

BRADSHAW: Yes, I can see that, I wasn't asking for your lifeblood, only –

EDGBASTON: We live very frugal here –

BRADSHAW: Oh, come on, where's your charity?

PYLE: Charity's for comrades.

BRADSHAW: With all respect, I don't think you have quite grasped the principle of charity, have you? The point, I think, is that it's undiscriminating, am I right? (*She looks at EDGBASTON. SCROPE mutters to her.*)

SCROPE: Come on, we'll get nothing here –

BRADSHAW: (*Hissing.*) I WANT A BUN. (*She turns back to EDGBASTON.*)

You're a preacher, aren't you? What is charity, isn't there a character of moral obligation in the word?

FEAK: You get none 'ere –

BRADSHAW: (*Turning on him.*) YOU GET NONE 'ERE! Well, what does the meaning matter, the offence is clear enough I SEE YOU KILL THE OLD REPUBLIC HERE and quite right, bury old equality, WHO SAID THAT! SHH! All these old dirty words, under the sod and stamp on them, come on – (*She turns to SCROPE.*)

EDGBASTON: We are wary of strangers –

BRADSHAW: No, no, don't be kind now, you will only suffer for it, keep your bun, a man must watch his bun nowadays, don't feed a stranger, what is this, the Commonwealth, WHO SAID THAT, not me!

SCROPE: (*Desperate.*) Take it!

BRADSHAW: Shut up! We can have the lot off them! (*She turns back to them.*)

I do respect your narrow eyes, your tight lip, very wise
now, hands in pockets, there are bun thieves about!
(*She makes as if to go.*)

FEAK: What were you, Mrs? With the Republic?
(*She stops, looks down at her garments.*)

BRADSHAW: Do I look a duchess? My husband gave the
king his death. Trembling somewhat. Well, wouldn't you?
He expected God to strike him dead. Sat on a ring of
rubber in case lightning struck his head.
(*Pause. Then PYLE flings herself at BRADSHAW's feet and
kisses her hand.*)

FEAK: Get buns!

BRADSHAW: (*As PYLE hurries off.*) With butter!

FEAK: An' beer!

BRADSHAW: Two bottles!

FEAK: Bring all the beer we got!

SCROPE: (*In joy.*) Oh, Christ, I hurt with hunger!

EDGBASTON: Our great rebels brought to this…there is
mud to your knees, sister…

BRADSHAW: So there is! You do see life without a carriage!
Has she any bacon?

EDGBASTON: (*Shouting off.*) Bacon, sis!

FEAK: We saw 'im, we was beside 'im when they axed the
bugger Stuart, weren't us, Bob?

BRADSHAW: Ask her to wrap a dinner up, in cloth or something –

EDGBASTON: (*Shouts.*) Make a dinner up! A dinner! Make
one up!

FEAK: Where you are standin', that's where we was, twelfth
footguard, battle-dress in case a' bother, trailin' pikes –

EDGBASTON: (*Shouting.*) In a cloth! A dinner! Yes!

FEAK: I said, that is the President a' Council, that is
Bradshaw, 'e was like from 'ere to there – remember, Bob?
An' 'e was pale, dead pale 'e was –

BRADSHAW: He had a very fair skin –

FEAK: Fuckin' right 'e did, an' when the blood spilt, did 'e
jump!

EDGBASTON: We all jumped –

FEAK: I jumped, you jumped, every bugger jumped!

EDGBASTON: KING'S BLOOD!

FEAK: An' I thought, Christ Almighty, it's the same as any other, it's the same red stuff...

EDGBASTON: Off came his shoe –

FEAK: An' the foot –

EDGBASTON: The foot without the shoe was going –

FEAK: On the wooden boards –

EDGBASTON: Bang – bang –

FEAK: On this frosty mornin' –

EDGBASTON: Bang – bang, the Stuart foot...

(*PYLE returns with a small parcel of food. They look at it disparagingly.*)

FEAK: What's this?

PYLE: It's little. Because they gave us little.

EDGBASTON: Sue –

PYLE: You give what you get –

EDGBASTON: Sue –

PYLE: DON'T YER, THOUGH? THAT'S LIFE!

(*Pause.*)

I thought, crossin' this field, this bloody field which is runnin' in our sweat an' our dad's sweat before us, what are yer doin', Sue, you silly bitch, why fetch for them?

BRADSHAW: Give us a bite.

PYLE: I thought, you are forgettin' something, girl, in your excitement you ain't thinking right.

BRADSHAW: Give us a bite.

PYLE: Because we came from 'ere, 'alf starved as usual out this bloody field to chuck the bastard Stuart over an' get Oliver an' Mr Bradshaw in, ten years of killin' Spaniards, Scots an' Irish, an' for what?

EDGBASTON: You are being most –

PYLE: To come back to this soddin' field again! This field of bloody clay, only this time it was buggered with the horses ridin' over it an' wouldn't take a crop –

FEAK: It was, Bob –

PYLE: But did they let us off the rent? Did they? I ask yer, did they give us one bloody little quarter off the rent?

FEAK: They never, Bob...

PYLE: An' we are still tryin' to wring a dinner out this mud! Commonwealth? Whose commonwealth? Give them dinner, I thought, fuck!

(*Pause. Then she holds out the food to BRADSHAW. She takes it, sits at once and starts eating. SCROPE watches anxiously.*)

SCROPE: I do think...with all respect...you are not being entirely fair...Mr Bradshaw...you may know...was highly critical...of the...slow progress...of agrarian...reform...the tenant question...very...memoranda...to...and...

(*He drops to his knees and grabs at the food, stuffing it in his mouth in ecstasy.*)

Oh! Oh!

(*The others watch them a few moments, then drift off. BRADSHAW stops eating, stares after them.*)

BRADSHAW: Listen –

SCROPE: Mm – mmm –

BRADSHAW: Oh, listen. I did something.

SCROPE: Mm – mmm –

BRADSHAW: Will you listen to me.

SCROPE: Mm –

BRADSHAW: Scrope, I did it. When he kissed me. I TOOK HIS WALLET. Get on your feet!

SCROPE: Wha'?

BRADSHAW: (*Showing it.*) I TOOK HIS WALLET! Oh, my lovely quick hands, look!

(*He stares at her in horror.*)

Congratulate me.

(*He just stares.*)

CONGRATULATE ME, THEN.

SCROPE: But they – they were our people –

BRADSHAW: CONGRATULATE ME, THEN!

(*Pause. He stares at her.*)

SCROPE: You cannot do it to them...

BRADSHAW: I did, you see, I did!

SCROPE: Listen –

BRADSHAW: Look at my fingers! Aren't they wonderful, and swift? They tremble in their little ecstasy, do look!

SCROPE: Please, listen –

BRADSHAW: (*Collecting the remaining bread.*) Hurry up, or
they'll discover it, and then it's noses slit and ears off, do be
quick!

SCROPE: I refuse to move until you hear me!

BRADSHAW: (*Stares.*) What, then? What?
(*Pause.*)

SCROPE: You must not injure people in their faith.

BRADSHAW: Why not? What's so precious about faith?
Why can't it take a kicking like anything else? I do them a
favour. They get an education, and I get a wallet. Cheap at
the price, there is fuckall in it –

SCROPE: You swear, I hate to hear you –

BRADSHAW: Ask a rat about his faith!
(*She starts to go.*)

SCROPE: Wait!

BRADSHAW: Scrope, your ears!

SCROPE: A man may be beaten, and his wife violated,
and his house burned, and his children murdered by his
enemies, and yet stay whole. But to be so treated by his
friends...you encourage madness.

BRADSHAW: I DO KNOW THAT. Do you think I found it easy?
It wasn't easy. But that's my triumph. Any fool can rob his
enemy. Where's the victory in that?

SCROPE: Mr. Bradshaw would suffer if he could see this...

BRADSHAW: It's a long time since he lost his eyes, if he ever
had any. What colour were they? I forget...
(*SCROPE begins to sob.*)
Oh, Scrope, you are a wet little sparrow of a man...

FEAK: (*Off, distantly.*) OI!

SCROPE: (*Grabbing his satchel.*) Oh, Christ!

BRADSHAW: Oh, Scrope, the argument...

FEAK: OI!

BRADSHAW: (*Grinning as he tears offstage.*) What about the
argument?

INTERLUDE

The vaults of the Bank of England. GAUKROGER beats a staff.
HAMBRO appears.

GAUKROGER: Oh – King – Charles – our – rightful – chief!

HAMBRO: I am the Governor.

GAUKROGER: I am the Officer.

HAMBRO: Give me the keys.

GAUKROGER: What is the password?

HAMBRO: The password is orange.

GAUKROGER: (*Holds out a bunch of keys.*) God save the monarch!

HAMBRO: His honour and his might!

    (*GAUKROGER marches out.*)

    Where are you, Frank?

    (*He jangles the keys.*)

    Oh, don't be a silly bugger.

MOBBERLEY: (*From hiding.*) 'is honour and 'is might…

HAMBRO: Quite.

MOBBERLEY: 'is bollocks and 'is conk…

HAMBRO: Very funny. Now, when you're ready, perhaps you'd help me get a table out.

MOBBERLEY: (*Stepping out the darkness.*) Gimme the keys…

HAMBRO: Because I'm not doing this all by myself…

MOBBERLEY: Give us 'em.

HAMBRO: (*Shifting a table.*) Frank, you are supposed to be the Minister for Public Works, I wish you'd –

MOBBERLEY: I WANNA LOOK AT ME GOLD.

HAMBRO: You can't. Bring over those chairs.

MOBBERLEY: SHOW US ME GOLD.

HAMBRO: I keep trying to explain to you, it is not your gold, it's everybody's gold.

MOBBERLEY: I WANNA SEE MY BIT, THEN.

HAMBRO: (*Pausing.*) Frank, one of these days you will have to come to grips with the principles of banking –

MOBBERLEY: (*Snatching the keys.*) GOT 'EM! HA, HA! GOT 'EM!

HAMBRO: Sooner or later focus the great beams of your intellect on the mobility of money –

(*He attempts to recover the keys.*)

GIVE THEM BACK.

MOBBERLEY: I DON'T TRUST YER!

HAMBRO: This is precisely why we have a bank.

(*Pause. MOBBERLEY leans on the table.*)

MOBBERLEY: Billy, I am a brickman with paws so clumsy I can 'ardly scratch my name. All the juice in the royal 'ores' cunts will never make my fingers soft. I 'ad one kiln I fired with my own furniture, an' one cart, which when the army took the 'orse off me, I stood in the shafts myself. I now 'ave fifty carts an' fifty drivers, an' there ain't one night my wagon lights ain't bumpin' down the London road, come snow or flood. Show us me gold and don't fog my 'ead with science.

(*He goes off to the vault. A man enters.*)

PARRY: I said velvet. Velvet, I said. Velvet, you silly arse. He thought the word was orange. I don't know about orange, I said, I only know velvet.

HAMBRO: (*Laying out glasses.*) Velvet was last night.

PARRY: I will talk to Coldstream about his fucking guards. If he thought it was orange why did he let me in?

UNDY: (*Entering.*) Oh, I love this place! I do love this place! I love its columns and its architraves, I love its Greekness! I could have been Romulus or Remus coming up them steps…

PARRY: They weren't Greeks, Ralph, they was Romans.

UNDY: The guard says 'what's the password?' Velvet, says I. No, he says, not velvet. It is fucking velvet, says I, if it's not velvet, what is it? Orange, he says –

PARRY: We have just been through this, Ralph.

UNDY: Oh, you have, have you?

PARRY: Where's Frank?

HAMBRO: Frank is in the vault.

PARRY: In the vault?

HAMBRO: He wants to – feel the ingots.

PARRY: Feel the ingots?

HAMBRO: Yes.

PARRY: FEEL THE INGOTS?

HAMBRO: That's what I said. I do think someone's got to talk to Frank.

UNDY: This is a palace you got here, Billy. The King will never have a better.

HAMBRO: No. He can't afford it, can he?

PARRY: Not on what we give him.

STREET/MONCRIEFF: (*Entering.*) Are we late?

HAMBRO: Marginally.

STREET: I cannot stay late. I am in a slight hurry.

HAMBRO: We don't have much to discuss that concerns the Navy.

UNDY: What slight hurry is this, Stan? We have not met for three weeks, have we?

STREET: A masque in Putney.

UNDY: (*Disbelief.*) A masque in Putney?

STREET: My wife is expecting me.

UNDY: His wife is expecting him. Well, if his wife is expecting him, what's it matter we have not met in three weeks?

STREET: Don't be silly, Ralph.

UNDY: I'm surprised he could make it at all, what with his wife expecting him.

HAMBRO: Ralph…

UNDY: A most commanding lady is Joanna…

PARRY: Are we ready for the oath?

UNDY: We govern, and are governed in our turn, it seems, all our conference must hang on Stanley's wife. Does she know she governs the country, Stanley, may I ask?

HAMBRO: Ralph.

UNDY: I thought we had got rid of absolute monarchy, but no, there is Stanley's wife more terrible than Louis le whatsname or the Tsar, kicking her heels in Putney, Christ help us –

PARRY: THE OATH, RALPH!

UNDY: Ludicrous.

HAMBRO: Please.

UNDY: It is.

(*They stand round the table, join hands over a bottle.*)

MONCRIEFF: Mobberley's not here.

PARRY: Fuck.

HAMBRO: F–R–A–N–K!

STREET: Leave him out of the oath.

UNDY: Can't.

HAMBRO: This once.

UNDY: Can't.

PARRY: As Stan's in a rush. Agreed?

UNDY: Bloody hell.

ALL: Agreed.

HAMBRO: Ralph?

UNDY: Stan's wife commandeth.

HAMBRO: Go on, then, Bob.

PARRY: (*Reciting the oath.*) To those whom God grants power grant honour, equity and conscience too –

ALL: Semper fidelis, Semper honorabilis, Semper, Semper –

UNDY: Oh, Christ, what has Frank –

ALL: Semper, Semper –

MOBBERLEY: (*Dragging some gold bars on a small trolley.*) GOT A BIT OF ENGLAND, SIR!

PARRY: Oh, put it back, Frank –

MOBBERLEY: (*Picking up a bar.*) In my grubby paw got boys and girls –

HAMBRO: Just give us the keys –

MOBBERLEY: GOT WOODS AND FIELDS AND SHOPS AND RIVERS –

HAMBRO: Put them on the table, there's a good –

MOBBERLEY: AN' FISH AN' FENCES, GARDENS, CRADLES, VIRGINS, COTS!

HAMBRO: Frank, I am the Governor of this place!

MONCRIEFF: Leave him.

MOBBERLEY: Leave me, Billy. I am hanging on to MY BIT.

(*He sits at the empty chair.*)

Did I miss anything?

UNDY: You missed the oath.

MOBBERLEY: (*Putting the gold bar on his lap.*) Fuck the oath.

(*He turns to his neighbour.*)

I am keeping my gold indoors.

PARRY: You can't

MOBBERLEY: 'ho says so?

47

PARRY: You can't because we lend it to people.

MOBBERLEY: I don't wanna lend it.

STREET: You've got to. It's the system.

MOBBERLEY: Whose system? Not my system!

UNDY: I thought Frank was *au fait* with economics.

HAMBRO: No…

UNDY: Frank, I thought we had a civil war to get this straight. I spent four years on horseback chasing over garden fences to sort this out. Four years! And now you want to take your gold home and rip up the floorboards. I HAVE A WOUND FIVE INCHES LONG IN MY GROIN SAYS ENGLAND'S GOT TO HAVE A BANK!

(*Pause. MOBBERLEY looks confused.*)

MOBBERLEY: I keep getting bits of paper.

HAMBRO: They are not bits of paper, they are credit notes…

MOBBERLEY: It's still paper, ain't it?

HAMBRO: IT'S GOT MY SIGNATURE ON!

UNDY: All right, Billy.

STREET: I'm in a slight hurry, if you remember, so may I suggest –

MONCRIEFF: (*Paternally.*) Hang aboot, hang aboot, will ye? Take your mind back to before the war. You may remember, before the war, the King told us to pay him money. Ordered us to, ye cud na argue with it. But we did na want to pay him money, so we had the war, all right? Now, we have a new King, an' he still wants money. He has to ha' the money from somewhere, it stands ta reason. But noo, instead o' givin' it to him, we lend it to him instead. Are ye clear on that, Frank? An' ye canna lend money if it's under the bed.

(*He smiles.*)

Now, goo an' put it back in the vaults, and when ye wanna see it, ye can see it, can't he, Billy, he can coom and look at his stuff. That's noo a lot to ask, is it?

HAMBRO: I suppose not.

MONCRIEFF: Of course he can. Okay?

(*Pause.*)

MOBBERLEY: Sorry, I am being dense.

48

MONCRIEFF: Noo, noo, not at all. It's a complicated subject. Off ye goo.

(*MOBBERLEY gets up, tows his trolley away.*)

STREET: Now, can we get down to business?

(*HAMBRO rises to his feet.*)

HAMBRO: I want to stop the terror.

PARRY: Why?

HAMBRO: Well, why not?

UNDY: Yes, why not, Bob? I think we've had enough of randy cavaliers knocking the eyeballs out of puritans. It's all right for a fortnight, but I had a Dutchman lose an ear last week and he was here to place a contract.

PARRY: They must have their fling.

UNDY: I think they've had it. Christ, all the republicans are still in hiding.

PARRY: No. Let 'em rampage a while yet, or they will turn their attention elsewhere. Let 'em beat the communists, and the pamphlet writers and the free love and the Christ-on-earth mob, let 'em carve the King's initials on their arses.

UNDY: I would be perfectly happy for that, but they are getting indiscriminate.

HAMBRO: They are getting out of hand, Bob.

PARRY: They are meant to be out of hand, they are cavaliers, aren't they? They have been rotting in foreign brothels for ten years, they are bound to be out of hand.

UNDY: They are blinding my customers.

PARRY: All right, and what do you intend to do with them?

HAMBRO: Enlist them in a regiment. Give them a uniform with lots of tassel and gold facing. Call them The King's Own and send them on an expedition from which they won't come back.

PARRY: They are too old for expeditions. They are antiquated thugs who lost their estates for monarchy and if we don't let 'em rollock they will sit about on doorsteps and start to think –

UNDY: What with, Bob?

PARRY: And they will think –

UNDY: What with, exactly?

PARRY: With what is left of their brains –

UNDY: Never had any –

PARRY: Whatever happened to their little estates, and they will look around and they will see who has 'em –

UNDY: Never –

PARRY: And it will be us –

UNDY: Oh, bollocks, Bob –

PARRY: And we will be in deep shit I tell you.

HAMBRO: Bob, you are governing England now. I do think, when a man is governing England, he oughtn't to shudder so much.

UNDY: 'ear, 'ear!

HAMBRO: No one will undo the settlement. Let them rot in taverns and piss their grievances down the sink.

UNDY: 'ear, 'ear!

STREET: Shall we vote?

UNDY: Why not? Stan's in a hurry, mustn't forget.

HAMBRO: Those in favour of calling them off?

(*A majority of hands are raised.*)

It's off.

CHARLES: (*Off.*) ORANGE, HE QUOTH!

UNDY: (*Jumping up.*) Fuck, it's the mad shagman!

HAMBRO: (*Clearing the desk.*) Look casual!

MOBBERLEY (*Entering.*) I put 'em back –

UNDY: Siddown!

HAMBRO: It's a drink – it's only a drink!

CHARLES: (*Entering.*) NOT ENTER MY BANK!

GAUKROGER: (*Entering abjectly.*) Did not know you, sir!

CHARLES: Did not know me! And have I not the conk? The conk which goes before me crying MONARCH? Orange or velvet, here's the conk!

(*He thrusts his face at GAUKROGER, catches sight of the bankers.*)

Oh, there's a do! There's a do in my bank!

HAMBRO: (*Bowing.*) Sir, a glass?

NODD (*Entering.*) 'ullo, Billy, workin' late?

CHARLES: An' Undy, an' Mobb'ley, what's this?

GWYNN: (*Entering.*) Men only.

CHARLES: Come to show Nelly me bank, an' there's a beano!

HAMBRO: A seat, madam?

GWYNN: No, give us the keys.

CHARLES: (*Peering.*) An' Parry! Well, fuck me, what's this?

PARRY: Well, we meet…

CHARLES: Oh, yer meet, do yer? An' who's that?

NODD: Dunno, 'ho is it?

(*STREET bows.*)

CHARLES: Oh, Stanley, you too?

NODD: 'ho is 'e? Somethin' legal ain't 'e?

CHARLES: Something legal, he says. He is Chief Justice, yer ass. Well, I'm buggered at this…

(*He sits in a chair.*)

GWYNN: Where's the gold, Charlie?

CHARLES: Give her the keys.

HAMBRO: (*Taking them off the table.*) There are three doors to the vault, each one with an eight-lever lock –

CHARLES: Don't blind her with science, she is after rubbing her bosoms over the bricks.

GWYNN: (*Taking the keys.*) Can I 'ave one?

HAMBRO: Can you have one?

GWYNN: A gold brick.

(*Pause. She looks at CHARLES.*)

NODD: Go on, give 'er one.

(*Pause.*)

HAMBRO: I should like nothing more, only –

NODD: No, no, stuff all that. Give 'er one.

HAMBRO: It isn't that simple.

CHARLES: Why ain't it?

HAMBRO: Each brick represents –

CHARLES: Represents what?

HAMBRO: The accumulation of other men's wealth.

NODD: Well, that's why she wants it. She ain't a nana. Give 'er one, then.

(*HAMBRO looks resolutely at the floor.*)

GWYNN: Oh, Charlie, 'e don't want to!

(*He looks at him.*)

Ain't you mean, when you got such a lot?

NODD: Take it. G'arn take it.

(*Pause. CHARLES gets up.*)

CHARLES: I may not. Do you see. Noddy? I may not.

NODD: (*To GAUKROGER.*) Oi, you! You git down there an'
bring us a brick!

(*GAUKROGER looks at HAMBRO.*)

Look smart, then!

(*He doesn't move.*)

CHARLES: No, I may not...

(*He moves away.*)

NODD: Oh, you crew of fuckers –

CHARLES: Nodd –

NODD: What's yer racket, eh? Down 'ere in the dead a' night,
what is it?

CHARLES: Nodd –

NODD: It's a conspiracy, ain't it? When two or three are
gathered together, charge 'em, it's treason an' you know
it –

CHARLES: Nodd, you will make enemies of powerful men –

NODD: Fucked if I care –

CHARLES: I can't save you. Even my dad – my dad who was
absolute and had God sitting in his eyeballs – could not
save his pals, his bumloves and his vicars – they look at
you so darkly, Nodd, take a warning from their looks!

(*He goes up to them mockingly.*)

Oh, do not hurt my Noddy, he is a slumboy, all cock and
prattle, do not murder him, you will make all Southwark
weep...

UNDY: His Majesty has had a long evening...

CHARLES: He thinks I'm tired –

UNDY: Perhaps a carriage –

CHARLES: No, Ralph, you are too kind, you are too
generous, he offers me a carriage, such a nice, nice man...
I do like Ralph...

(*He turns to go, stops.*)

What are you doing here?

(*They are silent.*)

Well, I can't bring charges, the chief lawyer's here himself!

NODD: Turn the mob out!

CHARLES: The mob – the mob – his touching adulation of the mob –

NODD: My mates –

CHARLES: Oh, Christ, spare us your mates –

NODD: Give over–

CHARLES: He thinks to terrorize you with his mates, the legion of the half cut, don't it touch you, Ralph, with its naivety?

NODD: All right, fuck yourself –

CHARLES: Mobs, no, SHOW 'EM THE LOOK THAT STOPS THEIR HEARTS!

(*He leans on the table, intimately.*)

You will like this, I know you will, and you Billy, you will love this –

(*He turns to NODD, who is feeling in a bag.*)

HURRY UP, WE'RE WAITING! Give it to Nell, she can handle flesh, Nell, show the gentlemen the way you kiss, there is no kissing like her, you would think all the kissin' I done there was nothing left to be discovered, but there is, there is!

(*GWYNN takes the head of BRADSHAW from NODD and holding it in both hands, kisses the mouth.*)

Watch her lip now! Can yer see, Ralph? Do come nearer, and you Mobberley, she has a kiss as long as the coast, oh, she makes yer faint, she does!

(*He goes close to HAMBRO.*)

Was he ever done like that, I ask yer, Billy, was he, do yer think?

HAMBRO: I don't know who kissed him.

CHARLES: Oh, Billy don't remember who lipped him, Robert, you would know!

(*PARRY shakes his head.*)

Nobody? And you were peas once in the pod of the Republic! Oh, look at his one eye, the single eyeball does look sad to be rejected, his one eye that says LONG COLD NIGHTS OF SERIOUS THOUGHT. Scaring, ain't it, Mobb'ley. THE MAN WHO THINKS US TO DEATH! Show Ralph!

UNDY: (*As GWYNN moves near him.*) 'ullo, Dick, 'ow are yer?

CHARLES: Oh, now, wit! Ralph's mordant wit! Look him in the eye, Ralph, the eye please, fix it…
UNDY: (*Looking.*) Been having late nights again, old son…
CHARLES: NO, LOOK AT HIM!
UNDY: I am looking at him.
CHARLES: I hear he never slept.
UNDY: Well, you can see that.
CHARLES: But worked all nights.
UNDY: So they tell me.
CHARLES: Planning new commonwealths.
UNDY: Very likely…
CHARLES: Ever more common. Ever less wealthy.
UNDY: He 'ad some funny ideas…
CHARLES: Writing constitutions in the starry night, while moths struck the window…
UNDY: Quite…
CHARLES: While the rain lashed, plotted the extinction of private property…
UNDY: Wouldn't put it past 'im…
CHARLES: PLOTTED THE EXTINCTION OF YOU, RALPH!
(*He leans closer, quoting from the 'Harmonia Britannia'.*)
'And there were some called rich, who gathered to themselves the labour and the inventiveness of others, and kept them brutally in place, but these were like a nightmare or bad memory, for in Harmonia there was neither gold nor money, but such things were laughed at as a superstition and a dead weight in the pocket…'
There, I know my Bradshaw, banned book but I got him in my library…
(*He tilts the head up and down.*)
Word perfect, ain't I? Yes, he says…
(*He tosses the head to NODD.*)
Stick him back in the bag, he makes their bowels go loose, or Ralph all witty, which is the same thing, same stink, ain't it? Nell, wish the gents goodnight…
GWYNN: Ta ta –
HAMBRO: (*Arising, bowing.*) Sire, good night –
CHARLES: Down poodles, down spaniels!
NODD: Woof, woof!

GWYNN: Ol' buggers, aincha?

CHARLES: (*To GAUKROGER.*) Orange or velvet?

GAUKROGER: Whatever you say, Sire –

CHARLES: Oh, you are too accommodating! And me only a monarch too!

(*They go out. HAMBRO etc. remain standing, silently. Pause.*)

UNDY: Billy…

HAMBRO: I know…

UNDY: No, let me say this –

HAMBRO: I know what you're going to say –

UNDY: I still wanna say it –

HAMBRO: If you must –

UNDY: I must. WHY IN CHRIST'S NAME DID WE BRING THAT BACK?

PARRY: Have a drink, Ralph –

UNDY: Fuck the drink –

PARRY: (*Offering MONCRIEFF.*) Andrew?

UNDY: WHY!

HAMBRO: I think you know why.

UNDY: OUT – FUCKING – RAGEOUS!

STREET: Sit down, Ralph…

UNDY: IMPERT – INENCE!

HAMBRO: Ralph, he knows. And that is all that matters.

UNDY: I got my pride!

HAMBRO: HE KNOWS.

(*Pause.*)

The rest is shrill and squealing. Never mind the squeal. I don't.

ACT TWO

SCENE ONE

Beside the Thames in Essex.

DEVONSHIRE, in a cloak, looks out. At a distance, a FOOTMAN.

DEVONSHIRE: I do feel clean here. I do feel clean. The wind off the estuary. The cockle-women shouting I can't hear. And the low cloud racing, and the grey flat water, the thin surf on the mudbank, really it is better than a marine landscape by Mr Van Oots and in any case I don't think I like sex.
(*Pause. She breathes.*)
Oh, this is pure, this is absolute life, I never felt so whole and so completely independent, this is the third letter in a week begging me back and in verse too! All very flattering but really it is pure dick, a woman should never forget a poem is actually dick, should she? I don't believe before Mr Van Oots anyone went near a beach, you can't smell the seaweed in a painting, can you?

FOOTMAN: OI, GET BACK!

BEGGARS: (*Throwing themselves before her.*) Alms, miss!

DEVONSHIRE: Or the beggars, for that matter…

FOOTMAN: (*Wading in among them.*) FUCK OFF!

DEVONSHIRE: You are in pain, I know you are, you don't have to tell me, and I tell you that I am too! Does that sound callous?
(*They look at her. She goes towards them.*)
To look at me you'd think she knows no pain, now, wouldn't you? I'm sure you say that, privately. Admit you say that.

BEGGARS: No –

DEVONSHIRE: Oh, you do, you do! Her lovely this, her lovely that, compared to us in our rags and shanties, you do, of course you do, you think I have no agonies. But there are pains and pains, aren't there?

(*They look blank.*)

No?

(*They look blank.*)

Pains of the mind?

BRADSHAW: Yes.

DEVONSHIRE: Somebody knows! And they are, if anything, worse than the pains of hunger or whatever you are on about, because there is no cure. No, no cure! I have a pain like that. Believe me. Now, hurry off before Sam gets awful –

(*She dips in a purse and throws small change about.*)

...and think of me sometimes, and see the pain is not all on your side, mm?

FOOTMAN: All right, scarper!

BRADSHAW: (*Not moving.*) Tell you about your pain.

FOOTMAN: Fuck off, I said –

BRADSHAW: Go on, let me –

FOOTMAN: (*To her face.*) OI!

DEVONSHIRE: (*Turning away.*) Don't kick her. I don't own the beach.

FOOTMAN: Above the tidemark –

DEVONSHIRE: Oh, sod that –

(*Pause. FOOTMAN stands away.*)

BRADSHAW: All my knowledge. Give it to you. All my life.

DEVONSHIRE: Why?

BRADSHAW: Because you're shallow.

DEVONSHIRE: Oh, I am, am I?

BRADSHAW: And a bit cruel with it.

DEVONSHIRE: Do watch it dear, Sam will kick you in the head.

BRADSHAW: Yes.

(*Pause.*)

DEVONSHIRE: This is my beach and so is everything else that you can see. I am twenty-four and have miscarried seven times. That is wicked, isn't it, of God? Have you miscarried?

BRADSHAW: Yes.

DEVONSHIRE: It is particularly cruel because I care for men. Last week I thought the floor of my body was being bitten out, by rats, by dogs, I thought my whole floor going, have you had that?

BRADSHAW: Yes.

DEVONSHIRE: I cannot keep a child in, absolutely cannot, yet I conceive from a look, what is the matter with God, my womb is only fit for a nun, or is He trying to tell me to be a nun, is that His way, do you think? I will die from one of these drops. I would keep away from dick if I could, but you cannot be as good as I am, looking as I do, and keep away from them, can you? I am trying to appreciate views instead, but he writes so beautifully, my rump, my rump, he goes on about, keeps him awake at nights, my whispering hair and so on, I go back tonight, I know all poems are dick but I go back, I will die of him, it is silly but he makes me feel alive. What's your advice? I believe in asking strangers for advice, you cannot trust your friends. I believe in essence all your friends wish you dead. Say yes or no.

BRADSHAW: Yes.

DEVONSHIRE: (*Turning on her.*) You only want to get me killed!

(*Pause.*)

Really, what kind of advice is that? Forty years old, are you, and you say one syllable. Get off my beach. Sam…

(*She goes to leave.*)

BRADSHAW: HOW DARE YOU TURN YOUR BACK, I HAVE GIVEN YOU THE EDUCATION OF A LIFETIME!

DEVONSHIRE: All you said was yes.

BRADSHAW: Yes was all you asked for.

DEVONSHIRE: I'm not to be taken literally.

BRADSHAW: I will tell you what yes means, shall I?

(*Pause.*)

Shall I?

DEVONSHIRE: Go on.

BRADSHAW: Yes means no resistance. Yes means going with the current. Yes means lying down when it rains and standing up when it's sunny. Yes urge. Yes womb. Yes power. I lived with a man whose no was in the middle of his heart, whose no kept him thin as a bone and stole the juices from him. No is pain and yes is pleasure, no is man and yes is nature. Yes is old age and no is early death. Yes is laughter, no is torture. I hate no. No is misery and lonely nights. Do you follow or shall I say it again?

(*Pause. Then DEVONSHIRE unclasps her cloak and lays it over BRADSHAW's shoulders.*)

DEVONSHIRE: Take all the cockles off the beach.

(*She turns to go.*)

BRADSHAW: Let me be your servant.

DEVONSHIRE: I don't need a servant.

BRADSHAW: (*Crawling to her feet.*) I will give you service of my life's blood though you are the worst bitch in the kingdom and pay me never. Employ me. I'll turn the kitchen spit with my teeth.

DEVONSHIRE: And you think me shallow?

BRADSHAW: Perfection.

(*Pause. She looks at FOOTMAN, who shakes his head. She smiles.*)

DEVONSHIRE: I live in Blackfriars.

(*She goes out, followed by FOOTMAN, who is barely offstage when he turns and runs back.*)

FOOTMAN: Yor're no skivvy! I seen you! All you old republicans, six months ago you wouldn't call no geezer master, now look at yer! I'M THE TRUE SKIVVY! YOU WILL KILL THE TRADE YOU BLEEDERS! Coming!

(*He runs off again. BRADSHAW is on her knees when SCROPE enters.*)

SCROPE: I do not, of the obscene career I've witnessed, care to specify which gave me the most horror, watching old women cheated from behind a bush, or in this instance tucked behind a dune, seeing you fondling the foot of the most callous whore to flounce in daft courts. TAKE OFF THAT PURPLE BADGE OF SHAME, PLEASE... I do believe I saw Mr Bradshaw thin and gaunt with pain creep over the water...his kind eyes in the candlelight while we planned constitutions and just wars...

BRADSHAW: Have a cockle...

SCROPE: I believe no woman came nearer to touching
    saintliness than you and you – do not eat with your mouth
    open, I do hate that doglike manner!

BRADSHAW: (*Opening the cloak.*) Come under with me,
    there's a cruel wind off the water…

SCROPE: I was thinking today just where his greatness lay,
    and it lay in this, that nothing was ever set firmly in his
    mind, but he would challenge every thought and beat it
    round his head like a bear set on by dogs, stagger it from
    corner into corner, was it good, was it proper, the bloody
    bear pit of his mind!
    (*He sits beside BRADSHAW. She covers him.*)
    And me…it is my misfortune to have served him, who
    blew out my little candle with his great light…when I
    might have written…might have… LOST MY CHANCE NOW!
    (*He begins to sob.*)

BRADSHAW: Oh, don't cry for Christ's sake –

SCROPE: I have to! I'm not ashamed of tears!

BRADSHAW: You only cry because you want to impress me.

SCROPE: Rubbish.

BRADSHAW: You do. To show how great your soul is. From
    now on I am banning crying. You've been snivelling on
    and off since Norwich.

SCROPE: I've not…!

BRADSHAW: A red eye in the wind, some wail coming out
    the hay at night. Tears are a rebuke, to man or nature.
    Protests, aren't they? I don't protest, and I'll be happy. See
    if I ever cry again.
    (*Suddenly BALL bursts out of cover, waving a sword.*)

BALL: You never paid your drink in Roxworth! Took the
    ale and scarpered! Oh, trail of scrounging and cruel little
    knocks, I AM ENTITLED TO PUNISH IN THE NAME OF THE
    STUART. GET OVER THERE YOU!

SCROPE: Oh God…!

BALL: OVER OR I CUT YER!
    (*SCROPE rolls into a ball, away from BRADSHAW.*)
    I have hunted you from your bed madam, from the smell
    of your sheets I have, show me your face, your thin, dry

lips, show me, you may not leave your domicile if you were of the rule of antichrist the Commonwealth, you broke the regulation, did you think I'd let my fancy go? I AM COME INTO MY RIGHTS!

(*He swings to SCROPE.*)

Stay there you ball of scrawn and bollock I AM THE GOVERNOR NOW!

(*He turns back to BRADSHAW.*)

Listen, I have been drinking and not paying either, but I may do 'cos I suffered, no publican gives me a cacky look I bust his lip for him, I have been drinking and I love you, stand up, it offends me to see a woman crouching, is he to do with you? What is he? Be my darling, I have a thing about you, you could be as rough as fifty hellbags, I still got a thing for you, I don't know what my passion's coming to, to be honest you are nothing to stare after, why am I fixed like this?

BRADSHAW: It happens.

BALL: Fuck, it does, and I shall love you on this shore, or stab you, I am that bewildered! Let me worship, God, your eyes are tired and yet full of secrets, I wrote you a poem, no, I tell a lie, I wrote thirty, thirty sonnets in one night, there is cavalier art for you, I was up to dawn and squinting by a candle in the guest-room of some inn, 'sir, your boots on the boards keep us awake' cries the publican, 'balls to your kip,' says I, 'I am creating, I am sonnet mad for Bradshaw!' Read this one, or shall I?

(*He takes a paper from his pocket.*)

This is the best, this is the cream, in the Italian manner, I should bawl it in palazzos but this stinking beach will do it, shall you read it or shall I?

BRADSHAW: You.

BALL: I am a poor reader –

BRADSHAW: Oh, don't say that –

BALL: All right –

(*He swings back to SCROPE.*)

DON'T SHIFT OR I'LL SPLIT YOUR LIVER!

(*He turns back.*)

It goes, I start – Christ, this beach stinks – I call it – 'A
Love Unexpected' – it is twelve lines in the Tuscan manner
– I DON'T THINK I CAN DO IT JUSTICE – notwithstanding
that, I – I – it –
(*He lets his hand droop.*)
I will fuck you or I shall go mad. You have given me hell
these last ten nights.

BRADSHAW: The poem.

BALL: No, no –

BRADSHAW: Perhaps I –

BALL: No, no, the poem, stuff it –
(*He thrusts it back in his pocket.*)
There is a hut over there, go into it –

BRADSHAW: You are going to force me –

BALL: Yes. Quick now.

BRADSHAW: I prefer you read the poem –

BALL: LOOK, I AM AN AGENT OF CHARLES STUART, ALL I DO IS
LEGAL, NAUGHT IS WRONG, SEE?
(*Pause.*)
I worship, I bring my poor love to the altar, over there out
the wind now…

BRADSHAW: God help me to do this…

BALL: He will, Christ knows you are perfect to me…
(*She seems to prepare herself, then goes out. BALL looks round
quickly, then follows her. SCROPE staring, quotes from the
'Harmonia Britannia'.*)

SCROPE: 'And there will be love betwixt man and woman
of a sort not known yet, founded on freedom of will and
desire, so that she shall not be hampered by false modesty
nor him by his cult manliness… '
(*He shudders with a paroxysm of impotent anger.*)
Oh, all you who come after, make your revolution right!
(*He takes the book from his pocket and flings it into the mud,
weeps. Pause. BALL returns.*)

BALL: It is a funny thing this, and I have never found it
otherwise, that I come off so miserable I could weep or
join a priesthood. I am off to fish in some pond, have an
awful need for some tranquility…
(*He goes a little way, stops, holds out the poem.*)

Will you give her this? I think love would be to come off
and be happy…

(*SCROPE takes the poem. BALL walks off. After a pause,
BRADSHAW returns, by a great effort of will she resumes exactly
the posture she occupied before his arrival. Pause.*)

BRADSHAW: You know, do you, for seven years Bradshaw
did not come near me?

SCROPE: How should I know?

BRADSHAW: Well, I tell you. Could not come near me
for the power of his thought, his nightmare. So I was
untouched.

SCROPE: Oh.

BRADSHAW: So this one licked me.

(*SCROPE turns away.*)

LICKED ME AND OPENED ME AGAIN.

(*Pause.*)

And I –

SCROPE: Go, shall we?

BRADSHAW: Felt sorry that he left me so depressed…

(*Long pause.*)

SCROPE: (*Bitterly.*) You seem – you take this – very – oh, I
don't know, cowlike, stand up to nothing now, but bend
down and so on, no tears or protest, wisdom of compliance
and so on, but – well, I –

(*He faces her.*)

Suppose I – what if I –

BRADSHAW: (*Seeing the direction.*) Scrope, I don't wish it –

SCROPE: Wish it? What's this wish it? What are wishes, what
are tears?

BRADSHAW: I don't –

SCROPE: You don't ? And how do you know I have not also
found you beautiful? What of my compulsion? I have slept
beside you on trestles and on bales in barns and never
once out of respect for him –

BRADSHAW: Him?

SCROPE: Him who was my master, yes, out of respect not
once lifted my hand to you, yet any coloured, drunken
royalist can take you and –

BRADSHAW: Oh, God…

SCROPE: And you regret he did not feel a pleasure! What of me, I have the same thing, don't I –

BRADSHAW: I saw you as a friend, I –

SCROPE: No friend, never! I am a man, too!
    (*Pause.*)

BRADSHAW: I could not keep him off. You I can easily push over…

SCROPE: WELL, WHERE'S THE JUSTICE IN THAT!

BRADSHAW: (*Standing up to go.*) Don't know the word…

SCROPE: (*Grabbing her roughly.*) Do it with me, now –

BRADSHAW: Look –

SCROPE: MUST! MUST!

BRADSHAW: You'll only hate me for it –

SCROPE: No –

BRADSHAW: What about your honour –

SCROPE: Never mind it –

BRADSHAW: You know what you'll be like, don't you, it'll be recrimination and –

SCROPE: NEVER MIND IT, I SAID, NEVER MIND!
    (*Pause. She turns to him. He buries his face in her breasts.*)
    Oh, my love, oh!

SCENE TWO

A garden in London. MILTON is staring blindly at a rose. CLEGG is watching him, with SCROPE.

CLEGG: I hide Mr Milton in my garden, though the penalty for concealing him is death, and me, who is court poet, double death of some description. I do this for literature, though I hate his views, though his politics offend me and his poetry upset my gut, I do it in case one day he writes a good thing in adversity. I am a very decent man, especially since I am so minor I will be forgotten quicker than my eyes melt into muck and no one prints my plays. I could happily denounce him out of envy, but I don't, Mr Milton always knew how to cultivate his enemies, didn't you, John, in case the Commonwealth collapsed? He doesn't

answer, but then he is chock-a-block with cunning. This is
Mr Scrope, who is educated, persecuted, and all the rest.
He won't answer yet.
(*Pause. They wander.*)
I am a King's man, and a property man, and a Bishops'
man, and everything John hates man, yet I hide him in
my roses, I do believe I am the best that England makes,
and have tolerance, which is more than John does. I am
the author of a tragedy, 'Mayhem in Attica', in which the
moral strength of the nation is shown to be inseparably
linked to its respect for property. I have shown this to
John, who says the Commonwealth was not opposed to
property, on the contrary, John has a little bit himself. It
is a fine play, but I warrant I will be unknown to posterity,
unlike John's stuff. I shall be buried in some obscure grave
and no one will traipse to visit me, I don't know why I save
him from execution, I must be mad, but you see I have my
envy under firm control, it was envy brought on the Civil
War, though John calls it justice, no, it was envy and it
could not last...

SCROPE: I'm afraid I am not acquainted with your work, Mr
Clegg...

CLEGG: What a surprise! He has not heard of me! You hear
that, John?

SCROPE: I have heard of you –

CLEGG: He *has* heard of me! Well, more surprising still, I
am heard of! Forget the name, don't waste a useful space
inside your memory for such a mediocre talent, there is Mr
Milton there –

SCROPE: Of course I know Mr Milton –

CLEGG: Oh, you do, do you? Well, fancy, heard of Mr
Milton, John, your luck is in! How well do you know my
plays?

SCROPE: I am not a play-going man –

CLEGG: Well, no surprise, there has been a slight dearth
of theatre the last twenty years! You shall see 'Mayhem
in Attica', I have been promised a production, I cannot

say when, but the promise is there, for what a promise is worth, not a lot in the theatre, I assure you, but it exists.
(*He grins at SCROPE.*)
No, I tease you, don't waste your time on a man whose statue there is no subscription for, dogs will shit on my grave and lovers grapple on it, and none will say 'Here lies Clegg who spared Milton and had a mediocre talent.' No, stay at home and read John. Do you care for roses?

SCROPE: Yes.

CLEGG: I hope I shall not be sent any more of you atheistic wretches to shelter, I am a King's man after all and fought your lot at Worcester, cut a man's arm off and nearly fainted, where were you?

SCROPE: I was at no battles.

CLEGG: No more was John, but then you do well with a pamphlet, do you?

SCROPE: I was Secretary to the Council...

CLEGG: Oh, and took down all their evil in a book! I have a garden full of enemies! Am I not the best of men? I dread to think the boot were on the other foot, you would put my eyes out. Want a cordial, John? Look, I wait on him and yet I hate his views.
(*He goes out to fetch drinks. SCROPE nervously advances to MILTON, stops, hesitates.*)

SCROPE: I wonder, sir, if you feel able to elucidate us...as to the failure of our struggle...
(*He ignores this.*)
The errors in our calculation and –

MILTON: Shit and God.
(*Pause.*)

SCROPE: Yes?

MILTON: Man.

SCROPE: Yes?

MILTON: SHIT AND GOD.
(*BRADSHAW enters.*)

BRADSHAW: I had forgot the peeing you do with a child –

SCROPE: Shh!

BRADSHAW: What?

SCROPE: This is Milton.

BRADSHAW: Don't he know a woman pisses?

SCROPE: NO, HE DOESN'T. PLEASE SHUT UP.

BRADSHAW: He must do, didn't he go to bed with one?

SCROPE: I BEG YOU DON'T EMBARRASS ME.

(*Pause. She goes to MILTON, who has not moved.*)

BRADSHAW: I had a husband sat by you, and hatched
a thing or two together, 'De Rerum Magisterium' or
something, you would know Latin, on our lawn one
summer, side by side in deckchairs with cloud scudding
over Suffolk, in the sunshine writing revolution, now I kip
in barns or gutters, there's a turn-up for you, your name
is a good excuse for knifing and my old man's hanging on
Blackfriars, oh, don't look so tragic, you are all right, they
don't kill poets –

SCROPE: Our primary task must be – in my estimation – the
examination of our errors –

BRADSHAW: Bradshaw left his bed in dead of night – did
you do this – grappling for a pencil – mutter, mutter
– kicks the pisspot over – wakes the house –

SCROPE: All is not wasted if error can be the educator of the
future –

BRADSHAW: Night after night this – I said for all the warmth
you bring, you might sleep in your study – and dropped
his linen everywhere – are you like that – found items of
his underwear on stairs – shitty drawers he could not bring
himself to part with –

SCROPE: This is not true –

BRADSHAW: And scratching! You never saw a barmy cat
more vicious with itself, could bleed sometimes from some
raw eczema itch – here – behind the ear – look – mad
fingers – ARE YOU WATCHING!

SCROPE: THIS IS JOHN MILTON, YOU BITCH.

(*Pause. She looks at MILTON.*)

BRADSHAW: Put your fingers on me. Read my face. I'm not
the woman I was, am I? Tell me I'm not!

(*He does not move.*)

Thank you.

(*Pause. She looks at him.*)

I do think it's impossible to respect a genius when he's out of luck. I do. I quailed before you once, couldn't bring myself to speak – not that Bradshaw wanted me to, did he – just cart the sandwiches this way and that – but really, you made me tremble, and now you move me so little I could –

(*With a sudden inspiration, she slaps his face.*)

MILTON: AAAGGGHHH!

CLEGG: (*Returning with a tray.*) Oh, don't do that…

MILTON: AAAGGGHHH!

SCROPE: (*To BRADSHAW.*) I HATE YOU FOR THAT!

BRADSHAW: (*In delight.*) No, look –

SCROPE: HATE YOU FOR THAT!

BRADSHAW: See what I did!

SCROPE: UGLY! UGLY!

MILTON: AAAGGGHHH!

CLEGG: I always said, you need not fight the rebels, just lock them in a chamber and they will die of arguing within a week –

SCROPE: UGLY! UGLY!

CLEGG: Have a cordial…

BRADSHAW: (*Going to MILTON.*) Oh, don't cry. I didn't hurt you –

SCROPE: HURT SHE SAYS!

BRADSHAW: (*Turning to him.*) I didn't!

(*And to MILTON.*) Listen, if you knew how it mattered I could do that! You don't, do you? You have no idea! I feel so grateful I could slap you again!

(*To SCROPE.*) DON'T WORRY I SHAN'T!

(*To MILTON.*) Try to understand me. I have broken myself into pieces to do this…

MILTON: I do not like women.

BRADSHAW: No, of course…

(*Pause. She looks at CLEGG.*)

Find Scrope some little task. He will copy out your Latin, and feel his honour is all safe. And when the shout dies down, get him in some college –

SCROPE: DO NOT DARE TO INTERCEDE FOR ME!

(*Pause. She turns to him.*)

BRADSHAW: Good bye.

(*She holds out a hand.*)

SCROPE: I will not shake your hand.

BRADSHAW: (*Fondly.*) Oh, my little lover –

SCROPE: DO NOT SAY THAT, PLEASE!

(*Pause. She goes out.*)

MILTON: She slapped my face because her heart is broken. I find that comprehensible. When the war is won, wage war on the victors. Every civil war must be the parent of another. Those given laurels praise then execute. And their executioners, when the time comes, execute them too. Any amount of war a man will take, will acquiesce in his own destruction even, provided that he knows the change takes place. That is the God in him. But if after the first war, you only heap praise on the victors, they will make themselves your masters, even ape the first oppressor and invite him back. Any amount of power a man will take, provided we permit it. That is the shit in him. Next time, should we start there must be no finish, or we shall slap one another's faces in the gardens of our enemies...

SCENE THREE

A gate in Blackfriars. BRADSHAW is looking up at something black and shapeless on a spike. Long pause. She conquers herself.

BRADSHAW: I was deceived. Bradshaw was an African. I never stripped in daylight, nor him either. How was I to know he was an African? NO WONDER WE HAD REVOLUTION, THE MOORS HAD GOT INTO OUR BEDS. I can't think why there's flesh on it, the birds here are so finicky. WHAT'S THE MATTER, ISN'T THE MEAT GOOD ENOUGH FOR YOU?

(*A soldier appears.*)

THAT IS PERFECTLY GOOD MAN, YOU FUSSY BUGGERS!

SHADE: Now, then.

BRADSHAW: Why is he black?

SHADE: Sunshine, ain't it?

BRADSHAW: It's a bit well done for me, but never mind. I can find a use for it, get it down, ducks.

SHADE: You wouldn't be the fuss to ask...

BRADSHAW: Well no, there is a wicked shortage of cagmag, isn't there? People will use anything to make a stew. And they call this a restoration! A restoration of what, starvation? WHO SAID THAT!

(*She pretends to look behind her.*)

Come on, give us it, he was my husband.

SHADE: And I'm Father Christmas.

BRADSHAW: What do you expect, the cock to rise? Look, I have the other quarters in the bag –

(*She opens a large bag.*)

SHADE: Oh, fuckin' 'ell...

BRADSHAW: Nip up and get it, there's a love. They were so good to me at Moorgate, they even wrapped it up, like butchers –

SHADE: (*Moving her on.*) Come on, darling, get along –

BRADSHAW: Don't hustle me –

SHADE: Move, then –

BRADSHAW: Who owns the pavement –

SHADE: I do –

BRADSHAW: Get it for me – listen – WHO ARE YOU SHOVING – WILL SOMEBODY WITNESS THIS!

SHADE: You barmy bitch –

BRADSHAW: SOMEBODY WITNESS THIS –

(*She is pushed to the ground. The SOLDIER walks off. BRADSHAW remains on her knees. DEVONSHIRE appears, with the FOOTMAN. She looks at her.*)

DEVONSHIRE: I was shagged. You were shagged. I am pregnant. You are pregnant. I do not know the father, and I warrant, no more do you. It is a shambles being a woman. I would chuck it all up if I met a doctor who could do the trick.

(*She starts to go.*)

BRADSHAW: Use me.

DEVONSHIRE: How, dear? I have no need of a skivy.

BRADSHAW: I have a lifetime's cunning.

DEVONSHIRE: You were not cunning enough to keep someone's cock out of your purse.

BRADSHAW: Give me one month as your housekeeper, and I will save you my wages by cutting the rest.

DEVONSHIRE: You could not pay them less than me. They'd scarper.

BRADSHAW: People will always go beyond the point they say they stick at. I will bring you change on payday, watch.

DEVONSHIRE: You are certainly persistent.

BRADSHAW: I will manage servants as only one who's grovelled knows how to. A duchess really has no idea how to use a servant. Even her blows are full of charity. Trust me.

(*Pause. DEVONSHIRE scrutinizes her.*)

DEVONSHIRE: If you give birth I will not have it on the premises. I hate the sound, you see.

BRADSHAW: If I'm lucky it'll die.

DEVONSHIRE: And take you with it, darling.

BRADSHAW: Chuck me on the dungheap if it do.

DEVONSHIRE: You have what I most appreciate in servants, a complete lack of self esteem. Follow us, and when we reach home, kick someone out an attic.

(*She turns to go.*)

What's in the bag?

BRADSHAW: Only a few bits.

DEVONSHIRE: You're not fond of possessions?

BRADSHAW: No.

DEVONSHIRE: I like my servants very Christian, who see the world as futile tinsel. Otherwise they're nicking. Sam, take her bag.

(*DEVONSHIRE walks off.*)

FOOTMAN: You cut my wage like fuck, darling. I am a sodding Christmas tree, dangling with grandads and crippled kids.

BRADSHAW: Make it up from your subordinates.

FOOTMAN: Like fuck I –

BRADSHAW: Sam, be realistic.

FOOTMAN: I AIN'T SAM TO YOU.

BRADSHAW: Or find another situation. I am the bitch now, and you're only pussy. Find a mouse to torture.

(*She goes out, watched by SHADE and the FOOTMAN. BALL enters, with a bottle.*)

BALL: Quick, pink bum, or I'll crack your arse...

(*FOOTMAN takes up the bag and goes.*)

Oh, this is a country for shit lickers now. There is more lace than dinner. WHOSE DOG ARE YOU!

SHADE: Stuff it, Andy.

BALL: Stuff yerself, I'm pissed on misery.

SHADE: Nothin' new.

BALL: Nothin' new, nothin' new! Oh, you skinny little shivering hound, lock yer teeth for Christ's sake, I crave a decent conversation, even the conversation has deteriorated since I came back –

SHADE: Oh, yeah–

BALL: IT HAS, YOU SPUNK, IT HAS! And half the soldiers are in spectacles, some manhood has vanished –

SHADE: Oh, yeah –

BALL: FORESKIN IT HAS!

SHADE: (*Turning to go.*) Go under the bridge and have a kip with all the other pissed ol' cavaliers, I got a job to do –

BALL: THEY HAVE WITHDRAWN OUR CERTIFICATES!

SHADE: I know, mate.

BALL: I AM NO LONGER A KING'S MAN, WHAT OF THAT! No, it is a weird thing but I loved this fucking nation, and what is it –

SHADE: Good question –

BALL: COME 'ERE I SAID WHAT IS IT!

SHADE: (*Stops.*) What?

BALL: The nation, you tit hair, what is it? Is it hills? Is it rivers? Is it scenery? You answer me.

SHADE: Buggered if I –

BALL: You answer me! Because it can't be people, can it? It can't be you. Because I wouldn't raise a fart for you. They have gone off, they have, I mean just look at YOU –

SHADE: Yer pissed, mate –

BALL: I am pissed, but I can look at you, and really you are a shambles of an English man, I say that – no offence intended – but to my mind you are not a man at all, you are something –

(*He waves his hand vaguely.*)

– altogether–

(*SHADE goes to leave.*)

I lost some lovely comrades in the war you cunt!

(*SHADE stops again.*)

The nation, you see, is going down. Got to save the King, see? CUT THE GANGRENE OUT.

SHADE: (*Nodding at him.*) Okay, mate...

BALL: (*Suddenly tossing his bottle at the spike.*) Oh, you bleeders, where's my race?

(*The bottle strikes the spike and dislodges the trunk. It has barely touched the ground before BRADSHAW appears, issuing a fine scream. She scoops up the remains and runs off with them. SHADE makes a futile gesture of resistance.*)

SHADE: Hey – Hey –

BALL: Hey he says! OH, YOU GREAT ENGLISH BASTARD. Hey, he says!

(*He jeers.*)

SCENE FOUR

A banquet. Guests, music, a wedding cake.

DEVONSHIRE: I do not want a husband.

CHARLES: No, but baby wants a dad.

DEVONSHIRE: You are the dad.

CHARLES: Oh, you'd believe any old rumour! I must say I can imagine nothing nicer than you and Hambro locked together in the bed. It takes the edge off my misery to inflict him with a bitch like you...

DEVONSHIRE: I hate you, Charles.

CHARLES: No, it's only passion back to front...

NODD: (*Passing.*) Cheer up, darlin', Charlie'll still slip yer one, won't yer, Charlie, if yer good. Chin up!

DEVONSHIRE: If there is one thing I hate above all others it is cheerful cockneys. Go into a corner and get pissed.

HAMPSHIRE: Gloria, you were never more beautiful.

DEVONSHIRE: Oh, don't be a silly old liar.

(*She turns to CHARLES.*)

Charlie, call it off.

CHARLES: Who says I ain't a mighty mover of destinies, flinging coldbummed bankers down with Lady Roaring Hips? These old republicans will fuck shears for an earldom.

DEVONSHIRE: Call it off.

CHARLES: I could lie beneath the mattress just to hear old Hambro grieve. Will he shove sovereigns up your slit? Tell all, won't you, and call the infant Ajax, you must admire its tenacity, no prod or quinine's shaken it, nor baths in boiling cowshit, I believe.

DEVONSHIRE: I hate its guts.

CHARLES: No!

DEVONSHIRE: I tell you I do.

CHARLES: Wait till it's grinning at your tits.

DEVONSHIRE: I will pinch its little pink bum.

CHARLES: (*Drifting away.*) Oh blimey, Gloria, what pleases you?

BRADSHAW: Don't be angry with me. You look beautiful.

DEVONSHIRE: I don't want Hambro touching me. Has he promised? Has he sworn?

BRADSHAW: I have his assurance.

DEVONSHIRE: Good.

BRADSHAW: You are so perfect I could kiss you myself.

DEVONSHIRE: Do, then.

(*BRADSHAW kisses her.*)

Do you like me very much?

BRADSHAW: Yes.

DEVONSHIRE: I sometimes think I am unloved.

BRADSHAW: How could you?

DEVONSHIRE: And my life stinks.

BRADSHAW: Never.

DEVONSHIRE: I have no bloody friend but you. It is my day and I never felt more like hanging myself.

BRADSHAW: Wedding nerves. I wanted to hang myself.

DEVONSHIRE: Really? Promise me!

BRADSHAW: Oh, yes, hanging wasn't half of it! And you are so lucky, he promises he will not pester you. This is a wedding you can really enjoy!

CLEGG: (*Passing.*) Her radiance doth dim the stars,

Come Hymen, banish Mars,

In splendid nuptial forget our wars,

Oh, lucky fate of Royal Whores!

DEVONSHIRE: Sam, one of these days, I shall have you daggered in an alley…

(*She turns, moves off.*)

CLEGG: (*To BRADSHAW.*) Well, ain't you done well, miss, for an old red?

BRADSHAW: I get by, Mr. Clegg, thank you.

CLEGG: Visit me again, and we'll piss over courts and all this lark, I got some lovely satires.

BRADSHAW: No.

CLEGG: Go on, I love your belly.

BRADSHAW: Very well. I have to be consistent.

CLEGG: Good.

(*As he moves off.*) By the way, they took your Mr Scrope for calling God a liar. But Milton's safe.

(*He advances towards HAMBRO who enters.*)

Bring gold, bring silver to her feet,

Dives of our day we humbly greet!

CHARLES: (*Greeting HAMBRO and his best man, McCONOCHIE.*) Oh, Billy, ain't you smart and passionate! Let me kiss your hungry face!

(*He embraces him.*)

Be sweet to my daughter – AND DON'T SODOMIZE HER YOU FLOPPY CATKIN – I call her my daughter, well, why not, I'M GIVING HER AWAY, AIN'T I? Yer earldom don't give access to all her crevices –

(*He sees McCONOCHIE.*)

Oh, and you brought your best man! Clegg, got some verses for my favourite Scot?

McCONOCHIE: (*Bowing.*) Good day, sir.

CHARLES: Sam, lines for the great specialist!

CLEGG: Willingly – only – off the top of my head, I didn't come prepared –

NODD: Ain't that what yer paid for?

CLEGG: (*With aplomb.*) Where should we be,
    If from Dundee,
    Had not appeared this prodigy?
    (*Cheers and applause.*)
    To banish drips from sickly cocks,
    McConochie, we kiss thy socks!
    (*Boos and applause.*)
    Top of my head, I said, didn't I!

McCONOCHIE: Sir, I am deeply honoured by yer verse…

CHARLES: McConochie knows the pattern of our underneaths like a general knows a map of the terrain, don't you, know our INS AND OUTS? No court in Europe's got the like of him. THANK THE PRODIGY, TED!

HAMPSHIRE: I do thank him –

CHARLES: No, thank him properly, down on yer knees –

McCONOCHIE: Noo, noo, there is noo need –

HAMPSHIRE: (*Kneeling.*) I thank him, I thank him –

CHARLES: WHAT IS THIS RUMOUR THEY WANT MCCONOCHIE IN HANOVER!

McCONOCHIE: Oh, it's no a temptation to me, I –

CHARLES: I SHALL HAVE YOU IN CHAINS FIRST!
    (*He turns away.*)
    Oh, Gloria hangs back, sweet virgin, hurry to your husband's side! It brings tears to your eyes, don't it, I do think there is no better union than beauty and success!
    (*He draws her by the hand.*)
    I've seen weddings where the couple was both beautiful, no, rubbish, this is the RAW OLD UNION OF GAIN AND EXPEDIENCY!

HAMBRO: She moves with the grace of ten heifers…

CLEGG: They come like angels out the cloud,
    Breathless meeting of the shy and proud,

In aristocracy unite the nation,

Flesh and gold's infatuation!

(*The couple offer a dry kiss. Applause.*)

PONTING: Speech! Speech!

CHARLES: Nodd! Fetch it! Fetch my present!

McCONOCHIE: I call upon the Right Honourable, Sir William Hambro!

CHARLES: Oh, Gloria, do smile you bitch!

PONTING: Her uncle swears she is a virgin!

SOUTHWARK: Billy, I can hear a baby crying!

CHARLES: Yer speech! Yer speech!

SOUTHWARK: Wah, wah, wah! Wah, wah!

HAMBRO: (*Staggering.*) I hate this – cock out – big balled – shagging lot –

PONTING: Christ, Hambro's pissed –

HAMBRO: I hope they all die of burst livers in some SNOBBY BRAWL! Knocked down in some – vomit bucket –

(*Cheers and abuse.*)

Die like – bullocks rolling in the gore – eyes wild and – out of focus –

SOUTHWARK: Billy, watcha on about?

HAMBRO: I'M SPEAKIN', AREN'T I? Their old shag history going past their eyes – and dirty boots –

PONTING: Shuddup!

(*Something is thrown.*)

HAMBRO: And dirty boots – going in – and in –

SOUTHWARK: Yer pissin' down yer leg, banker!

HAMBRO: DIRTY LIFE AND DIRTY DEATH!

(*Roars of abuse.*)

I HATE BIG ARSED MEN WHO LIVE LIKE CATTLE!

(*Roars.*)

CHARLES: Billy's language comes out like the old red agitators, no wonder he don't drink too much...

HAMBRO: I LIKE MY LIFE –

HAMPSHIRE: Yer like to poke where yer mates have been –

HAMBRO: NO, YOU SILLY BUGGER, DO YOU THINK I'M MOCKED?

PONTING: I can hear a baby!

HAMBRO: OH, YOU GREAT BULLOCK, DO YOU THINK I'M
MOCKED BY THAT? YOU AREN'T IN YOUR TIME AND I AM,
SEE? All that happens is as I want it, and everything suits
me!

McCONOCHIE: I think we cud move on now –

HAMBRO: EVERY DAY I PICK UP THE PAPER I SHALL SAY
'GOOD', SEE? The smoothness of my time. My life without
rage, SEE?

(*He collapses into his chair as NODD brings in a large, wrapped object.*)

CLEGG: This gift to you from he who reigns,

Reminder of old times and gains,

The spirit of lost dreams retrieves,

The muse of History giggles in her sleeve!

DEVONSHIRE: This is something horrible.

CHARLES: Nobody say that Billy made it easy, he did not!
While others passed him, spraying brilliance, Billy crawled,
fly on the pane, silent progress of his sticky feet, the rockets
fell back past him, spent, but did not shake him. The Fly in
History. Nobody laugh at flies.

DEVONSHIRE: What is this?

CHARLES: Open it.

DEVONSHIRE: I don't want to –

CHARLES: Open it!

(*HAMBRO takes the string from DEVONSHIRE, and pulls it.
The wrapping falls from the figure of SCROPE, his lips cut off,
around his neck a massive copy of 'Harmonia Britannia'.*)

DEVONSHIRE: Is that supposed to be funny?

CHARLES: Funny? I did not say it was funny. I said it was
a present. Does a present have to be funny? It is a SAD
PRESENT. I have invented the SAD PRESENT. Thank me,
Billy, for inviting an old colleague whose name was
somehow left off the list of guests.

(*He turns to SCROPE.*)

If you can't come as a guest, you shall come as a present.
He was caught saying God did not exist. HE DOES EXISTS,
HE'S OVER THERE!

(*He looks at HAMBRO.*)

Billy, do welcome him, he is the most famous note-taker
in history. There will be girls with books of shorthand on
their knees and ignorant, oh, ignorant, of what a great
forebear they had in him! THIS WAS ENGLAND'S GREATEST
SECRETARY, wrote down in his copperplate OFF WITH MY
OLD DAD'S HEAD. Remember, Billy, you was there…?

DEVONSHIRE: Get him out.

CHARLES: (*To SCROPE.*) Speak, can you? Tell us what you
know of the filthy act of History?
(*He cups his hand to hear. SCROPE hesitates.*)
Mmm? Can't hear yer, mm?

SCROPE: a – a – er – ee –

CHARLES: Mmm?

SCROPE: Arr – the –

CHARLES: Come again?

SCROPE: LONG LIFF THE COMMONWEALTH OHH EQUALS!

CHARLES: Oh, no, that's old stuff, ain't it –

SCROPE: DOWN WIFF THE SIN OHH MONEY AND MONARCHY!

CHARLES: Oh, dear, I never asked him to say this!

SCROPE: LONG LIFF THE ATHEIST RE – HUB – LIC!

CHARLES: Stop spoiling Billy's banquet with all this old stuff,
really, it was a youthful abberation, wasn't it, THIS OLD RED
MUCK!

SCROPE: (*In tears and frustration.*) THE SIN OFF KINGS
– DISEASE OF RICHES –

BRADSHAW: Shut up.

SCROPE: (*Seeing her.*) AAAGGGHHHEDDAWAY!

BRADSHAW: Just shut up.

SCROPE: (*Recoiling from her.*) AAAGGGHHHHEDDAWAY!

BRADSHAW: What do you think you've got there, dignity?
Really, I have seen some idiots, crashing about the
doorposts of time and history, shouting out their old abuse,
but you, what have you discovered, your MANHOOD or
something? You absurd thing, you should be nailed to a
board. SHUT UP.
(*She looks around.*)
Excuse me. No. I'm perfectly all right. Well, I am, aren't
I? Look, I have clean drawers on, courtesy of madam,

starched underthings. And lips. Not rose bud. Not what they were, of course, but lips.

(*She curtsies, turns away.*)

CHARLES: Kiss the bride, then, Billy –

BRADSHAW: Lips…

CLEGG: Of such unions as this,

Shall spring the race none can resist,

Throughout the globe, all under heaven,

Raise the cry, the Earl of Devon!

ALL: (*Toasting.*) The Earl of Devon!

HAMBRO: It's my thing in her belly.

(*Pause. He looks around.*)

It's my thing in her belly.

(*Pause. Then CHARLES leads a cheer. HAMBRO smiles. Suddenly one of the servants flings off his wig and is revealed as BALL. He rushes forward and stabs HAMBRO in the back. HAMBRO falls across the table.*)

BALL: I SAVE THE KING! I SAVE THE KING! CAVALIERS AND STUARTS, HO!

(*Uproar. BALL climbs on the table.*)

I STAND IN BLOOD OF RUBBISH! CHURCH AND KING! PARLIAMENT IS ABOLISHED, WE HAVE STRUCK FOR ENGLAND AND THE MONARCHY. KEEP STILL THERE, PLAY THE ANTHEM, SEND OUT MESSENGERS TO EVERY VILLAGE, RING THE BELLS!

(*Nobody moves.*)

RING THE BELLS, THEN!

(*There is no response.*)

CHARLES STUART, BE A KING!

(*CHARLES doesn't move.*)

ENGLAND CALLS YOU! BE A KING!

(*Silence.*)

Come on, then.

(*Pause.*)

Come on, I have liberated yer.

(*Pause.*)

Oh, come on, be a FUCKING MONARCHIST.

(*There is no response. BALL lets out a terrible wail.*)

CHARLES: Drink my health and get off the table.

(*BALL sways, closing his eyes, he drops the dagger. Men close round him and haul him off the table.*)

DEVONSHIRE: Oh, God! Susan! I miscarry, oh!

(*A second uproar. BALL is hauled out. CHARLES sweeps from the room, followed by the assembly, who remove HAMBRO's body.*)

(*As she is borne away.*) Susan!

(*BRADSHAW does not move. She finds herself alone in the room but for McCONOCHIE. He stares at her.*)

McCONOCHIE: A'm dooin' verry well here, as ye can see…

(*Pause.*)

Ye ken A noo relish the idea o' discovery…

(*Pause.*)

It's noo more than a –

(*Suddenly BRADSHAW flings herself into his arms, crushing him in an embrace.*)

A'd be grateful therefore, if ye –

(*She sobs.*)

Wuld ye be so kind as –

(*She kisses him.*)

A have noo desire to be –

(*Suddenly he dissolves into tears.*)

Noo – noo – noo –

BRADSHAW: Shh…

McCONOCHIE: A canna – canna –

BRADSHAW: Shh…

McCONOCHIE: A want a muther, A want a muther!

BRADSHAW: You mustn't, no –

McCONOCHIE: A do! A do!

BRADSHAW: You must not weaken, you must not weaken –

(*She weakens herself, kissing him.*)

McCONOCHIE: A HATE THIS PLACE…

(*CHARLES enters, unaware of them. BRADSHAW puts her hand over McCONOCHIE's mouth, pushes him off. CHARLES holds up BRADSHAW's head in his hands.*)

CHARLES: Oh, Billy, we are standing in your blood…

(*He kneels by it.*)

Drink, Dick, at the puddle of yer enemies…
(*He holds the head to the blood. He begins to weep, then to laugh.*)
This ain't remorse, only when I'm depressed it looks like
it…
(*BRADSHAW makes a movement. CHARLES turns.*)
WHO'S THAT!

BRADSHAW: Me…

CHARLES: The cavalier, he thought he stabbed for me…he
loved something I'm only pretending…
(*He goes towards her. BRADSHAW winces at the sight of the
head, recoils a moment.*)
Don't be like Gloria…if you listen to me I'll give you a
bit of Surrey… I am terribly cold, hold my fingers in your
lap…
(*She takes his hand. They sit on the floor.*)
Have you a child there? I have no children I dare
acknowledge, the Queen's womb's like a walnut, I felt
it with my tip once, have you heard I got a melancholy
character?

BRADSHAW: Yes…

CHARLES: So I never know if I am talking sense or it's the
membranes shifting, there must be some truth, mustn't
there, or is it all biology? I don't think anybody cares
whether monarchs live or die now –

BRADSHAW: (*Recovering.*) Oh, don't say that –

CHARLES: No, no, don't be shallow, don't make soft
replies, the cavalier, he knew after my dad there would
be no English monarch would do anything but tickle
crowds for bankers, I looked in that man's eyes and I
was all humiliation, may I touch your belly? It's round as
a football. I think a woman in late life and pregnant is a
precious sight, look, the light is going, say no if you want
to, I am sick of forcing women…
(*She strokes his head.*)
Pity me, will you? I make you very gently, I am no rocking
billy, overlook my shallowness if I say that I love you, but I
do now, you kind woman…

(*CHARLES falls asleep on her. With infinite caution,*
BRADSHAW extricates herself, covers the sleeping figure with
a cloak. She is about to pick up the head when she is aware of
McCONOCHIE looking at her. He seems to shudder, then turns
away in disgust, and slowly walks off. BRADSHAW takes up the
head, covers it and is about to leave when the sound of jangling
keys is heard. The FOOTMAN, now a janitor, appears.)

FOOTMAN: Lockin' up.

(*Looking away, BRADSHAW attempts to pass.*)

Oi.

(*She stops.*)

For six months I 'ave 'ad no work, you cow.

(*She looks at him. Suddenly, he strikes her violently.*
BRADSHAW forces her hand to her mouth to prevent a cry. He
forces her to the ground and beats her. She utters no sound. He
finishes, jangling the key.)

Lockin' up.

(*BRADSHAW staggers out.*)

SCENE FIVE

The garden in Suffolk. CROPPER is standing in an apron.
BRADSHAW enters carrying a sleeping baby in her arms. She leads,
by a rope, the broken figure of BALL, who himself is carrying the bag
of remains. They halt.

BRADSHAW: What have they done to my house?

CROPPER: Burned it.

(*Pause. She looks at BALL.*)

Who is that?

BRADSHAW: My husband.

(*She shrugs.*)

He wasn't always like that, but they put him on a rack.
Well, they had to find out, didn't they, if he was a
conspiracy? He was a conspiracy, but a conspiracy of
one. In some ways I prefer him now. He was awfully
– boisterous – before. I came here because – because there
is nowhere to go in the end, but where you came from, is
there?

CROPPER: (*Going to BALL.*) Welcome. Would you care for a drink?

BRADSHAW: They had his tongue out, by special order of the King. It was very good of him, the magistrates were out to get him chopped. I mean, he killed a banker. All the bankers were…frothing…you can imagine…

CROPPER: Forgive me if I –

BRADSHAW: Yes –

CROPPER: If I – rather hate you for a minute –

BRADSHAW: Yes –

CROPPER: To go away and then –

BRADSHAW: Come back –

CROPPER: As if –

BRADSHAW: Absolutely, yes – do get him a drink, having no tongue his mouth gets all –

    (*CROPPER goes out. BRADSHAW goes to fetch the bag off BALL, who makes a clumsy grab for her.*)

    Yes…yes…

    (*She laughs, he grunts. CROPPER reappears with a glass. She watches, uneasy.*)

    Oh, don't be frightened, it's me he loves.

    (*She gives him the water. BRADSHAW drops the bag down.*)

    I brought Bradshaw back.

    (*CROPPER turns in horror. Pause.*) –

CROPPER: You –

BRADSHAW: In the bag. The dad.

    (*Pause.*)

    Well, look at it.

    (*CROPPER shakes her head.*)

    Oh, listen, I have been put to some little inconvenience retrieving that –

    (*She shakes it again.*)

    Look at it, then!

    (*Pause. CROPPER concedes, looks in the bag. Closes it again.*)

CROPPER: It is not him.

BRADSHAW: Who is it then?

CROPPER: It is not –

BRADSHAW: It's not? It is! Don't tell me I don't know my own –

CROPPER: It's bones!

BRADSHAW: Yes, of course it's bones, what did you expect? It's bones, obviously. Naturally, it's bones –

CROPPER: And he –

BRADSHAW: What's wrong with bones?

(*Pause.*)

CROPPER: I learned Latin.

BRADSHAW: Latin. What's that?

CROPPER: I read his book. By night. Run my dirty finger through the words. Mice in the skirting. Husband groaning in his kip. The sentence coming to me like a birth in the pale morning. I am translating it. 'Harmonia Britannia'. I am printing it.

(*Pause.*)

BRADSHAW: Oh, look, it's raining…

CROPPER: Quickly, come to the house.

(*Thunder. BRADSHAW doesn't move.*)

Give me the child, quick…!

(*BRADSHAW does not move. CROPPER takes the baby from her, hurries away. After a few moments BRADSHAW goes to BALL, puts her arm round him. She pulls a scarf over his head, then they go, clasped together, towards the house.*)

THE EUROPEANS

Struggles to Love

Characters

LEOPOLD, Emperor of Austria

OFFICERS, of the Imperial Army

TURKISH CAPTIVES

THE PAINTER, of the Imperial Court

STARHEMBERG, an Imperial General

THE EMPRESS, of Austria

KATRIN, a Wounded Citizen

ORPHULS, a Priest

SUSANNAH, Sister of Katrin

IPSTEIN, an Imperial Minister

HARDENSTEIN, an Imperial Minister

FALLENGOTT, an Imperial Minister

GRUNDFELT, an Anatomist

PUPILS OF ANATOMY

FIRST MOTHER, Parent of Orphuls

SECOND MOTHER, Parent of Starhemberg

FIRST BEGGAR

SECOND BEGGAR

THIRD BEGGAR

FOURTH BEGGAR

FIRST WOMAN BEGGAR

SECOND WOMAN BEGGAR

SERVANT, to the Empress

SHYBAL, a Common Soldier

McNOY, a Common Soldier

ARST, an Academician

FELIKS, an Academician

STENSH, an Academician

BOMBERG, an Academician

MIDWIFE

LABOURERS

JEMAL PASHA, a Turkish Commander

NUNS

ACT ONE

SCENE ONE

A plain, following a battle.

LEOPOLD: I LAUGH

> I LAUGH
>
> (*He walks towards some squatting prisoners.*)
>
> I LAUGH
>
> I LAUGH
>
> WHERE'S THE PAINTER?
>
> (*A figure enters with an easel and board.*)
>
> I LAUGH
>
> I LAUGH
>
> (*The PAINTER sketches.*)
>
> THIS PAIN WHICH SODDENS EVERY TURF
>
> THIS BOWEL WHICH DROOPS FROM EVERY BUSH
>
> THIS CROP OF WIDOWS AND ORPHANS
>
> I LAUGH

OFFICER: (*Observing.*) The Turks! The Turks!

LEOPOLD: (*Unmoved.*) Fuck them.

> (*Some fire. The OFFICERS sheath their swords. The PAINTER paints. LEOPOLD kneels.*)
>
> Oh, God, I thank, oh, God, I stoop, let all this Muslim flesh manure Christian ground, oh, God, I bow, let all this scrag of Islam bring forth crops to feed the lowest labourer and he shall situate the crucifix above the lintel of the door and hang his weapon on its hook, and in the frosty fields his child shall kick the Tartar skull that ploughs dislodged –

OFFICERS: (*Unsheathing their weapons.*) The Turks! The Turks!

LEOPOLD: Fuck them –

> (*Shellfire. The PAINTER rises anxiously.*)
>
> Are you afraid of dying?

PAINTER: No.

LEOPOLD: You don't mean no.

PAINTER: I do mean –

LEOPOLD: You say no, but you mean yes. You are afraid of dying, why?

PAINTER: I have this – I am under this – terrible illusion I am a decent painter and – as yet have little evidence – so –

LEOPOLD: I LAUGH

I LAUGH

PAINTER: Quite rightly but –

LEOPOLD: You think I am mad but the mad are the speakers of our time –

PAINTER: Yes –

LEOPOLD: Why?

PAINTER: Why –

LEOPOLD: Are they, yes?

PAINTER: I –

LEOPOLD: You say yes to everything I say, how will you ever be a decent painter?

PAINTER: I don't know –

LEOPOLD: Look at the prisoners, how they tremble like reeds on the lakeside as soon as their brothers come near, like a wind they come and go –

YOU LOST

YOU LOST

No fucking Seljuk lancer will cut you free, Ali! Draw them, record their bewilderment, they cannot understand why their god's quit, draw them!

OFFICER: The Turks! The Turks!

LEOPOLD: Oh, fuck your alarums, I am discussing art! (*Returning to his subject.*) This one in particular, who sports the topknot of his native land, squats with the distant look of one who senses execution in the offing, capture that. Though how you keep a pencil still in fingers that tremble as yours do, I can't imagine –

PAINTER: It's cold –

LEOPOLD: IT IS COLD, IT IS EUROPE!

(*A general hurrah breaks out among the OFFICERS.*)

OFFICERS: STARHEMBERG! STARHEMBERG!

LEOPOLD: Oh, Starhemberg, they do so love the bastard, they love the bag of bones who showed no terror, who

sat out the siege when emperors fled, this moment I have
dreamed of, I kneel, I kneel to thee who saved Christian
Europe, I kneel and lick thy paws and here's a painter
will catch my homage for all time and so on, Leopold the
stooping, Leopold the supplicant!

OFFICERS: STAR – HEMBERG!

(*STARHEMBERG enters, goes to LEOPOLD, kneels.*)

STAR – HEMBERG!

LEOPOLD: They do go on, they do adore you more than me –

STARHEMBERG: No, never –

OFFICERS: STAR – HEMBERG!

LEOPOLD: I LAUGH

I LAUGH

I slept in lovely beds while you thrust corpses into
breaches of the walls, I do most humbly thank you and of
course simultaneously hate you for showing the dignity of
character I was not endowed with but how was I to know
the Europeans would suddenly unite? It is the first and I
daresay the last occasion we have managed so fuck you
and thank you!

(*They embrace, swiftly, and separate.*)

Now slaughter this lot.

(*He indicates the Turkish prisoners.*)

Or their brothers back in Anatolia will say the Christians
are merciful and take prisoners, no, this is a spot no Turk
will stagger back to but as doormen, dustbin porters, café
keepers and the like, AWAY!

(*The prisoners are kicked offstage.*)

I LAUGH

I LAUGH

(*To the PAINTER.*) Did you capture this? I will not embrace
the mighty bonebag twice.

PAINTER: Yes –

LEOPOLD: Into Vienna now for all the sarcasm of the
survivors.

STARHEMBERG: No, surely –

LEOPOLD: Yes, indeed, and if they toss cabbages –

STARHEMBERG: There are no cabbages in Vienna, we
have been eating dogs –

LEOPOLD: Dogs, have you? And not the last time dogs will stand in for pastry, is the palace swept out? If so chuck the rubble back, it's right we should return to chaos, the arms askew, the monograms a shambles etcetera, and cannon holes above the bed, I think Vienna will know the crack of field guns more than once and bury babies of starvation. (*He falls, kneels, as if in a paroxysm of exhaustion. The OFFICERS watch, confused. The EMPRESS enters, gestures for them to stand away. She goes to him, rests her hands on his shoulders.*)

EMPRESS: Five hundred disembowelled women are lying in the Wienerwald.

The stench.

Of all classes.

The stench.

Of all degrees.

Islam's *au revoir.*

The Poles have saved Paris.

LEOPOLD: Paris…?

EMPRESS: Rome.

LEOPOLD: Rome…?

EMPRESS: London. Copenhagen. Amsterdam. The Poles have saved five million women, at this moment dreaming, knitting, wiping the arses of their infants, sucking the cocks of their husbands' friends, writing novels, hemming curtains, get up now, the wind will change and here's a cloth soaked in eau de Cologne, it has my monogram in lace which took the embroiderer twenty-seven hours, that is a waste of life some would argue, but no more fatuous than writing novels or what passes now for freedom in progressive circles and at least she has her bowels in, no Turkish dagger in her parts, get up you dear and sensitive soul, I sometimes think the barmy imaginings of the progressive rest on bayonets, do you follow? I mean the very fatuous pattering in Paris is predicated on the Poles, the spears of superstitious peasants keep their words aloft, the Turks would soon shut down their salons, in the harem with the bitches says the Seljuk, oh, you are getting up, we

have to make an entry to the city and give thanks, God
knocked Allah over this time…
(*She sinks down beside him.*)
We have in one day an Empire back which stretches from
the Alps to the Baltic, I thought, I fully thought, we would
die in a seaside hotel, Leopold, kiss my ugly mouth and I'll
kiss yours –

LEOPOLD: They're looking – the staff are –

EMPRESS: I do not give a piss for them, kiss me in this
screaming sea, this swamp of horrid dead, we have Europe
back…
(*He kisses her. The OFFICERS draw their swords.*)

OFFICERS: THE HAPSBURG! THE HAPSBURG!

SCENE TWO

A convent. A girl in a chair.

KATRIN: In my own words.
(*Pause.*)
Words of my own.
(*Pause.*)
The poor have neither words nor drawers.
(*Pause.*)
Oh, for literacy, oh, for numeracy, oh, for any pack of lies!
(*Pause.*)
So the four soldiers said –
(*Pause.*)
No.
No. There may not have been four. And they may not
have been soldiers. But they did have weapons and the
Turk does not wear uniform so for the sake of.
(*Pause.*)
Let's say four.
(*Pause.*)
The four soldiers said lie down – well, they didn't say
it, no, they did not say the words they indicated by very
simple gestures this was expected of me, words were
dispensed with, words were superfluous though much

language was expressed on either side, by me, by them, but words not really, no.
(*Pause.*)
Consequently I lay my face down in the relatively sympathetic grass. OF COURSE I AM NOT IN THE LEAST ASHAMED DESCRIPTION COMES EASILY TO ME but can I have a glass of water? The dryness of my mouth suggests anxiety but I have had a dry mouth since my throat was cut, some channel or some duct was severed, something irreparable and anatomical.
(*A NUN places a glass of water by the chair and withdraws.*)
It's you who are ashamed not me but I forgive in all directions then one of them threw up my skirt excuse me –
(*She drinks.*)
Or several of them, from now on I talk of them as plural, as many-headed, as many-legged and a mass of mouths and of course I had no drawers, to be precise –
(*Pause.*)
I owned a pair but for special occasions. This was indeed special but on rising in the morning I was not aware of it, and I thought many things, but first I thought – no, I exaggerate, I claim to know the order of my thoughts WHAT A PREPOSTEROUS CLAIM – strike that out, no, among the CASCADE OF IMPRESSIONS – that's better – that's accurate – cascade of impressions – came the idea at least I DID NOT HAVE TO KISS.
(*Pause.*)
The lips being holy, the lips being sacred, the orifice from which I uttered my most perfect and religious thoughts only the grass would smear them but no.
(*Pause.*)
Can you keep up? Sometimes I find a flow and then the words go – torrent – cascade – cascade again, I used that word just now! I like that word now I have discovered it, I shall use it, probably ad nauseam, cascading! But you –
(*Pause.*)
And then they turned me over like a side of beef, the way the butcher flings the carcass, not without a certain

familiarity, coarse-handling but with the very vaguest
element of warmth, oh, no, the words are going, that isn't
what I meant at all, precision is so – precision slips even as
you reach for it, goes out of grasp and I was flung over and
this MANY MOUTHED THING –

(*She shudders as if taken by a fit, emitting an appalling cry and
sending the water flying. The NUN supports her. She recovers.*)

Now I've spilled the water – don't say there's more where
that came from – so it is with life – don't mop the floor, I
can take it from the floor, so my mouth –

(*Pause. The NUN withdraws.*)

My mouth which I had held to be the very shape and seat
of intimacy they smothered with wet and fluid – I don't
think you could call them kisses – YES, YES, KISSES, THEY
WERE KISSES I try to hide behind the language, oh, the
language I do twist like bars of brass to shelter in, no, they
were kisses because a kiss can be made of hatred – kisses,
yes, oh, yes…

(*Pause.*)

They soaked, they drenched, they swilled me with their
kisses, and bruised my lips and bit my mouth and thrust
these thousand tongues into my throat AND THIS WAS ONLY
THE BEGINNING ONLY THE BEGINNING YOU WITH THE
BOOK AND PENCIL WAIT!

(*Pause. She controls her horror. A PRIEST appears from the
darkness.*)

ORPHULS: I think, for today, we leave it there –
KATRIN: Why –
ORPHULS: The tension of –
KATRIN: The tension, yes –
ORPHULS: Is making you –
KATRIN: Obviously –
ORPHULS: And us for that matter, we are also –
KATRIN: You also, yes, quite rightly, suffer as I –
ORPHULS: Greatly, and –
KATRIN: Greatly, yes, why shouldn't you –

(*She sees the NUN leaving.*)

DON'T GO AWAY!

(*The NUN continues her way. Pause.*)

I'm mad, aren't I? I hate the word but technically it does seem suitable. Please call me mad I wish for it. I long for madness to be ascribed to me. I thirst for such a title.

ORPHULS: I don't believe you are at all insane, only –

KATRIN: OH, COME ON!

(*With a sudden inspiration.*)

Listen, this is madness, this is proof! I dream, I passionately dream, of some pretty valley in the Danube where a Muslim girl is kneeling to the East. She bows to Mecca, she spreads her Turkish things, her Turkish mirror, her Turkish mat, and threads the Transylvanian flowers through her hair when down like wind swoop Christian troopers rancid with the saddle and STAKE HER TO THE GROUND WITH KNIVES, her naked haunches, her perfect breasts they slash into a running sieve of blood, all channels red, all drain of horror, what satisfaction could I have from dreaming only my Turks die? No, revenge must be upon the innocent. Now, am I mad?

ORPHULS: No...

(*She laughs.*)

KATRIN: I have no breasts! I have no breasts!

(*She laughs and sobs. ORPHULS holds her in his arms. A woman enters.*)

SUSANNAH: Is my sister there?

(*The sobbing stops.*)

Katrin?

ORPHULS: Yes.

SUSANNAH: It's so dark –

ORPHULS: It is dark. It must be dark.

SUSANNAH: (*Appearing in the shaft of light.*) Yes...

(*She extends a hand to KATRIN.*)

Come home, now.

KATRIN: No.

SUSANNAH: Come home and –

KATRIN: HOME WHAT'S THAT.

(*Pause.*)

It's your peremptory tone I hate.

SUSANNAH: My tone's as kind as I can make it –

KATRIN: It's peremptory –

SUSANNAH: What a funny word, you do –

KATRIN: Love funny words, yes, give me a new word and I'll thank you, but home, stuff that, take home and bite it like a cold, raw egg, muck, ugh, spew, ugh, and sharp shell in the gums, no, you are peremptory and always were, beautiful, peremptory and unhappy, at least you are unhappy, thank God for that, I could like you, given time.

SUSANNAH: How much time? I carried you about, little sister.

KATRIN: I'm so cruel, aren't I? It comes of having a vocabulary and no breasts DON'T TOUCH.

(*SUSANNAH draws back.*)

I can't bear to be touched now, even by those who claim their touch is pity.

SUSANNAH: I don't pity you, Katrin.

KATRIN: Why don't you? Everybody else does.

SUSANNAH: I think you are more cruel than any clot of raping mercenaries.

(*Pause.*)

Now, you made me say that. You made me utter sentiments which in any case I do not feel. You do that to people. Let's go home.

KATRIN: I have finished with home, for which, all gratitude to Islam's infantry –

SUSANNAH: Silly –

KATRIN: DON'T CALL ME SILLY IN THAT WAY YOU DO.

(*Pause.*)

I can't go home because – and do listen, this will be difficult for you, perhaps beyond your grasp – home is the instrument of reconciliation, the means through which all crime is rinsed in streams of sympathy and outrage doused, and blame is swallowed in upholstery, home is the suffocator of all temper, the place where the preposterous becomes the tolerable and hell itself is stacked on shelves, I wish to hold on to my agony, it's all I have.

(*Pause.*)

SUSANNAH: I had such a pleasant room prepared for you...

KATRIN: Use it to fuck in.

(*She bursts out.*)

to girls' miseries? Inform me, I am your servant and no matter what the sins I absolve you, I would be skewered on Islamic daggers but for you, make me your confessor, I would be honoured not only to hear but share your pains. And thank you for the bun, I was in hell there.

(*Pause. STARHEMBERG raises him, kisses him, and goes out.*)

SCENE THREE

A palace. Courtiers. A chair. LEOPOLD enters. He topples the chair and perches on the result. The courtiers shift uncomfortably.

LEOPOLD: Sometimes, you will want to laugh. And you will feel, no, I must not laugh. Sometimes you will suffer the embarrassment of one who feels exposed to an obnoxious privacy. You will feel, he should never have shown me that. And sometimes you will experience the terrible nausea that accompanies an idiocy performed by one for whom you felt respect. As if the world had lost its balance. I can only tell you, all these feelings I permit. So laugh when the urge seizes you, and then, be ashamed of the laugh. The Emperor only acts the insecurity of all order. Do you accept the truth of that?

(*The courtiers shift uncomfortably.*)

No one understands! *Nihil comprehensa!* Now, you may turn the chair up.

(*The chair is put on its legs. LEOPOLD sprawls.*)

IPSTEIN: Morality.

LEOPOLD: Mm.

IPSTEIN: Has utterly collapsed.

LEOPOLD: It does in sieges. Like cakes left in the rain. And humour also, that deteriorates. The sort of joke you would not twitch a muscle for in peacetime sets crowds of starving rocking in a siege.

IPSTEIN: Humour I think, we can leave aside for –

LEOPOLD: WHY LEAVE HUMOUR OUT!

(*Pause. IPSTEIN shrugs.*)

Do I bully you? Don't shudder, no one will hack your hand off, this is not Rome or Russia.

HARDENSTEIN: Women are selling themselves and the bourgeoises are the worst.

LEOPOLD: You should pity the privileged, how they suffer in adversity. See the best shops are stocked first. Next.

FALLENGOTT: The currency is unstable.

LEOPOLD: The currency is always unstable.

FALLENGOTT: Not like this.

LEOPOLD: I am sick of currency and its instability. I shrink to think a single life, a dog's or pigeon's even, should be warped by currency and its antics. Hang currency from trees.

FALLENGOTT: We might as well, it is that useless.

LEOPOLD: I sense the coinage has found a friend in you.

FALLENGOTT: Not a bit, but –

LEOPOLD: OFF YOUR KNEES TO COINS, it is a despicable sight. Are the bankers back yet?

HARDENSTEIN: The Jews never left.

LEOPOLD: The fall of shells is like a passing shower to them. Where is the Turkish treasure?

FALLENGOTT: Lying in ravines.

LEOPOLD: Then float the new economy on that. Enough, and thank you for your opinions, I weigh them all, I seem brusque, I seem shallow but in privacy I meditate profoundly, you must take that on trust, of course.
(*They start to leave. LEOPOLD places his hand on the PAINTER's sleeve.*)
Not you.
(*The COURTIERS depart. Pause.*)
I speak everything, like one variety of idiot. And you are silent, like the other. Draw me now. I pose.
(*He kneels on the floor like a dog.*)
I pose. And thus cheat your imagination.

PAINTER: (*Turning to a fresh page.*) How?

LEOPOLD: Because the artist hopes his portrait shows a secret truth, and I show my secret. Call this 'He Comes Back to Vienna'.

PAINTER: Must I?

LEOPOLD: Yes.
(*The PAINTER begins drawing.*)

PAINTER: I think, by discarding the formality of monarchy, you think you disrupt criticism, and by playing the fool, disarm any who would dare call you so, and thereby flatter your intelligence. I hope I am not offending you.

LEOPOLD: You were never this perceptive on the battlefield.

PAINTER: I was too cold.

LEOPOLD: IT IS COLD, THIS IS EUROPE...!

PAINTER: Yes...yes...so you said...at every foggy ditch and burial –

(*He throws down the book.*)

It's – really it's – impossible! You cannot – an artist cannot hope to paint an act! Find another – find a –

LEOPOLD: (*Abandoning his absurd pose, and sitting on the floor.*) No, no, you are the one...you are...

(*Pause. He is weeping. STARHEMBERG enters, looks at them.*)

I'm crying again...Starhemberg...crying again...

(*STARHEMBERG goes to him, cradles his head.*)

Why? Why this weeping all the time?

(*The PAINTER sketches this, furtively.*)

Don't you weep? You don't, do you? WHY IS IT, THEN, IT INFURIATES ME –

(*The PAINTER goes to leave discreetly.*)

Don't slip away with that!

(*He stops.*)

Show me the book.

(*He offers the book.*)

You see, he gets it down, the moment of despair, his fingers work like lightning to capture that, how well he seizes that –

(*He tears out the page, gives the book back. The PAINTER leaves.*)

Where do you go at nights? You are unobtainable.

STARHEMBERG: Am I not free? I have no titles which are not honorary now.

LEOPOLD: No, none, and at your own request. But half the time you are not in your premises, and the messengers say the state of the windows suggests the genius has quit. Four times I have left messages. You are a hero and yet you creep around in hats, we need our hero, we are afraid you will be discovered lying in some alley and then the word will go around Starhemberg is out of favour, there's gratitude for you, when nothing could be further from the truth!

STARHEMBERG: During the siege I had half the cannon turned to face in.

LEOPOLD: In? Why in?

STARHEMBERG: Every night a dozen citizens slipped out with handkerchiefs on which were written WE LOVE ISLAM in mis-shapen Arab script. I must tell you, at the lowest point I received a delegation who proposed the burning of all effigies of Christ, and as for the Imperial standard, I saw it stuffed inside a drain-pipe. Officers were tearing off their epaulets, and priests lurked in wigs. I forced freedom on them, and when they applaud me, their claps are drowning out the shame which roars inside their ears. I loathe the crowd. I love big hats.

LEOPOLD: They are only frail...they are only frail... I cannot criticize them...how can I, the arch-deserter, criticize? You must help us to restore ourselves. Be a mirror in which we dwarves may see the possibility of godlike self.

STARHEMBERG: No.

LEOPOLD: Restore us, Starhemberg, who has no flaws –
(*STARHEMBERG turns to leave.*)
WHO SAID YER CAN GO!
(*He stops.*)
I think you are a selfish and self-loving fantasist or you would have surrendered months ago.
(*Pause.*)
No, no, listen, I owe you everything and don't despise me I can have you made a saint, do you want to be a saint? It can be done, the long grey jaw and hooded eye, excellent, try that if you are tired of soldiering, but not this anonymity, or do you hate us?
(*Pause.*)
You do...so that's your burden...you are thin with hate... Oh, Starhemberg, you are crueller than the worst Arab butcher, who stabs with childlike relish and then grows

tired, and waking in the morning, plays with the infants he
forgot to slay. Starhemberg, my maker, you are ill…
(*He goes to him, holds him.*)

STARHEMBERG: The innocent are not innocent…

LEOPOLD: I LAUGH! I LAUGH!

EMPRESS: (*Entering.*) Starhemberg! How rarely he! Oh, his
unfamiliar! Kiss me, then!
(*He kisses her hand.*)
Cold mouth. Have you a mistress?

STARHEMBERG: I love a woman.

EMPRESS: But your mouth is cold!

LEOPOLD: He holds us all in spite.

EMPRESS: Not me.

LEOPOLD: Yes, you included! Someone is writing his
biography, but he will give no evidence. And the city
architect has sculpted him for Starhemberg Square but
without a face! It is ridiculous, when can he do the face?

STARHEMBERG: Let it have no face.

LEOPOLD: I LAUGH. I LAUGH.

EMPRESS: Are you loyal to the Hapsburgs?

STARHEMBERG: I can conceive of no improvement in the
nature of the government.

LEOPOLD: You see! That is how he is!

EMPRESS: (*Looking at STARHEMBERG.*) He thinks his
boldness will win our admiration. He is very near offence,
and thinks we will admire his subtlety. I do admire it, so
there! Do sit, or won't you?

STARHEMBERG: No.

EMPRESS: Of course not! To sit would end his
condescension, I do admire all your moves, I think you
are a cold and wonderfully imagined man, I mean, you are
your own invention, isn't that so?

LEOPOLD: My wife is so perceptive, her gaze melts snow.

STARHEMBERG: Yes.

EMPRESS: There you are! And a reply of one syllable, for
more would only spoil the effect. I feel such attraction
for you, Starhemberg, I would run away with you to a
pigman's hut and fuck the rest of my existence out!

LEOPOLD: I LAUGH!

EMPRESS: You see, I can match all your gestures. No real
man is worth the effort, but one who invents, and re-
invents himself! He can keep us heated!

LEOPOLD: I LAUGH!

EMPRESS: (*To LEOPOLD.*) As you do, as you also do…
(*She kisses LEOPOLD.*)
Starhemberg, we must invent the European now, from
broken bits. Glue head to womb and so on. And fasten hair
to cracked, mad craniums. And stop being ashamed. Now,
go, you excellent actor, do go…
(*He bows.*)

SCENE FOUR

*An Institute of Science. A semi-circle of physicians. KATRIN naked to
the waist. SUSANNAH and STARHEMBERG in the audience.*

GRUNDFELT: She is nineteen. She is from the agricultural
district of Thuringia. She is one of nine children. She is
literate. She suffered on the twenty-third of August. She
was without benefit of surgeons. She is pregnant and in
the fourth month of her term. She gave testimony to the
Bishop's Commission on Atrocity.

KATRIN: I volunteer my disfigurement.

GRUNDFELT: She comes of her own free will.

KATRIN: I needed no persuasion.

GRUNDFELT: She welcomes the scrutiny of the Institute.

KATRIN: I rejoice in it.

GRUNDFELT: We are grateful to this courageous and
patriotic woman.

KATRIN: And I am grateful to you.

GRUNDFELT: Drawing is permitted.
(*The audience rises and surrounds KATRIN, with books and
pencils.*)

STARHEMBERG: They cluster her… How thick they are on
her, and urgent…

SUSANNAH: Are you a surgeon? Hurry along with your
pencil or you will miss the itemizing of the wounds.

STARHEMBERG: I shall see her…

SUSANNAH: Everyone will see her. She is determined her misery will go into print, and colour, too, you are staring at me in a way which at one time would have been thought offensive…

STARHEMBERG: Her absent breasts, and yours so very present…

SUSANNAH: It is peculiar, we would have thought at one time, to have such intellectual symposia among men who cannot muster a sandwich between them…

STARHEMBERG: Your succulence, and her aridity…

SUSANNAH: But we swiftly become used to anything, don't you find? All right, what have you got? I don't want pig fat, oh, God, you are Starhemberg –

STARHEMBERG: Introduce me to her.

SUSANNAH: Aren't you, you are Starhemberg, I am bathed in confusion –

STARHEMBERG: You honour me quite unnecessarily –

SUSANNAH: I bite my words –

STARHEMBERG: The world has dropped several rungs, and us with it, when will you speak to her?

SUSANNAH: Now, if you command it –

STARHEMBERG: I command nothing any more –

(*She turns to go.*)

Wait – I also love women –

SUSANNAH: What are you asking me?

STARHEMBERG: On the floor here, show me –

SUSANNAH: Show you?

STARHEMBERG: I have seen you fucked –

SUSANNAH: Impossible –

STARHEMBERG: No, it's so – go down and let me look at you – your hair – your crevices –

SUSANNAH: I prefer we –

STARHEMBERG: I ask only to gaze, there's no complication –

SUSANNAH: I must, since you saved Vienna.

(*She lies down among the benches, draws up her skirts. The voice of GRUNDFELT drones. STARHEMBERG stares down at her, and up occasionally.*)

STARHEMBERG: Up now, they're quitting –

(*She rises again, straightening her skirt.*)

Introduce me, then wait in the Ballgasse.

(*She makes her way to the front.*)

GRUNDFELT: Our feelings of sympathy are not less profound for the objectivity we have attempted here in detailing your condition –

OTHERS: Hear, hear –

KATRIN: Nor is my modesty less whole for the intensity of your examination –

OTHERS: Hear, hear –

GRUNDFELT: We thank you both for this and for your gracious manner.

KATRIN: I thank you equally, shall this be printed and in colour?

(*The physicians hesitate.*)

BRUSTEIN: At this moment we had only thought to record your terrible misfortune for the archive of the Institute…

KATRIN: Oh, no, I understood there was a publication –

BRUSTEIN: In learned journals, some details might –

KATRIN: No, no, but in the shops, I mean –

BRUSTEIN: I – did we –

KATRIN: Oh, certainly!

GRUNDFELT: I have no recollection we –

KATRIN: Assuredly, some six thousand copies!

GRUNDFELT: I don't think any –

KATRIN: YES, SIX THOUSAND. I don't dream these figures. They printed fifteen thousand of Duke Starhemberg, he hangs in every pub, and eighteen thousand of the Emperor, why not, there is a vast supply of cartridge in the city, and ink's no problem, some have taken to drinking it –

SUSANNAH: (*Advancing with a shawl.*) My sister is –

KATRIN: NOTHING. My sister is.

(*Pause.*)

STARHEMBERG: (*Walking down.*) Is there a drawing?

PAINTER: A preliminary sketch –

STARHEMBERG: Then tint it, and add her face.

SUSANNAH: My sister is –

KATRIN: Nothing. My sister is. Do arrange and hurry with the proofs. If you have not my face, I'll sit here longer.

PAINTER: If the Duke commissions this, I –

KATRIN: What duke? It's me has all the copyright.

STARHEMBERG: Please, ask her to be covered…

(*Pause. KATRIN allows SUSANNAH to draw a shawl over her naked shoulders. STARHEMBERG goes to the front.*)

Arrange a sitting. She is staying in a convent.

KATRIN: And another, later, like this…!

(*She pretends to feed a child.*)

I raise my infant, who is crying for his feed, but to the absent breasts, where no milk flows! His arms reach out, his tiny hands…! Imagine my expression! Imagine his!

STARHEMBERG: Sketch as she says.

KATRIN: Ten thousand copies.

GRUNDFELT: I doubt this would achieve a sale of tens –

KATRIN: YOU MISJUDGE.

(*Pause.*)

And if they don't, then post them through the doors…

(*GRUNDFELT bows, withdraws, with the physicians.*)

SUSANNAH: This is Duke Starhemberg.

(*KATRIN looks at him.*)

KATRIN: The birth is for the seventeenth. I want it public in the square, and banks of seats. No awnings, even if it rains, and let actresses be midwives if nurses have their scruples. (*To STARHEMBERG.*) Why would you not look at me?

STARHEMBERG: I only look when I am certain I shall see.

KATRIN: You will see.

(*She gets up, falls against SUSANNAH, who holds her. With an effort of will, KATRIN rids herself of SUSANNAH.*)

Oh, you all so want me to be spoiled! Kiss me!

(*SUSANNAH goes to kiss her. KATRIN removes her cheek.*)

I don't trust kisses! Embrace me!

(*SUSANNAH goes to hold her, she arches away.*)

I suffocate! You only rub your grief against my flesh, as if it would come off, as a cow will back itself against the thorn and scrape its hide. That's how we kiss, that's how we hold! Where is my nun, I want to go now. Mother!

(*She pulls on a gown.*)

This was no endurance, do you know why? None would look me in the eye, and I have such lovely eyes. Are my eyes so dangerous? No Turk did either.

(*The NUN enters.*)

My eyes remain unravished, Mother, like unentered rooms…

(*The NUN encloses her, leads her to the door. ORPHULS enters, bows to her.*)

STARHEMBERG: Let me father your child…

(*Pause. KATRIN stops.*)

KATRIN: But it won't live!

(*She goes out. Pause.*)

SUSANNAH: I think we live in Hell, but something makes Hell tolerable. What is it? Anger? I am so bad at anger.

ORPHULS: This is not Hell.

SUSANNAH: Not Hell? What's Hell, then?

ORPHULS: Absence.

SUSANNAH: I assure you, this is absence.

ORPHULS: Of God.

(*Pause.*)

SUSANNAH: (*To STARHEMBERG.*) Take me to the café. You said you would, for showing you God's absence…

(*She goes out.*)

ORPHULS: The siege was simultaneously a moment of degeneracy and of the highest moral order. On the one hand, every fence to immorality was torn down, and on the other, peculiar sacrifices were made in the spirit of human love. Did you find this?

(*STARHEMBERG does not reply.*)

Every morning when we awoke, we felt the possibility of UTTER TRANSFORMATION rising with the sun. Death, obviously, but worse, enslavement to all things foreign… the crying of the mullahs in their tents…shall we never hear again the crying of the mullahs in their tents? How tightly I did hold the woman's arse to me, her warmth, our miserable thin blanket and I kissed her hollowed neck with tears all down my face, RING THE BELLS I SAID, WHERE ARE

OUR BELLS TODAY? And then at last, the bells crashed back, drowning, waves of drowning, seas of booming iron, and she stirred slowly, some widow, some pale, inconsequential widow who held in her thin body all that was ours, all culture, all effigy in her broken lips. We pulled on our drawers under the dirty sheets, ice on the windows, and on the table, last night's greasy plate…

STARHEMBERG: Hearing you I know I could only love a corrupt priest…

ORPHULS: Don't betray me. I am ambitious.

STARHEMBERG: Never.

ORPHULS: Once you were seen in every street, on every barricade, I heard people swear you had been seen in seven quarters simultaneously, and though I never saw you, I imagined I did, and children pointed to your profile in the clouds and said 'I know that beak…!'

STARHEMBERG: I love the plumpness of your face. I know when you serve mass, you rarely think of Christ.

ORPHULS: I think of Him, but –

(*Pause.*)

No, I hardly think of Christ, rather, I think – I am Him.

STARHEMBERG: Yes…

ORPHULS: I tell you this! I tell you, God knows why, why do I tell you? Don't betray me, I am so ambitious!

STARHEMBERG: I would rather take your blessing than a thousand cardinals stinking of celibacy shook their absolution over me.

(*An old woman enters.*)

FIRST MOTHER: Is it him? Is it his voice crying love?

ORPHULS: No.

FIRST MOTHER: I find him everywhere!

STARHEMBERG: Yes, he is an itinerant priest.

(*He goes out.*)

FIRST MOTHER: His long words, his lovely words, all his lovely education licks the ceiling and –

ORPHULS: I've no more bread.

(*Pause.*)

I mean –

I have a bit but –

I need that for –

Oh, fuck you, take it!

(*He pulls some bread from under his cassock.*)

FIRST MOTHER: (*Taking it.*) Don't swear so, you'll make enemies.

ORPHULS: I have only one enemy and that is you. I take that back.

FIRST MOTHER: You take everything back but only after you've said it.

ORPHULS: I hope you will not eat that here, it scalds my soul to think I might have fucked a woman for it and all it does is extend your burdensome life, I take that back, but you know what I mean.

FIRST MOTHER: I wouldn't burden you if your sisters were more like daughters.

ORPHULS: You have a miraculous appetite and thrive on bird shit. Most of the old collapsed and died in the first month of the siege. I looked in all their faces, but where were you? Take her swift, I prayed to God, but no, claw at the door before the morning guns…

FIRST MOTHER: You love me, that's what kept me whole.

ORPHULS: So you say.

FIRST MOTHER: You must do or you wouldn't tolerate me. You are kind and I am so demanding, you are busy and I pester you –

ORPHULS: Yes, well, I –

FIRST MOTHER: Oh, yes, but I shall be no trouble to you soon, my life's as good as chucked –

ORPHULS: So you keep on saying, but –

FIRST MOTHER: I live for you –

ORPHULS: For me, but –

FIRST MOTHER: My little one –

ORPHULS: Oh, God in Heaven –

FIRST MOTHER: His tiny arms went round me once, he hid his darling face in my poor skirt –

ORPHULS: PLEASE! OH, PLEASE!

(*She is silent. She chews bread. Pause.*)

I try, I do try, to eradicate you from my life, to erase you, every morning like a butcher rubbing down his bench...

FIRST MOTHER: Too deep a groove...

(*He nods.*)

Too deep a stain...

(*He turns his back. Pause.*)

Mind all these women.

ORPHULS: Yes.

(*She starts to move away, stops.*)

FIRST MOTHER: I see you in that bishop's hat.

ORPHULS: You always did. Since I first joined the choir.

FIRST MOTHER: My son, almighty in his bishop's hat –

ORPHULS: IF I WANT TO BE A BISHOP IT WILL BE MY DECISION.

FIRST MOTHER: Of course it will.

ORPHULS: I am not ambitious. It is you who is ambitious. Sickeningly so. I am happy as a pastor here. Happy and fulfilled.

FIRST MOTHER: Good. I won't keep you, then. You must have such a lot to do –

ORPHULS: Stay as long as you like, I – stay if you –

FIRST MOTHER: No, I must get on –

ORPHULS: Must you? Well, if you must, you –

FIRST MOTHER: Don't grieve for me.

ORPHULS: YOU TALK ABOUT DYING ALL THE TIME BUT DO YOU!

FIRST MOTHER: (*With infinite patience.*) You will, of course. You will grieve for me.

ORPHULS: I hate the way you eat. Half the crumbs are on the floor.

FIRST MOTHER: Always ate this way.

ORPHULS: I know and it always horrified me.

FIRST MOTHER: I thought you liked the common people. We are common –

ORPHULS: SOMETIMES I THINK I COULD MURDER YOU.

FIRST MOTHER: (*Kneeling, brushing up the crumbs.*) I know. It's love.

ORPHULS: Stop that! Get up!

(*She finishes, gets up.*)

Go away, now.

FIRST MOTHER: (*Looking at him.*) My own son.

(*She goes out. Pause.*)

ORPHULS: I love you! I do love you!

(*Pause.*)

If everything remains the same, why did we suffer? I buried thirty in a day and still I imitate!

(*He examines himself.*)

Other self. Other self unborn. Wrist inside my wrist. Lung inside my lung.

(*Pause.*)

And in the hospitals they said – the young but not only the young – the injustice of my death so sours me, I have not been, I have not been yet what I might have been. But looking at them I thought, had you been, what would you have been? What magnificence? And I concluded, none. A gift of years they would have squandered in casual repetition and in servile acts. Clay, therefore. Complaining clay.

(*He looks aside, sees SUSANNAH, who has returned, watching him.*)

SUSANNAH: Do you talk to yourself? Another madman of the siege?

(*Pause.*)

You blush! Wonderful blush!

ORPHULS: I was – I was –

SUSANNAH: Praying?

ORPHULS: Not praying, no.

(*Pause. He looks at her.*)

I have no bread today.

SUSANNAH: I've eaten.

ORPHULS: Eaten? Oh…

(*Pause. Then with immense will.*)

Be my mistress, then.

(*A prolonged pause.*)

SUSANNAH: Yes.

ORPHULS: Oh, my own bitch, yes…!

(*She goes towards him. He recoils.*) No.

SUSANNAH: (*Stopped.*) No?

ORPHULS: You must not – simply –

SUSANNAH: No –

ORPHULS: Do you understand? Not simply, but –

SUSANNAH: Yes.

> (*Pause.*)

ORPHULS: Suffer.

> (*Pause.*)
>
> It.
>
> (*SUSANNAH goes out. ORPHULS collapses to the floor, a ball of ecstasy.*)

SCENE FIVE

A cellar in Vienna. STARHEMBERG among the outcasts.

STARHEMBERG: In all calamity, the persistence of the destitute! In all catastrophe, the resilience of the poor! The tolerant, the semi-tolerant, CRUSHED TO DEATH! The educated, the semi-educated, TROD TO DUST! The cruel, the semi-cruel, SCORCHED TO ASHES, but the carriers of neither hope nor property, THEY SHALL INHERIT THE EARTH! That's you! (*He holds one tightly.*) Who are your true loves, those who drop small coins in your paw?

FIRST BEGGAR: No –

STARHEMBERG: No – those who come with leaflets preaching revolution?

FIRST BEGGAR: No –

STARHEMBERG: No – those who offer beds at Christmas, do you love those?

FIRST BEGGAR: No –

STARHEMBERG: No, the ones who drive their iron wheels over your splitting shins, they are your brothers!

FIRST BEGGAR: I don't see what –

STARHEMBERG: YES, THE FRATERNITY OF BASTARDY!

> (*He releases him.*)
>
> Yes, very few of you died, I notice, my dear friends, very few, oh, very few, and had Islam burst the gates they would not have stooped to hack your noses, those who have some

gristle left, no, the beggar attracts so little violence, we must learn from him DON'T STAND BEHIND ME I HATE THAT do I lecture you, I don't mean to, I am in search of education, I clown, I misinform, I lick the oily effusion that trickles from your gut DON'T COME UP BEHIND ME –

SECOND BEGGAR: You are a mad and vicious fucker, Starhemberg –

STARHEMBERG: DON'T COME UP BEHIND ME I LOVE TO SEE YOUR FACE IN WHICH IS WRITTEN SURVIVAL OF THE FITTEST, up you monarch!
(*He hoists the BEGGAR onto his back, and parades with him.*)
I am the horse to him! Spur me, you cannibal! Whip me, you angel!

SECOND BEGGAR: Put us down, yer cunt…!

STARHEMBERG: I CAUGHT HIM WITH HIS GOB IN THE CORPSE'S BELLY!

SECOND BEGGAR: Fuck off, you mouth and arsehole bastard –

STARHEMBERG: I did! And excellent! Withold respect? Not me! I canter, I perform my dressage, I am as perfect as the carriage horse, the hearse animal, oh, master, oh, genius in self-perpetuation, I CAUGHT HIM WITH HIS GOB IN THE ENTRAILS!

SECOND BEGGAR: Who the fuck are –

STARHEMBERG: NOT YOU? THEN IT WAS YOUR DOUBLE!

SECOND BEGGAR: Down or I'll kick the kidneys out yer arse –

STARHEMBERG: Down? To the humble soil? Tread pavements, you? Oh, no, not you, MONARCH!
(*He tips him brutally to the floor.*)

FIRST WOMAN BEGGAR: You should watch it, how you hurt the feelings of these gentlemen.

STARHEMBERG: (*Sitting.*) Their sensitivity engulfs me.

FIRST WOMAN BEGGAR: They also breathe.

STARHEMBERG: Yes, I smell it.

FIRST WOMAN BEGGAR: They also suffer.

STARHEMBERG: What, the indigestion caused by human meat? No, I bow to such persistence, you know I do, I am your student, I am your novice, and my tongue hangs out

to the dribble of your wit like the putti in the fountain, piss
your life to me, I drink!

SECOND WOMAN BEGGAR: You are no fucking angel –

STARHEMBERG: No angel yet – but trying –

SECOND WOMAN BEGGAR: WHO FED YOU?

STARHEMBERG: The army commissariat.

SECOND WOMAN BEGGAR: I SPIT ON THAT.

STARHEMBERG: I feel your spit, a cool and perfect fluid…

FIRST WOMAN BEGGAR: Why do you come down here?

STARHEMBERG: To swim your gratitude! To bathe in your
eternal thanks, why else? What's the gift of monarchy to
your applause? The gratitude of wealth is pure selfishness,
but those who only own the gutter, to be praised by them!
(*He mockingly cups his ear.*)
Deliverer, did you say?
Redeemer, over there?
No, didn't catch it, so deafening is the accolade –
(*He fondles the FIRST WOMAN BEGGAR.*)
Fuck with me, I'll kiss your scabs, I'll be a Christ to you, an
ageing Christ who slipped the crucifixion –

FIRST WOMAN BEGGAR: Oh, slag yerself, I done with
rubbing –

STARHEMBERG: Rubbing, she calls love…!

SECOND BEGGAR: (*Threatening him closely.*) Nothing fills me
with more violence, mister, than a punctured snob who
spunks from squalor –

STARHEMBERG: He identifies me –

SECOND BEGGAR: Lock yer gob, you shit picnic –

STARHEMBERG: How my lip swells from your compliments –
(*SECOND BEGGAR goes to attack STARHEMBERG, but
STARHEMBERG is the swifter and takes the BEGGAR in a
terrible embrace.*)
Oh, dance you terrible hater, dance, sick-with-life, NOT
DANCING!
(*He jerks the BEGGAR.*)
Oh, he shifts in some gavotte, some mockery of civil
manners, teach me, I can't follow –
(*He jerks him again.*)

Oh, your movements, are these the VEILED MESSAGES OF
LOVE –

SECOND BEGGAR: You – hurt – you –

STARHEMBERG: Or symbols of the hierarchy? I can't
imitate!

SECOND BEGGAR: Oh – fuck and –

STARHEMBERG: (*Lowering him in a hold.*) Down now, piss-
odour, to your loved level…
(*He pushes the BEGGAR's mouth to the flagstones. A silence. He
releases him, moves away, shuddering.*)

THIRD BEGGAR: You will end up eye-gouged, or nose-
spiked, I dare suggest, the wretched harbour grievances,
having little else to harbour…
(*STARHEMBERG looks at him.*)
I think it possible we are related…

STARHEMBERG: So's all humanity, if we could excavate the
bedrooms.

THIRD BEGGAR: Touché, but I am an Esterhazy of the
excluded line.

STARHEMBERG: I knew the nose.

THIRD BEGGAR: I am not after favours, have you seen my
sister, I am not after favours, obviously, she was put in the
asylum at Estragom –

STARHEMBERG: Go away, now –

THIRD BEGGAR: In a room, and chained, how could she
write poetry in such a posture, the manacles were bolted
to the ceiling, impossible I should have thought, she was
committed for no other reason than her poetry, it did not
rhyme, you see, I ask no favours, why have they dimmed,
your eyes?
(*He sits at STARHEMBERG's feet silent.*)

FIRST WOMAN BEGGAR: You have hurt Larry's throat,
you mad cat…

STARHEMBERG: Then he can shake his bowl for two
defects instead of one.

FIRST WOMAN BEGGAR: You are a proper pig melt in this
mood…

SECOND BEGGAR: (*Roaring at a distance.*) I WILL BLIND 'IS
EYES!

BEGGARS: Down, Larry, down, son…

SECOND BEGGAR: BLIND 'IM, EVERYONE!

STARHEMBERG: You could not blind a pigeon if it sat
trussed in your fingers…

SECOND BEGGAR: PISS IN YER MOUTH!

BEGGARS: Steady, Larry…

SECOND WOMAN BEGGAR: 'ho asked you here in any
case?

STARHEMBERG: Nobody asked, you once perfect, breath-
stopping excellence – for whom I would have crawled
whole avenues of rotting butchery…

SECOND WOMAN BEGGAR: Piss in yer mouth.

STARHEMBERG: So you say.

FOURTH BEGGAR: (*Sitting by STARHEMBERG.*) You know,
so tell me, shall there ever be a system with no poor?

STARHEMBERG: Never. Unless they gaol the poor in
palaces. I don't rule that out.

FOURTH BEGGAR: And shall the poor men burn the rich
men's houses?

STARHEMBERG: Yes, again, and again, or how else could
the rich feel happy?

FOURTH BEGGAR: I follow nothing 'e says! Nothing!

SECOND BEGGAR: POKE 'IM IN THE EYEBALLS, THEN!

FOURTH BEGGAR: SHUDDUP!

STARHEMBERG: (*Grabbing the FOURTH BEGGAR by the
collar.*) Describe what hope you have, your hope, what is it?

FOURTH BEGGAR: Hope?

STARHEMBERG: Yes, you know the stuff, it came in with
the mother's milk, had you no mother?

FOURTH BEGGAR: Yes –

STARHEMBERG: What, then?
(*Pause.*)

FOURTH BEGGAR: Dinner!

STARHEMBERG: NO, AFTER DINNER!
(*Pause.*)

FOURTH BEGGAR: None, after dinner…
(*STARHEMBERG gets up.*)

FIRST WOMAN BEGGAR: I don't think you should visit us. Let us be vicious, as we are, and you be vicious, as you are, and piss in all mouths, but no trespass.
   (*Pause. STARHEMBERG starts to go.*)
FOURTH BEGGAR: Take me…!
   (*STARHEMBERG stops, looks at the FOURTH BEGGAR, shakes his head, goes out. The FOURTH BEGGAR rushes after him.*)

SCENE SIX

A darkened room. An arid and dusty old woman in a chair. STARHEMBERG enters.

SECOND MOTHER: Why are you here?
STARHEMBERG: God knows.
SECOND MOTHER: Here again, and don't know why. Dux. Imperator. Have you aged?
STARHEMBERG: Yes.
SECOND MOTHER: Deliverer. Defender. One day you will enter and I shan't be here. A woman with a baby will be here, and the shutters open, all sunlight and diapers.
STARHEMBERG: Obviously.
SECOND MOTHER: I have nothing more to say and you keep coming here.
STARHEMBERG: Yes.
SECOND MOTHER: Do you love me so much?
STARHEMBERG: It would appear so.
SECOND MOTHER: It would. Tribune. Liberator.
STARHEMBERG: Once I saw you naked. But only once.
SECOND MOTHER: You want to talk of these things, but I have nothing to say.
STARHEMBERG: You have nothing to say but I have much to ask.
SECOND MOTHER: Speak your questions to my grave.
STARHEMBERG: I will do.
SECOND MOTHER: Why do I need to hear?

STARHEMBERG: I would have been your child. How I lay and wished I was your child. If I had been your child none of this would be necessary.

SECOND MOTHER: Generalissimus, you cannot know how tired I am.

STARHEMBERG: I also. And your breasts were like the breasts of a witch.

SECOND MOTHER: Is that the mid-day bell?

STARHEMBERG: The antithesis of sculpture.

SECOND MOTHER: It is. And now I wind my watch.

STARHEMBERG: The antithesis of abundance.

SECOND MOTHER: Thus is my day divided. Only at night do I open the shutter. On the eight o'clock bell. Thus is my day divided.

STARHEMBERG: I come as rarely as I can. Often I wish to come, and refuse myself.

SECOND MOTHER: Yes, rarely, Gloriosus Austriae.

STARHEMBERG: Naked, only once, and I believe you knew that I was there.

SECOND MOTHER: My teeth are falling.

STARHEMBERG: Mine also.

SECOND MOTHER: Sometimes I hear a tinkle as one strikes the tiles. I have been asleep and open-mouthed. The saliva stains my shoulder. My head goes always to the left.

STARHEMBERG: I came behind you and –

SECOND MOTHER: So the left collar of my dress is pale.

STARHEMBERG: I MUST COME HERE ALL THE SAME.

(*He sits. A long silence. He rocks, head in hands.*)

SECOND MOTHER: Oh, my darling one, oh, my little son, my darling one…

(*A long pause.*)

STARHEMBERG: Do they bring you food?

SECOND MOTHER: At one.

STARHEMBERG: Eat, then. Do eat.

SECOND MOTHER: Why?

(*He shrugs.*)

STARHEMBERG: Cease eating, then. And my visits could cease, also.

SECOND MOTHER: Deus Imperator. My lip is thin as
    paper and it spontaneously bleeds…
    (*He rises to his feet.*)
    Deus…
    Deus…
    (*He goes to her. The interruption of a loud voice on the stairs.*)
EMPRESS: LE SIXIÈME ÉTAGE!
    (*Footsteps on the boards.*)
    THIS IS HER ROOM!
    (*The door opens.*)
    I enter! I burst in! A clumsy and unwelcome mound of
    governing flesh!
    LIGHTS!
    OPEN THE SHUTTERS!
    (*A SERVANT enters.*)
    Is she here? I did not knock, I might surprise her straddling
    the commode, but I am a woman of the world and more,
    where are you, Mother of Deliverance? And why this
    hatred of *la clarté, das licht,* are you afraid to witness your
    own decay?
    (*The SERVANT throws back the shutters.*)
    I understand, I also have abolished mirrors and am half
    your age –
    (*The light shows STARHEMBERG and the SECOND
    MOTHER. The EMPRESS stops.*)
    Starhemberg. The filial obligation.
    (*Pause. She bows to the SECOND MOTHER.*)
    Madam, you have more magnetism for this man than all
    five hundred rooms of the Kaiserhof. I think your son is a
    remarkable swine.
SECOND MOTHER: He is not my son. I never suffered him,
    nor any other infant.
EMPRESS: The light is cruel…does no one sweep in here?
    My shoes crack biscuits and the skeletons of gorged
    mice…it is a thoroughfare of rodents and merciless to the
    nostrils, leave the door wide, *je souffre, ich ersticke.*
    (*To STARHEMBERG.*) Why are you here, I am
    embarrassed.
STARHEMBERG: I don't know.

EMPRESS: And why am I, you wonder, you cogitate behind
your level and perceptive gaze, I find he makes me stutter,
as if my head were suddenly a void! Does he do this to
you, unbrain you, my skull is like – well, what – an old
woman's room, does he do this to you?

SECOND MOTHER: Never –

EMPRESS: Well, you are lucky in all ways...

(*Pause. No sound but from the street below.*)

Can you explain to me what sexual preference is?

(*Pause.*)

Its arbitrary –

(*Pause.*)

Its pitiless arbitrariness –

(*Pause.*)

Its –

(*Pause.*)

Well, I longed to see you. I had to see you. And I have!
Tell the coach, get lost, I walk home unattended and may
take hours.

(*The SERVANT leaves. To STARHEMBERG.*)

You must talk more. You force the most undigested vomit
of dissonance and trash from those surrounding you, which
is a gambit on your part, like everything, I believe nothing
you do is not calculated in utter coldness, and you let your
mother stink.

(*She turns, stops.*)

They want to name a regiment The Starhemberg but
someone must present the colours. Do it. In the knowledge
they will splash their flesh against some wall in Hungary.

(*He bows.*)

The Turks chop off their genitals, why is that? And the
noses, why is that?

STARHEMBERG: They are afraid to love.

EMPRESS: Aren't we?

(*To SECOND MOTHER.*) I was so curious to meet you. And
of course, it all makes sense.

(*She turns to leave.*)

SECOND MOTHER: He came up behind me, on a hill.

EMPRESS: Who did?

SECOND MOTHER: And he – so wanted to touch me
– such suffering – it marked me – like a disfigurement – I
could not turn but felt his awful stare – I felt my entire
body flush with blood – the kidneys gush – the whole
length of my bowel – hot rush of blood…

EMPRESS: That is a poem –

(*Pause. She looks at STARHEMBERG.*)

She did not think that. It is a poem. By Ady. ABSURD! I
know the poem by heart.

(*She goes out.*)

SCENE SEVEN

*A park in Vienna. KATRIN sits for the PAINTER. SUSANNAH
watches.*

SUSANNAH: My throbbing priest. My cogent and distended
priest I LOVE HIM TERRIBLY AND ALL HE DOES IS WRITE ME
NOTES.

(*Pause.*)

He is addicted to these little notes which are surely – which
are half-hearted penetrations, surely? I don't understand a
word of them, I hold them this way up, and that way up, I
read them diagonally, I cut them up with scissors, scatter
them and pick them up again I HAVE STRUCK HIM TWICE
ACROSS THE JAW and do you blame me? And oh, he was
white! White with pride and reticence and then forgave
me. He wanted to hit me but he didn't, he forgave me
instead. What is all this DIDN'T with him? I want a child.
God knows why. What do I want a child for?

KATRIN: (*Maintaining her pose.*) It is not a matter of you
wanting a child. It is the child wanting. I know. I never
wanted a child. But the child wanted. All this 'I never
asked to be born' etcetera, piss and nonsense! I know. The
unborn, the unconceived, force the act upon the parents
GET HER ON THE GROUND IT SAYS. GET HIM IN YOUR
BODY IT SAYS. I know. I do know all this. You must get
knowledge, Susannah, from anywhere, but get it.

SUSANNAH: Knowledge?

KATRIN: Yes, and make yourself again! There, now I've given you all this time, and all the time I've given you is time lost for myself, what am I, a charity?
(*She holds her belly.*)
It moves, my master…
(*Pause.*)
Do feel him…he is every bit as violent as his fathers…
(*SUSANNAH touches her belly.*)
He is perfectly loathesome the way he shoves. He longs to be out and about and intent on damage! HE RAMPAGES!
(*SUSANNAH withdraws.*)
Pity the land when he is out. Do you think I will be proud of him, and secretly gloat at every little crime he does? Mums do, they worship their terrors, their stabbings they collect like exam certificates. I know. I dread the criminality of motherhood. It is a criminal relation.

PAINTER: From here on a good day you can see to Transylvania…
(*He peers, holding his brush.*)

KATRIN: (*Inspired.*) Imagine a room, crowded, locked and barred, in which a poison cloud has drifted…! Imagine the mother of the infant trampling the occupants, her heels, her spikes, go into eyes and cheeks as she climbs the dying mound for the last cubic inch of oxygen, the infant stretched aloft, SPARE MINE! Oh, I have blinded you with my heel, oh, I have punctured your face, SPARE MINE!
(*She smiles.*)
Accurate. Oh, so accurate…
(*She closes her eyes.*)

SUSANNAH: (*To PAINTER.*) You're a man. You're a man, aren't you? Why should a man not wish to make love?

PAINTER: (*Staring, off.*) Europe, how it shines! As if a grimy sheet were lifted off, and sunlight fell on all its fields and forests!

KATRIN: And its graves. Its wonderful acres of graves!

SUSANNAH: Is it to torture me? As for fidelity, he asks for none, which makes it worse. I WANT TO BE FORCED TO BE FAITHFUL.

PAINTER: The war, how tedious it was! I ached to paint
women.

KATRIN: Women are in wars. Where were you?

SUSANNAH: And his thing is hard against me. A branch of
maleness. So it is not impotence, surely?

PAINTER: I do so adore the company of women…!

SUSANNAH: He had me once, of course. But that was
prostitution. That was opportunism. That was not love, or
if it was love, love of a different –
(*She stops, following his distracted gaze.*)
What are you looking at? I am short-sighted, what?

PAINTER: (*Putting aside his brush, taking up his sketchbook as if
by habit.*) They are executing a man…
(*He drifts away, drawn inexorably to the scene.*)

KATRIN: Who? Who!
(*She prepares to follow him.*)
I must watch.

SUSANNAH: Why?

KATRIN: I must, that's all.
(*She drifts a little way.*)
It's a park. This is a park, and they –
(*She goes out. SUSANNAH, alone, goes to the canvas. Slowly.
Her body is convulsed by shuddering. She grasps the easel for
support, embracing it. The front of her dress is smothered in paint.
She recovers. KATRIN returns.*)
The head fell…no…it did not fall… it spun…it whirled
away like a top…and the blood was four fountains…four
geysers…but…obviously, he could still see…the head
could see as it flew and he knew…he both knew himself to
be decapitated and also registered the crazy nature of his
flight…his confusion…and his…clarity…!
(*She sees SUSANNAH's dress.*)
You have ruined your dress…
(*The PAINTER appears with a head.*)

PAINTER: The consciousness is draining out of him…
(*SUSANNAH turns away.*)

KATRIN: He can still see…

PAINTER: Yes…he sees us…as through a telescope reversed…

KATRIN: Down tunnels which are darkening…

PAINTER: Our hostile stares are –

KATRIN: Not hostile –

PAINTER: Our curious stares…

KATRIN: Peer down from daylight, as if into a darkening cell…

(*The PAINTER puts the head on the grass and begins sketching.*)

PAINTER: Unfortunately he lopped his tartar hair, the better to conceal himself –

KATRIN: Absurd!

PAINTER: Absurd, with eyes like those –

KATRIN: Which proclaim his distant origins…

(*He sketches feverishly.*)

PAINTER: He was captured in an alley.

KATRIN: (*Plucking flowers.*) The alley is the European thing the silly horseman could not hope to navigate. Oh, silly horseman, I do feel such contempt for him…!

(*She drapes the flowers round the head.*)

SUSANNAH: Do stop it…

KATRIN: Stop it, why?

SUSANNAH: STOP IT, I SAID.

(*The PAINTER looks up, sees her dress, then the canvas.*)

PAINTER: Oh, bloody God, you've –

(*He throws down his pencil as two executioners enter, one with a sword, the other lumbering a crucifix.*)

SHYBAL: I can't let you keep the head.

KATRIN: That's all right, we don't want the head.

SHYBAL: Which is peculiar, when the country is so head-choked…

KATRIN: (*Handing it to him.*) Oh, but rules are rules…

McNOY: (*Popping the head in a sack.*) He was not bad, Johnny the Turk…

KATRIN: Oh, really, wasn't he?

McNOY: The women liked him.

KATRIN: Did they? Peculiar, the female nature. Deep as a pool. Or shallow as a puddle, arguably. What do you say?

McNOY: We're country boys.

KATRIN: No, female nature, though?

McNOY: Yokels, I say…

KATRIN: DON'T SAY YOKELS why did they like him YOKELS MY ARSE do say what it is with women that they do so swiftly turn themselves upside down for strangers –

SUSANNAH: Katrin –

KATRIN: COUNTRY BOYS no, they do so lurk inside their ignorance, they do so skulk inside their illiteracy as if it were a cave LIKE TURKS WHY DID THEY LIKE THEM SAY. (*Pause. SHYBAL stares at her.*)

SHYBAL: I found it in a Turkish trench, this crucifix. They had chopped bits off it, and it bled.

McNOY: And wept. It does at times, still bleed and weep… (*KATRIN looks at it.*)

KATRIN: Yes, I can see it does…

SHYBAL: And now we carry it, down all the lines, gun on left shoulder, Christ on right!

KATRIN: Yes…good… LOVE CHRIST AND WRECK HIS ENEMIES!

SHYBAL: (*Looking into her.*) I think you were one of them.

KATRIN: What?

SHYBAL: Turks' woman…
(*They go off, passing STARHEMBERG. KATRIN turns to him, sudden and brittle.*)

KATRIN: We only meet in public places! Is that because you follow me? Or do you feel you can be more familiar in a park? Why not? What's a park, in any case, a rather dirty place BLOOD ON THE GRASS.
(*Pause.*)
Starhemberg, I am frightened of everyone, especially you, and I would not be otherwise, I am so alive with fear, I am skinless, I am flayed and the nerves tremble on the slightest passage of a man like leaves on birches flutter at the poorest breeze…

STARHEMBERG: I feel them.

KATRIN: Good. To fear is to be alive. Of course I shan't live to be old, the body cannot take the strain.

STARHEMBERG: I dog you.

KATRIN: Yes, you do, and I find your face terrible. You know
you have a terrible face DON'T TOUCH ME I would shudder
if you touched me and some cry would issue from the
very bottom of my gut like afterbirth sings in the grate or a
green log screams, no, I wish to marry a young man of no
character whose good looks charm my mother and whose
manners are immaculate, a lover of families who will
spend all Christmas round the fire, perhaps a teacher at
the university when they open it again, and so ambitious,
SO VERY AMBITIOUS! He will know how to demolish any
argument, his humour will be infectious and –

STARHEMBERG: You have no mother.

KATRIN: So what –

STARHEMBERG: Your mother perished the same day as
you.

KATRIN: I did not perish –

STARHEMBERG: Yes.

KATRIN: You see, he must know everything, HOW DID I
PERISH I WAS MADE.

(*Pause.*)

Let us leave the park – Susannah –

(*She extends a hand to her.*)

The park fills me with despair – Susannah – hardly have
the howitzers ceased and the prams are out – look, they
are pulling a gun out of its pit and the nanny rushes in to
spread the picnic cloth, THE SPEED OF OBLIVION!

(*She shudders, her hand still stretched.*)

All right, kiss me if it helps you, press your thin mouth to
my thin mouth, all cracked with wind…

(*STARHEMBERG does not move. SUSANNAH gets up, takes
her hand.*)

How well am I known? Is it selling, my print?

(*They start to go.*)

STARHEMBERG: Help me, or I think we'll die alone…

KATRIN: Why not? Why not die alone? How would you
die? To the sound of violins, with your children clinging to
your feet as if your soul could be pulled back through the
ceiling? HELP YOU HOW.

*(Pause, she looks at him, laughs, then the women go out…
STARHEMBERG is left alone on a darkening stage, which
fills with members of the Academy, clapping the entrance of
LEOPOLD.)*

SCENE EIGHT

*A circle of critics at The Imperial Academy of Art. LEOPOLD enters
to polite applause.*

LEOPOLD: Not the room as we would want it. Not the salon
we would choose, the swags being somewhat chipped and
the putti lacking gilt, but in such pock-marked landscapes
imagination might erupt, I call upon you to elucidate the
principles of a new art, because the stir of Europe from its
sleep commands a terrible and unrelenting movement of
the soul. I have only half an hour. What shall the art be like
now, you say!
(He sits. Pause.)
Yes, you say.
(Pause.)

ARST: A People's Art.

LEOPOLD: No. Anybody else?
(ARST sits. Another rises.)

FELIKS: An art of celebration.

LEOPOLD: What do you want to celebrate?

FELIKS: Us, of course!

LEOPOLD: You? What is there to celebrate in you? The
fact you are alive and not a stinking thing among the pine
trees? Well, you go and celebrate that, but don't ask us to
join you.

STENSH: A celebration of the heroism of the –

LEOPOLD: No, no, leave out the heroism, please, the
heroism was not conspicuous, in my own case barely
perceptible, and much as we have reason to be grateful to
the Polish cavalry I think an art based on lancers is likely
to become repetitive, debased, mechanical, and pleading
muslims just as bad, we must move on, CELEBRATE WHAT

EXACTLY, Bomberg, you speak, your dark face is full of
irritation, which is inspiration, surely?

(*Pause. BOMBERG does not rise.*)

BOMBERG: Shame. An art of shame.

LEOPOLD: Elucidate.

BOMBERG: That's all.

ARST: What is there to be ashamed of?

(*BOMBERG shakes his head.*)

No, don't just shake your head, that is appalling
arrogance…

(*He shakes it again.*)

I think that gesture is typical of Professor Bomberg, who is
needless to say, not among the most popular of teachers –

LEOPOLD: WHO CARES IF HE IS POPULAR?

(*Pause. ARST concedes with a movement of the shoulders.*)

ARST: The fact is the students are unwilling even to attend his
lectures which –

LEOPOLD: WHO CARES ABOUT THE STUDENTS?

ARST: Well –

LEOPOLD: EVERYTHING YOU SAY IS MEANINGLESS.

(*Pause.*)

All that matters is whether he is right.

(*Pause.*)

On the other hand, Bomberg, do speak.

(*Pause.*)

BOMBERG: First, we must know who we are. And to know
who we are, we must know who we were. I do not think at
this moment, we know who we were, and consequently –

FELIKS: You will depress the people with your introspection.

ARST: He knows nothing of the people, go into the street and
see the people, you talk to nobody –

FELIKS: Listen to the people –

BOMBERG: The people have a million mouths –

ARST: You see, you are a pessimist –

BOMBERG: YOU WANT TO CLAIM THE PEOPLE. YOU WANT TO
OWN THE PEOPLE. NONE OF YOU TRUSTS THE PEOPLE.

ARST: This is why his lectures are so ill-attended –

BOMBERG: YOU SUFFOCATE THE PEOPLE –

LEOPOLD: Bomberg –

BOMBERG: YOU INVENT THE PEOPLE –

LEOPOLD: Bomberg –

BOMBERG: SHUT UP ABOUT THE PEOPLE!

(*Pause.*)

ARST: The people clamour for solidarity –

BOMBERG: No, they ache for truth –

FELIKS: Happiness, surely –

BOMBERG: Fuck happiness –

FELIKS: You see? What's wrong with happiness?

LEOPOLD: BRING IN A HAPPY PAINTER! YOU!

(*He points out the PAINTER.*)

Stand up. Don't be intimidated by men with words, you can pick words out of the gutter.

ARST: It is where the best words are.

LEOPOLD: Rubbish. Rubbish and condescension.

(*ARST shrugs bitterly.*)

Shh!

(*To the PAINTER.*)

Are you a happy person?

ARST: This is not exactly what we had in mind –

LEOPOLD: Shh! You want to dominate everything! These also are the people. These are the ones whom we must trust.

(*ARST shrugs again.*)

I WISH YOU WOULD NOT SHRUG LIKE THAT.

(*To the PAINTER.*) Are you happy?

PAINTER: I –

(*Pause.*)

No.

LEOPOLD: Why not?

PAINTER: I – perhaps a defect in my character –

BOMBERG: IT'S NOT A DEFECT IT'S A QUALITY.

LEOPOLD: Shh! If only – may I say this and then forget it – how I wish you gentlemen had shown such viciousness when Islam thrust its bayonets between the city gates – if only – now forget it!

(*To the PAINTER.*) Can you paint happy pictures? And if not, why not?

PAINTER: It is not a happy time.

ARST: Then why not make it so?

FELIKS: I think that's asking a great deal of –

ARST: Is it? Why? He is a craftsman, isn't he, he has a duty to
the people –
(*BOMBERG lets out a long and terrible cry.*)
Yes – yes – a duty to – God lent him the skill and – what
he does with it is – yes –

LEOPOLD: Who do you love?

PAINTER: Who do I love?

LEOPOLD: Not woman. Artist. Which?

PAINTER: Giovanni Carpeta.

FELIKS: Be serious.

PAINTER: Giovanni Carpeta.

ARST: Miserable, satanic, gloom-sodden egoist of idiotically
unreal landscapes which –

PAINTER: I don't agree –

ARST: Which induce suicidal thoughts in those already
suicidal –

PAINTER: Nevertheless –

ARST: And sends you lurching for the sunlight – one looks
at Carpeta and sees at once why the young are turning in
their droves to the Spanish and Chinese Schools –

BOMBERG: So what –

ARST: What does Carpeta say, what does Carpeta lend to
people already crippled with despair –

PAINTER: He speaks to me –

ARST: I don't think a single canvas of the man would last two
minutes in the market square –

PAINTER: I REVERE HIM! I REVERE HIM!

ARST: It would be torn from its stretcher and the crowd
would say –

PAINTER: I REVERE HIM!

ARST: You insult us with your pessimism –
(*The PAINTER lets out a long moan.*)
Yes, your human loathing – end of speech!
(*He shows empty hands. The PAINTER sobs.*)

LEOPOLD: (*To the PAINTER.*) You have to – I'm afraid
– defend your soul against the bullies of the mind…

ARST: I must say I am extremely weary with souls, which as far as I can see are merely pretexts for self-adulation.

PAINTER: (*To ARST.*) I must tell you…if I meet you again, I'll kill you…

ARST: NOW WHO'S THE BULLY!

(*He laughs. The PAINTER leaves.*)

Soul, I assume? The passing of soul?

(*Pause, then to ARST's horror, BOMBERG grips him from behind about the throat. LEOPOLD bursts out laughing. FELIKS tries to unlock BOMBERG's manic grip. The EMPRESS appears.*)

LEOPOLD: I LAUGH! I LAUGH!

ARST: (*As BOMBERG releases him, falling back into his chair.*) Mad – man…!

LEOPOLD: Bomberg, I think you must join the church…

(*BOMBERG shakes his head. weeping into his hands.*)

Yes, he must take Orders, mustn't he?

FELIKS: This has been a foolish meeting –

STARHEMBERG: It is a very foolish time. The snake cut into seven pieces writhes absurdly as it tries to join itself, but in what order! How could it be otherwise…?

LEOPOLD: You speak. You've said nothing yet.

STARHEMBERG: Nothing I say will be true.

EMPRESS: We don't ask for miracles.

STARHEMBERG: Everything I say I will later retract.

LEOPOLD: We are familiar with this tendency.

STARHEMBERG: The apparent logic of my position is only the dressing of flagrant incompatibilities.

EMPRESS: Obviously. And that is why we trust you, Starhemberg.

(*Pause.*)

STARHEMBERG: What I need. And what there will be. I need an art which will recall pain. The art that will be will be all flourishes and celebration. I need an art that will plummet through the floor of consciousness and free the unborn self. The art that will be will be extravagant and dazzling. I need an art that will shatter the mirror in which we pose. The art that will be will be all mirrors. I want to make a new man and new woman but only from the pieces of the old. The new man and new woman will insist on their utter novelty. I ask a lot. The new art will ask nothing. And now I am going to bed…

EMPRESS: I do not think, Starhemberg, you have quite grasped the temper of the times, has he? I think what Europe needs is rococo and a little jazz!

(*STARHEMBERG gets up, bows, is about to leave, but stops.*)

STARHEMBERG: During the war, while the ground rose under the shellfire and the sky was black with rising and falling and rising clods, and rising and falling flesh, and everything was racing from itself, the eye from the socket and the arm from the joint, you heard in the fractional silences a singing record going round, deep in a cellar, and the lips of the soon-to-be-dead were mouthing sentiments of banal happiness…

EMPRESS: And why not…?

(*He bows, goes out.*)

WHY NOT.

(*The sound of a popular march played by a band, rising to a crescendo.*)

ACT TWO

SCENE ONE

A bed in a public square, overlooked by benches. STARHEMBERG watches an old woman dragging a sheet over the stage. She flings it on the bed.

STARHEMBERG: Have you given birth?

MIDWIFE: To a proper bastard.

STARHEMBERG: Tell me then, what to expect.

MIDWIFE: Abuse, ducks.

STARHEMBERG: Abuse? Why abuse? It's supposed to be a miracle.

MIDWIFE: So was the saving of Vienna, but all I heard was blasphemy.

STARHEMBERG: Birth's a thing of beauty, surely?

MIDWIFE: It's a thing of pain.

STARHEMBERG: Yes, but pain's divisible.

MIDWIFE: It divided me. I thought I'd never come together again.

STARHEMBERG: (*Turning away.*) Oh, choke on your wit, I'm sorry I bothered you.

(*ORPHULS appears.*)

HUMOUR! HUMOUR! They creep among jokes like the lonely sentry in fortifications! I say pain's divisible.

There's pain for something and pain for nothing, so birth's tolerable and torture's sheer disintegration, surely?

(*He looks at him.*)

I am thinner than yesterday, and you are even fatter.

ORPHULS: No, I am –

STARHEMBERG: Yes, you swell with gratification –

ORPHULS: On the contrary, I am deprived –

STARHEMBERG: Then you swell on that. Everything agrees with you.

(*He goes close to ORPHULS.*)

I think all teeth rotted in the siege but yours. THAT'S HER BED. Where are you sitting?

(*He goes to the woman.*)

Mother, how much are the benches?

MIDWIFE: I do the bed.

STARHEMBERG: Oh, she is bed specialist.

(*He calls off.*)

BENCH MAN!

ORPHULS: Is she – has her labour begun?

MIDWIFE: There's been some show, so I get on.

STARHEMBERG: BENCH MAN!

ORPHULS: I think this is – I know you are full of admiration
for her but –

STARHEMBERG: The benchman is elsewhere, making
humour from his cataracts –

ORPHULS: What is the virtue in it?

STARHEMBERG: Or showing his stumps and making fun of
the absent legs –

ORPHULS: I ask you, what –

STARHEMBERG: NO VIRTUE IN IT. NONE.

(*LEOPOLD enters. ORPHULS sits disconsolately on a bench.*)

LEOPOLD: It's cold, I shan't stay for all of it. And what's her
game, in any case? I told Elizabeth this had to be illegal.
No, she said, not yet!

(*The audience is drifting in. LEOPOLD spots the PAINTER.*)

Here is the vantage point!

(*He propels the PAINTER to the front.*)

This also is a battle! And now it rains! She gets all she asks
for!

(*He pulls up his collar. Umbrellas go up. KATRIN appears,
supported by the MIDWIFE. Silence descends. She looks into the
crowd. Pause.*)

KATRIN: Not as many as I'd hoped. Don't they like a
spectacle? Not the numbers I'd predicted, but –

(*A spasm of pain doubles her. The MIDWIFE goes to assist her.
KATRIN pushes her away.*)

NOBODY HELP ME BIRTH THE CHILD.

(*Pause. She steadies herself.*)

Can everybody see all right? Some people – over there
– the view's restricted, surely?

(*Pause. She stares into the audience.*)

I bring you hope.

I bring you History.

(*She is doubled again. The MIDWIFE goes to assist but is repelled.*)

WHAT ARE YOU –

MIDWIFE: Only helping, lady –

KATRIN: No, that isn't it –

MIDWIFE: Helping –

KATRIN: THAT'S NOT WHAT IT IS.

(*Pause. The MIDWIFE looks to LEOPOLD, to ORPHULS.*)

MIDWIFE: This is how we get in labour – all abusive, but we don't mean anything –

KATRIN: I DO MEAN SOMETHING.

MIDWIFE: I know darling, but –

(*A further spasm. KATRIN staggers.*)

LEOPOLD: I can't watch this!

(*He half-turns away.*)

I can't watch this! Do something, somebody!

(*ORPHULS goes to move, with the MIDWIFE, but STARHEMBERG blocks them, drawing a knife.*)

STARHEMBERG: I'll burst the spleen of anyone who nears her bed.

(*A pause.*)

ORPHULS: She is delirious.

STARHEMBERG: She is lucid.

ORPHULS: She is in agony!

STARHEMBERG: Her pain she needs. Her suffering she requires. NO THIEVING BY THE COMPASSIONATE!

(*Pause. KATRIN struggles on the bed.*)

LEOPOLD: Starhemberg, if she dies, you are responsible.

(*Pause.*)

MIDWIFE: You are in such a bad position, lady…!

KATRIN: Good! Let it find daylight through my arse!

MIDWIFE: You see, that's 'ow they go, let me –

STARHEMBERG: (*Threatening.*) Move and you die.

MIDWIFE: I'M A WOMAN, AREN'T I?

ORPHULS: Starhemberg, you are under some awful curse…

(*A cry from KATRIN. She clutches her belly.*)

LEOPOLD: END THIS! I CAN'T WATCH THIS!

(Men, and the MIDWIFE, rush forward, overwhelming STARHEMBERG, who is disarmed and held. KATRIN is covered with umbrellas. NUNS drape the scene of birth. The EMPRESS appears.)

EMPRESS: *(Going to STARHEMBERG, where he is still held.)* Starhemberg, was that real love?

(He looks at the ground.)

Not if love's caring, but maybe caring's base?

STARHEMBERG: They pretend to pity her, but they steal her pain. Don't chain her in some madhouse.

EMPRESS: It's you they wish to chain…

(She indicates with a move of her head that STARHEMBERG be released. A cry of joy and applause from the birth place.)

LEOPOLD: It's over, and alive!

(A baby is handed to LEOPOLD. He holds it high.)

What History spoiled, let History mend. I christen her – Concilia!

(Applause. The baby is handed to a SERVANT. LEOPOLD and the EMPRESS depart.)

ORPHULS: *(To STARHEMBERG.)* Come to Christ, now…

STARHEMBERG: I do. I come to you at all hours. I raise you from your bed and beg you reasons why I should love men.

ORPHULS: Christ also suffered the intensest hate, or He could never have found charity. The good have little purchase on the memory. Who would follow the innocent? No, you follow him who triumphs over himself, who boils within and in whose eyes all struggle rages. Him you follow to the water's edge, and no other…

(He kisses STARHEMBERG's hand.)

KATRIN: *(From the bed.)* Starhemberg!

(STARHEMBERG turns to go to her. ORPHULS clings to his hand.)

ORPHULS: I must become a bishop.

STARHEMBERG: You must, it's obvious.

(He goes to her.)

KATRIN: It's perfect, isn't it? Quite perfect?

STARHEMBERG: No loving husband could have made a better child in sheets of wedded honour.

KATRIN: They cheated me…

STARHEMBERG: Yes.

KATRIN: And made of my horrors reconciliation.

STARHEMBERG: Yes.

KATRIN: HISTORY THEY MADE OF ME.

STARHEMBERG: Yes, but we will deny them yet…

KATRIN: (*With a wail.*) How…? How…?

(*Pause, then STARHEMBERG walks away. The MIDWIFE accosts him.*)

MIDWIFE: You have some pain, mister…

STARHEMBERG: Pain? Me?

MIDWIFE: I think you will find death difficult.

STARHEMBERG: Yes. I won't have it near me.

MIDWIFE: You tease me, but I'd give you good advice if you would let me.

STARHEMBERG: Do! I like the fact your hands are caked in blood. So were mine until recently.

(*The MIDWIFE goes close to him, intimately.*)

MIDWIFE: Hang yourself.

(*Pause. STARHEMBERG nods, as if in appreciation. The MIDWIFE squeals with laughter. He seizes her hand. She senses danger.*)

STARHEMBERG: It's you that must hang.

MIDWIFE: Only a joke!

STARHEMBERG: Yes, but I have no sense of humour.

(*The EMPRESS appears. The MIDWIFE hurries away, off.*)

EMPRESS: Starhemberg…

STARHEMBERG: She is a witch, the midwife. She must hang.

(*Pause.*)

EMPRESS: If you say so.

STARHEMBERG: (*Calling.*) DON'T LET HER ESCAPE, THERE!

EMPRESS: Starhemberg, your mother's dead…

(*He looks at her.*)

STARHEMBERG: Once they are in the slums, it takes a regiment to find them…

(*Pause. ORPHULS goes to STARHEMBERG and embraces him swiftly.*)

Dead? But I hadn't finished with her yet…

ORPHULS: We shall bury her…

STARHEMBERG: I shall have to see her naked, shan't I? I shall have to wash her and she was not clean…

ORPHULS: We'll bury your mother…

STARHEMBERG: Together…

ORPHULS: Yes…

STARHEMBERG: And then, perhaps…kill yours…

(*Pause. He departs. ORPHULS is left alone as night falls.*)

SCENE TWO

A plot in the city. ORPHULS alone. SUSANNAH enters.

SUSANNAH: I would lick you all over if you'd let me. I would take your testicles in my mouth and roll them gently as if they were blown eggs of such rarity, of such fragility. I would take your arse in my hands if you'd let me and raise it like a sacrifice, oh, listen, I must tell you I will marry somewhere else if you don't give me your flesh to love. An officer with four cows has made me a proposal.

(*He turns to look at her.*)

ORPHULS: Marry him.

(*Pause.*)

SUSANNAH: I will. I will marry him.

ORPHULS: (*Turning away.*) And lie awake whole wretched nights with your brain bursting. I will crouch in your imagination like a bear in a crate. I will pace there all your hours.

SUSANNAH: I will have children, whose wailing will drown out your memory.

ORPHULS: It's a tempting prospect, I can see, red-armed on the acre and a basketful of screamers. Is he drunk, this officer? Drunk and poxed? As he climbs on you to satisfy some savagery the cows will bellow in the downstairs room, what perfection! And how far from the city? They say there is rough pasture eighty miles outside Vienna

where the old troopers are settling, though the bodies of
the Janissaries must be cleared from it, YOU CATACLYSMIC
BITCH, all you have will disintegrate in a single winter!
(*He turns to others offstage.*)
HERE!
(*He points to the earth. Cloaked figures enter with shovels.*)
And not deep.
(*They begin to excavate the spot.*)
SUSANNAH: What have you done…?
WORKMAN: HERE!
(*They dig faster.*)
SUSANNAH: What have you done…!
ORPHULS: I shall inhabit you. I shall swim your veins and
smile like a gargoyle from the walls of your womb…
SUSANNAH: (*As LEOPOLD and others enter.*) What has he
done!
(*ORPHULS laughs as SUSANNAH runs off.*)
LEOPOLD: Not funny! Where?
WORKMAN: Here!
(*The EMPRESS goes to look at the excavation.*)
LEOPOLD: Don't look!
(*She persists.*)
Hideous! Don't look!
(*She ignores him.*)
All right, look if you must.
(*LEOPOLD goes to ORPHULS.*)
Are you mad? COVER THE GRAVE! What is to become of
Vienna? You want to be a bishop and you kill your mother,
are you mad? COVER IT ENTIRELY! We are building a new
Europe and you do this, you are in love with Starhemberg,
he eats your soul, you horrify me!
(*The EMPRESS joins them.*)
We must arrest him and declare him mad. What else do
you suggest?
ORPHULS: I am not mad. I am perfectly normal, only more
so.
LEOPOLD: IN WHAT SENSE!
ORPHULS: I was never more fitted for my task.

LEOPOLD: WHAT TASK!
(*He turns to the EMPRESS.*)
He looks the perfect cleric, he exudes authority, who would not confess to him the most lurid sin and yet –
(*He turns to ORPHULS.*)
Do you want to be tried, is that what you want? Do you want to be hanged, is that what you want?

ORPHULS: Perhaps.

LEOPOLD: Perhaps? You require it, obviously!

ORPHULS: I require unhappiness, that's obvious.

EMPRESS: And this is such a happy age! There never was such happiness! All this happiness, and you go and bash your mother with a rock. Was it a rock?

ORPHULS: A plank.

EMPRESS: A plank.
(*LEOPOLD groans.*)

ORPHULS: She placed no value on her life. It was a burden to her. Whereas her death meant much to me. So all things pointed to her extinction.

LEOPOLD: Especially Starhemberg! His finger, especially. I might have wished to kill my mother. What if I had, what should I have been!

ORPHULS: Excessively alive.
(*He holds LEOPOLD.*)
It is a second birth, and like the first, induces such a rush of air to unopened lungs, I struggled on the ground red as an infant, my unused limbs thrashing the air, and he carried me, he bore me home like the maternal nurse! There!
(*He points.*)
There is the site of my nativity!
(*Pause.*)

LEOPOLD: A new morality we asked for. And we get this.

ORPHULS: Feel me! I'm NEW.

LEOPOLD: Take your claw off me! You should shrivel in a furnace, and the skull, as it popped, should invite spontaneous applause!

EMPRESS: Oh, do be quiet –

LEOPOLD: YOU SAY BE QUIET AND –

EMPRESS: Think. Think.

LEOPOLD: When I think of my mother –

EMPRESS: That is not thinking, is it? Stop generalising and
think.
(*She looks at ORPHULS, who smiles.*)
What have you learned?

ORPHULS: Learned…?

EMPRESS: Learned, yes, for neither you nor Starhemberg do
things except for learning. Deliver us your sermon. Not on
murder, but what came of it. Quick, now! And you!
(*She calls to the workmen.*)
Yes! Down your tools and gather, cluster the Bishop, who
will speak, cluster him, he knows things you do not.
(*She turns away, waiting. The men reluctantly form a circle.
ORPHULS prepares, and then with the force of inspiration, turns
to deliver his oration.*)

ORPHULS: All that occurs, does it not occur that I should
be its beneficiary, nourished on it, be it filth or excellence?
Even the death of love is food to the soul and therefore
what is evil? Is there evil except not to do? I do not
blaspheme when I say the gift of life is paltry and our best
service to God is not to thank Him, endless thanking, no,
but to enhance His offer, and yet you do not, I think if I
were God I would declare with some weariness or even
vehemence, how little they do with the breath I gave them,
they exhale repetitions, they applaud the lie, they sleep
even in their waking hours, why did I make them thus, I
erred in some respect, they fill me with disgust, have you
no notion of God's horror? I am thinking of the God in us
whose profound groan is the background to our clatter –
(*He identifies one of the uncomprehending workmen.*)
You shake your head in silence, is that freedom? If silence
was freedom it is so no longer, the word is volatile, am
I too difficult for you? LIAR! YOU HIDE BEHIND THE
SO-CALLED SIMPLICITY OF CHRIST, BUT IS THAT NOT A
BLASPHEMY?
(*Pause.*)

If I had not done evil, how could I address you who have
perhaps thought evil only? If I did not know cruelty could
I know pity, they are the twin towers of the soul? Do not
hold hands in false gestures as if by crowding you could
exclude the groan of God, no, you must hear the sound of
His despair, and we must learn from Judas whose Gospel
is not written, we must learn from him who stood alone,
for Judas did not sell Christ nor was he corrupt, but Judas
was cruel for knowledge, and without Judas there could be
no resurrection, Beauty, Cruelty, and Knowledge, these
are the triple order of the Groaning God, I speak as your
adviser in whose pain you may see beauty, I praise my
beauty and you must praise yours!
(*Pause.*)
I end here, in a proper and terrible exhaustion. I have laid
myself before you, which is the duty of a priest.
(*Pause.*)
EMPRESS: How wonderful you are…I shall not forget one
word you said. How wonderful you are, I could truly love
you. But we can't know that, and you must die…mustn't
he?
(*She looks at LEOPOLD. The bell of a great church.*)

SCENE THREE

*A room in Vienna, shuttered. The bell ceases. Into the obscurity,
STARHEMBERG walks slowly. He removes his clothing, item by
item. He goes to a chair, and sits. KATRIN is discovered, already
naked, in a chair distantly opposite his own. They gaze, unfalteringly.*

KATRIN: I show myself to you. I show myself, and it is an act
of love. Stay in your place!
STARHEMBERG: I was not moving. Only looking.
KATRIN: You were not moving, no…
(*Pause.*)
I am in such a torment it would be an act of pity to
approach me, pure pity, but you will not, will you? I
know because you are not kind, thank God, you spare
us kindness, and your body is quite grey, it is so far from

146

perfect, spare us perfection also! You are a beautiful man, so beautiful my breath is stiff as mud to breathe, don't come near me.

STARHEMBERG: You shudder...

KATRIN: Yes, may I call you my love, whether or not you love me I must call you my love, DON'T GET UP!

STARHEMBERG: I shan't get up...

KATRIN: I am in the most beautiful Hell. Praise me a little, mutter me a bit, describe, describe for Christ in Heaven's sake, I could gnaw your knees to blood, and you mine, I know you could –

STARHEMBERG: Yes...

KATRIN: I would rather take one look from you than pulp a night in hopeless effort, there, I'm better now, much better...

(*Pause.*)

It's odd, but though I have done all that suggested itself to me, I never looked at any man but you, I think. Looked, I mean. I never knew to look was love.

(*Pause.*)

WHAT DO YOU SEE?

WHAT DO YOU SEE?

(*SUSANNAH enters, opening the shutters one by one.*)

SUSANNAH: My priest is dead.

(*Pause. Light floods in.*)

With all Vienna watching.

(*STARHEMBERG and KATRIN are still.*)

My priest is dead, and I am marrying a farmer.

(*She freezes.*)

NOT DIFFICULT IF YOU TRY.

(*Pause, then STARHEMBERG rises, pulls a long coat over himself. A child's cries distantly.*)

STARHEMBERG: We are going to Wallachia.

SUSANNAH: Wallachia? Why?

STARHEMBERG: To inspect the forts.

SUSANNAH: What forts?

STARHEMBERG: Within whose compass New Europe is to breathe. Under whose benign regard the vines may ripen undisturbed, and marriages be blessed with endlessness…
(*He leans his head on SUSANNAH's shoulder.*)

KATRIN: Yes! Show me the frontier! I will study the trajectory of shells, and arcs, dead grounds and fields of fire, I have Holbein, Durer, Montecucculi in my library! What don't I know of wars!
(*She pulls a gown over herself as a nurse enters holding CONCILIA, crying and swaddled. STARHEMBERG goes to the nurse and takes the child in his arms.*)

STARHEMBERG: And Concilia! Concilia, obviously!
(*He lifts her in the air. A fortress wall descends. The sound of knocking on a door.*)

SCENE FOUR

The fort in Wallachia. STARHEMBERG alone, half-dressed.

STARHEMBERG: Come in!
(*An OFFICER enters.*)

OFFICER: There is a Turkish regiment two miles off.

STARHEMBERG: Whose?

OFFICER: Jemal Pasha's Lancers.

STARHEMBERG: Show Jemal my standard.

OFFICER: That's done already. We think it most unlikely they will attack a fort.

STARHEMBERG: That's my opinion also.
(*The OFFICER bows, goes to leave.*)
Tell Jemal I have a gift for him. Hostages, safe conduct and the rest of it.
(*The OFFICER bows and is about to leave when STARHEMBERG grabs him violently.*)
Talk to me! Talk!

OFFICER: Talk…?

STARHEMBERG: Yes, yes, my gorgeous one, lie down and tell me your life.

OFFICER: Lie down?

STARHEMBERG: (*Propelling him towards a chair.*) There – yes –

OFFICER: But that's your –

STARHEMBERG: My cot, yes, but you have it, you spread,
you luxuriate, and off with lovely tunics –

OFFICER: I'm rather cold –

STARHEMBERG: (*Unbuttoning him.*) Forget the cold, and
I will come to you as a child to a long-lost relative, I will
place my head just – there – forget the cold, the cold is not
our enemy –

OFFICER: No, I suppose –

STARHEMBERG: Not in the least our enemy, and tell me
in a child-like way, for my infant ears, the beauty of your
life…

(*He lays his head in the OFFICER's lap, and draws his hand to
his head.*)

OFFICER: Beauty of it…

STARHEMBERG: Yes, do –

OFFICER: I don't know that it's –

STARHEMBERG: Mmm…

OFFICER: That it's very –

STARHEMBERG: Mmm…

OFFICER: Beautiful – I wouldn't –

STARHEMBERG: No, no, make me adore you –

OFFICER: Well, I –

STARHEMBERG: Go on –

OFFICER: I er – I er –

STARHEMBERG: Mmm…

OFFICER: I was –

STARHEMBERG: Mmmm…?

OFFICER: One of – seven children –

STARHEMBERG: Seven! Really? Seven?

OFFICER: And er – was born in Lombardy –

STARHEMBERG: Lombardy?

OFFICER: Yes – land of – er – many poplars there and – I
can't remember much of it but –

STARHEMBERG: No, no, paint it! Paint it! Make me love
you.

OFFICER: Poplars and – and –

STARHEMBERG: Say, do say…

(*The OFFICER dries, holds his head in despair.*)
Must. Must.
(*The OFFICER is in agony.*)
Must.

OFFICER: (*With sudden invention.*) I got up one morning
– before anybody else – I don't know why – got up and
crept downstairs – the sun was brilliant and –

STARHEMBERG: Mmm...

OFFICER: Walked down the street – it's not true, this – the
streets were full of – were full of – horses!

STARHEMBERG: Mmmm...

OFFICER: A cavalry brigade were tethered there and – I
took one and unbridled it – and rode it – clattering across
a bridge – the water was all – chopped and sparkling with
sunlight – I rode and rode – up four hills and down four
valleys – and when the horse stopped, so did I and I – slid
off and –

STARHEMBERG: Yes –

OFFICER: And –

STARHEMBERG: Don't stop! Don't stop!

OFFICER: I saw – a – beautiful girl –

STARHEMBERG: Make it an old man.

OFFICER: What?

STARHEMBERG: An old man. Make it an old man, please.

OFFICER: This old man, and he –

STARHEMBERG: Yes –

OFFICER: He – er –

(*KATRIN enters, silently. He observes her. She perches, silently,
on a chair.*)

He – er – had a long beard – and –

STARHEMBERG: How long?

OFFICER: RIDICULOUSLY LONG!

STARHEMBERG: Are you sure?

OFFICER: Yes!

STARHEMBERG: Go on...

OFFICER: Which reached to the ground – and he took my
hand – and his hand was – bleeding –

STARHEMBERG: Why?

OFFICER: I don't know why – it was anyway and – I put my
    little hand in his wet hand –

STARHEMBERG: Why though?

OFFICER: DON'T INTERRUPT! And led me – willingly – I did
    not protest to a – a –

    (*His eyes meet KATRIN's. He perseveres.*)

    Well – which when I looked was –

STARHEMBERG: What was in the well?

OFFICER: I'm coming to that –

STARHEMBERG: Forgive me, I –

OFFICER: Was – absolutely –

STARHEMBERG: Yes? Yes?

OFFICER: FULL OF BRICKS!

STARHEMBERG: Bricks?

OFFICER: Full of bricks, why not bricks!

STARHEMBERG: No reason, I –

OFFICER: Bricks, yes –

STARHEMBERG: That was why his hands were bleeding!

OFFICER: Obviously!

STARHEMBERG: I do like you! I like you very much!

OFFICER: And these bricks were so deep and so jumbled
    – so chaotic and so – arid –

STARHEMBERG: Yes –

OFFICER: They had caused the death of many animals…

    (*Pause.*)

    …whose bodies…lay littered round the rim…

STARHEMBERG: They couldn't reach the –

OFFICER: Not a drop…

    (*Pause. He holds STARHEMBERG's hand.*)

STARHEMBERG: Go on…

OFFICER: And the old man begged me – No, he didn't beg
    me, actually, he – insisted – most cruelly insisted that I
    – unblock the well… And I was only ten…

STARHEMBERG: Ten…

OFFICER: And the sun beat down, and the smell of
    decomposing sheep was…

STARHEMBERG: Poor boy…

OFFICER: Vile and – I thought – climbing in all that rubble thought – shifting the bricks, thought…

STARHEMBERG: What?

OFFICER: Many things, but – he was so severe – his ugly face over the rim was going – FASTER! FASTER!

STARHEMBERG: Vile man –

OFFICER: Vile man, yes –

STARHEMBERG: Thirsty, too!

OFFICER: Yes, that must have been – partly the explanation for his vileness, but – I felt – his beard hung over – hideous beard hanging right over – and I –

STARHEMBERG: Yes –

OFFICER: Instead of just throwing the bricks out I –

STARHEMBERG: YOU DIDN'T –

OFFICER: Yes –

STARHEMBERG: YOU HIT HIM WITH THE BRICK.

(*Long pause.*)

A terrible, terrible, story…

(*Pause. The OFFICER gets up, does up his tunic.*)

OFFICER: If I am to reach Jemal, I ought to…was that all right?

STARHEMBERG: So you never drank?

OFFICER: What?

STARHEMBERG: You never drank…

OFFICER: I…no, I suppose not… no…

(*He goes out. STARHEMBERG dresses in fresh clothes.*)

STARHEMBERG: Bring Concilia… Bring the child of impeccable origins…

KATRIN: It's late.

STARHEMBERG: Yes. Bring her from her little bed.

KATRIN: (*Puzzled.*) Why…?

STARHEMBERG: Concilia, whose forehead is a little swamp of Imperial kisses, and whose ears are tiny basins of kind sentiment…bring her here…

KATRIN: Why, Starhemberg?

STARHEMBERG: (*Finishing his dress.*) Because we must love each other, now.

(*KATRIN looks at him.*)

I don't think she has ever seen the stars!
(*KATRIN goes out. A cry is heard on the fortifications, which is repeated nearer.*)
THE WATCH: One bo – dy! One bo – dy!
(*Pause, then a Turkish officer enters, and stands.*)
STARHEMBERG: Why have your attacks all fallen off? You are good at rushing things but bad at standing under fire. Is that the personality of Turks, or the poor quality of officers?
(*Pause.*)
And always you maim. Coolly, maim. This sickened me for some years, because I thought a cruel act done in temper has its own excuse, but this slow hacking has not even the decent motive of a butcher.
JEMAL: The ceaseless propaganda of the Christian church has stirred up subject races, some of whom we have convincing proof are cutting off parts of their bodies to discredit the Ottoman authorities.
STARHEMBERG: I think it is to do with fear of love. I think in the very moment of the cruellest torture, the perpertrator suffocates the possibility of freedom in himself. And thus it becomes habitual, a narcotic.
JEMAL: You persist in identifying me with all atrocity which is –
STARHEMBERG: No, no, I was merely being philosophical…
(*KATRIN enters, holding the child in a shawl. She stops, horrified. STARHEMBERG looks at her.*)
Oh, the great chaos of this continent. The beating of lives in the bowl of obscure quarrels, the batter of perpetual and necessary horror. Who would not be a European if he could? I have a present for Jemal.
(*Pause.*)
KATRIN: Starhemberg.
(*Pause.*)
STARHEMBERG: Yes.
(*Pause.*)
KATRIN: She wants to stay in Austria!
(*JEMAL looks at STARHEMBERG, confused.*)

STARHEMBERG: Yes, but what has that to do with anything?

KATRIN: She loves us and –

SUSANNAH: (*Entering.*) Shh…

> (*KATRIN looks with bewilderment, first at SUSANNAH, then at STARHEMBERG.*)

KATRIN: I REFUSE WHATEVER YOU ARE –

SUSANNAH: Shh…

> (*Pause, then suddenly KATRIN attempts to leave with the child, but STARHEMBERG blocks her, holding her firmly. She is still.*)

KATRIN: Love? Did I say love?

JEMAL: This is a most unpleasant thing to witness in a State called civilized and I –

STARHEMBERG: The child's a Turk.

> (*Pause.*)

JEMAL: A Turk?

STARHEMBERG: Of Turkish fathers whose untimely executions left her stranded in this foreign territory…
> (*KATRIN shudders. STARHEMBERG holds her closer.*)
How do we escape from History? We reproduce its mayhem in our lives…

JEMAL: I refuse your gift!

STARHEMBERG: Refuse and you die. And my hostage officer, him too.
> (*STARHEMBERG takes the child from KATRIN, who is as if petrified. Suddenly she is seized by a physical delirium. SUSANNAH embraces her, overcomes her, stills her. She emerges, smiling, from the ordeal.*)

KATRIN: In any case, she might so easily have been seized in a raid.

STARHEMBERG: (*Giving the child to JEMAL, who hesitates.*) It happens all the time…
> (*He holds the baby out.*)
You will convert her to the true faith, obviously…

KATRIN: And who knows what might have befallen her if she stayed in Vienna? Smallpox? Carriage accidents? Anything!
> (*JEMAL takes the child.*)

And in a year, it will be as if I never knew her!
(*She looks at JEMAL. He returns her look, then turns on his heel and goes out. The cry of the sentries is heard.*)

THE WATCH: One bo – dy and a child! One bo – dy and a child!

KATRIN: (*To STARHEMBERG.*) Look at me. What do you see?
(*He gazes at her. Suddenly, an eruption of fireworks, explosions and coloured lights, cheering from the entire fort. The EMPRESS enters with the court, in riding cloaks.*)

EMPRESS: Starhemberg, who never answers the Imperial Despatch! Starhemberg, obscure in Wallachia! But we will not be deprived!
(*She embraces him. LEOPOLD enters.*)

LEOPOLD: (*Greeting KATRIN.*) The Mother! And the Child! Where is the Child?
(*He looks from KATRIN to SUSANNAH.*)
Concilia, where's she?
(*A burst of fireworks.*)

SUSANNAH: She's been returned.

LEOPOLD: Returned?

KATRIN: To her creators. She's with them.
(*The EMPRESS looks from KATRIN to STARHEMBERG.*)

EMPRESS: Starhemberg –

KATRIN: He –

EMPRESS: Starhemberg…?

KATRIN: Wait!
(*A firework trickles down the sky.*)
Let me finish it.
(*She speaks with infinite calculation.*)
He has – made – restitution – of – their property –
(*Pause.*)
for which – I – merely was –
(*Pause. She grins.*)
Curator…
(*She grips LEOPOLD by the arm. He is horrified.*)
Congratulate me!

LEOPOLD: Concilia…!

KATRIN: Congratulate me, then!
LEOPOLD: CON – CIL – IA!

CON – CIL – IA!

(*Lights rise and fall. KATRIN walks unsteadily to STARHEMBERG. They embrace. They kiss.*)

I LAUGH!

I LAUGH!

THE POSSIBILITIES

The Weaver's Ecstasy at the Discovery of New Colour

CHARACTERS

WOMAN

MAN

GIRL

BOY

FIRST SOLDIER

SECOND SOLDIER

•

A family of Turks are weaving a rug. The noise of a bombardment.
They concentrate.

WOMAN: My nerves...! I try, but my nerves...!

MAN: I am ahead of you now... Now, because of your nerves,
   I must wait.

WOMAN: The needle goes all –

MAN: The needle goes where you command it.
   (*A shell lands.*)

WOMAN: (*Throwing down the needle.*) YOU SEE, MY NERVES!

GIRL: It's God's will, where the shell falls, and our nerves can
   neither encourage nor deflect it.

WOMAN: I know... I know...

MAN: Pick up the needle.

GIRL: If we stop for the shells, when the siege is over and
   trade picks up, we shall be short of stock.

WOMAN: These are all things I know.

GIRL: I know you do. I am not lecturing you.

MAN: There are many terrible things, but the worst thing of
   all is to be short of stock.

WOMAN: I know. Even my death would not be worse.

BOY: Nor mine.

WOMAN: Nor yours, either. But I cannot hold the needle when these –

BOY: (*Looking.*) Our army is retreating!

MAN: God has his reasons.

BOY: But the Christians will enter the city!

MAN: Then it was obviously God's intention.

(*A shell falls. There is a cry near. Pause.*)

You have stopped. Why have you stopped?

BOY: I should take a rifle from a dead man and I should –

MAN: YOU SHOULD FINISH THE RUG.

BOY: And if the Christians hang us?

GIRL: They won't hang us. They will look at the rug and say, as they always do, what a weave you put in your rugs!

BOY: They will tip you on your front and pull up your skirt, on the rug or off it!

GIRL: How can I weave if he says that! HOW CAN I WEAVE!

MAN: You have lost a row of stitches.

BOY: AND YOU THEY'LL DISEMBOWEL FOR JESUS!

MAN: And another row. We are allowing the winds of passing struggles to break our family down. Look, I still work, my fingers are as rapid as ever, or as slow as ever, but I persist, I have not dropped one stitch for fear or history.

GIRL: I will make up my lost row.

MAN: She knows! She knows all pain will be smothered in the rug. The rug is the rug my father taught me, and his taught him, back to the beginning. All Christians, and all Tartars, and all Kurds, and neither Genghis nor the Tsar have changed its features. In you, boy thirsting for a rifle, the people live, you see the message in the threads.

BOY: I know.

MAN: You say you know but you still prefer the rifle.

BOY: Because without the rifle there's no rug! I don't know why, but the rug and rifle are the same.

(*A shell falls near. The WOMAN rises to her feet, shocked, and lets out a cry which does not distract the MAN.*)

WOMAN: Don't stop – don't take any notice of me –

(*Another shell. She screeches again.*)

It's all right, you carry on, I –

GIRL: Just sit. If you stand you will be hit by flying splinters.

BOY: A horse is hit!

(*A flood of blood swiftly spreads across the stage.*)

MAN: Perhaps the siege is nearly over. Then we shall eat again, but to eat costs money, and we shall have nothing to trade if we do not have stock. Stock is all. Stock is life.

GIRL: My fingers go more quickly when I think of food!

WOMAN: Forgive me, my nerves threaten us all. Forgive me and my nerves…

GIRL: We understand, you aren't as young as you were.

WOMAN: I was always delicate…

MAN: But your fingers worked like ants! Impeccable, relentless fingers which I saw and admired –

WOMAN: I was the fastest in the city!

MAN: She was, and I did not hesitate, I said, this woman must be my wife…!

WOMAN: It is only shells that spoil my concentration.

(*A shell falls near.*)

BOY: A MAN IS DEAD IN THE GARDEN!

(*A flood of blood swiftly spreads over the stage.*)

I should take his place…!

MAN: If you abandon the fringes we will never do the rug –

BOY: The Christians will take the city!

MAN: They have taken it before.

BOY: That is the attitude, if I might say, the very attitude that allows them back. I do not criticize, I am doing the fringes.

MAN: More wool. You see, I am through my skein. More wool.

(*The GIRL gets up to fetch wool.*)

I admit, this assault has unsettled even me, or I should have had it by me.

(*The GIRL returns with a skein. A shell explodes. She slips in the blood and falls.*)

BOY: Are you all right?

GIRL: I'm all right! Don't stop working, I'm all right. But I have fallen in the horse's blood.

BOY: Or the man's blood, is it?

GIRL: Don't stand up! The flying splinters…!

(*She crawls to them.*)

I'm sorry, I slipped.

MAN: We are working to eat. We are weaving not only for the
   rug, but for what the rug will buy us. Give me the wool.

GIRL: I'm sorry, the wool is ruined. When I slipped it fell in
   the horse's blood.

BOY: The man's blood, surely?

GIRL: I must go back.

WOMAN: Mind the flying splinters!

MAN: Show me...

   (*Pause.*)

   Look, the colour! The wool was pale, but the paleness has
   been coloured by the blood...

GIRL: I'll fetch another –

MAN: Wait. Look, as soon as this is dry, we shall have a
   different red. I feel certain this is a different red.

GIRL: Bring more, shall I?

MAN: Bring more, and soak it in the blood!

BOY: But it's man's blood!

MAN: Yes... So when this is gone, run to the hospital!

GIRL: The hospital?

MAN: Ask to take a bucket from the wounds –

BOY: The wounds?

MAN: From those who haemorrhage! You see, it has a tone
   which is not the same as ox's blood –

WOMAN: It is a beautiful and unusual red...

MAN: And it will bring us customers. They will gasp and say
   no other weaver has such reds!

BOY: But that is –

MAN: YOU QUARREL WITH A GIFT FROM GOD. You quibble
   at his miracles. Go, if you want, and be shot by the
   Christians. Die in the trenches and let their cannons grind
   your face –

WOMAN: Shh, shh –

MAN: I tell you, in the great cities of the world, they will bid
   and bicker for this stock...

BOY: It is not even Christian blood...

MAN: Would that improve its colour?

GIRL: My brother does not know how to take a gift...

BOY: I do, but –

MAN: It will end, this war, because they always do, and then we shall have no more of this colour.

BOY: Cut a throat, why don't you?

MAN: WHAT USE ARE YOU WITH YOUR INDIGNATIONS AND YOUR LIP ALL OUT AT ME? You have not done a stitch.

WOMAN: The guns have stopped...

BOY: The crescent flag is coming down...!

THE MAN. Needle, quick...

WOMAN: The guns have stopped...

BOY: We've lost!

MAN: Some have.

GIRL: The Christians, will they give us bread?

WOMAN: Give? Give bread? Their own soldiers are half-starving.

MAN: (*To the BOY.*) Hurry, to the hospital!
(*He goes out. Pause. The weavers work. Two SOLDIERS appear. They stare at the weavers.*)

FIRST SOLDIER: We took the city. And we found our soldiers crucified. Some with no eyes. Some castrated and with their pieces in their mouths.

SECOND SOLDIER: So now all bestiality is okay. All looting. And all opening of girls also okay.

FIRST SOLDIER: I'll take that rug.
(*The MAN grasps it defensively.*)

SECOND SOLDIER: Don't be an idiot.

MAN: My stock!

SECOND SOLDIER: What's that? An insult in his lingo? Oi!
(*He proceeds to stab the MAN, who dies. The WOMEN watch transfixed.*)

FIRST SOLDIER: (*To the GIRL.*) You – with me – I am looking for a servant to wash my things – etcetera –
(*The GIRL gets up. The SECOND SOLDIER rolls up the rug.*)
Don't look so scared. I am relatively kind, which is more than you lot manage...
(*They go off. The WOMAN tries to scream, but is dumb and only her mouth opens. The BOY returns with the bucket, looks.*)

BOY: The rug...
(*He looks.*)
THE RUG!

Kiss My Hands

CHARACTERS

WOMAN

FIRST TERRORIST

SECOND TERRORIST

THIRD TERRORIST

HUSBAND

CHILD

•

A knocking on a door at night, repeated. A WOMAN in night clothes appears from a room.

WOMAN: We never open the door at night!

VOICE: We have been ambushed and a friend is shot!

WOMAN: Ambushed by whom?

VOICE: The terrorists!

WOMAN: Which terrorists?

VOICE: Trust us!

WOMAN: How can I?

VOICE: Because you are a human being and not a dog.

WOMAN: I am not a dog, but you might be.

VOICE: Then we have to find another house and our friend
will die…!

WOMAN: All right.

VOICE: God praise your humanity!

WOMAN: I hope so.

(*She unbolts the door. TERRORISTS burst in.*)

FIRST TERRORIST: Where is he!

SECOND TERRORIST: Bedrooms!

THIRD TERRORIST: Kitchen!

WOMAN: Oh, Christ make me deaf and you speechless ever
more, you have murdered every decent impulse, you have
killed all language, you are the terrorists!

FIRST TERRORIST: We are, and it's a pity to have to work this way but your husband and his ilk must be cut out of our lives like warts, and then we shall bring back good neighbours, then you'll need no bolts I promise you!
(*The TERRORISTS drag her HUSBAND in, naked and roped.*)

HUSBAND: You let them in...

WOMAN: Forgive me, I only –

HUSBAND: You helped our enemies to murder me...

WOMAN: I was not – I had not killed the instinct of a neighbour – I apologize –

HUSBAND: Now I will die because you were so ordinary...

WOMAN: Let him go. You cheated me!

SECOND TERRORIST: One day, all normal again, and when the door is knocked on, open it...

WOMAN: NEVER OPEN A DOOR AGAIN.

THIRD TERRORIST: But then the genuine will suffer.

FIRST TERRORIST: Take him to the wood and shoot him there.

WOMAN: NEVER OPEN A DOOR AGAIN.

HUSBAND: You have made me hate my wife...in my last minutes, feel terrible anger for my wife...

SECOND TERRORIST: Good. You should suffer everything for your sins. I hope your child spits on your grave.

FIRST TERRORIST: When we have gone, shut the door.

WOMAN: Leave us alone...give us a minute on our own...

FIRST TERRORIST: If we did that, you would deceive us.

WOMAN: I swear not.

FIRST TERRORIST: How can I believe your oath? Because we cruelly cheated you, you would be justified in betraying us. This struggle wrecks the old relations! Outside with him.

WOMAN: Forgive me!

HUSBAND: I want to – I want to, but – I am dying for your error! And I had such work to do, who will replace me in the village? I might have served so many, and I perish for your error...

SECOND TERRORIST: I love this. I had never reckoned this.

WOMAN: Struggle! Struggle to forgive!

HUSBAND: I WANT TO!

WOMAN: Struggle, then…

HUSBAND: Don't move me yet!

   (*They stare at him.*)

   To survive, we must learn everything we had forgotten, and
   unlearn everything we were taught, and being inhuman,
   overcome inhumanity. Now, kiss my hands…

   (*He holds out his roped hands. She kisses them.*)

   All's well between us, then…

   (*They take him out. She is still, then she kneels on the floor, in a
   ball. Pause. A child's voice.*)

CHILD'S VOICE: Mummy…

   (*Pause. The CHILD enters.*)

   What was that noise?

   (*THE WOMAN stares at THE CHILD.*)

WOMAN: Killers.

CHILD: Mummy, don't be –

WOMAN: Fetch the pillow from your bed.

   (*He goes off, returns with the pillow.*)

   Give me the pillow.

   (*He gives her the pillow. She puts it over his face. He struggles.
   They grapple, as if endlessly. Suddenly she casts away the pillow
   and takes him in her arms.*)

   I will open the door… I WILL OPEN THE DOOR…!

The Necessity for Prostitution in Advanced Societies

CHARACTERS

OLD WOMAN

YOUNG WOMAN

YOUNG MAN

•

An OLD WOMAN in a chair. A YOUNG WOMAN dressing.

OLD WOMAN: I thought, treading through the broken glass of rich men's houses, how simple this is…! Picking through the bonfires of their letters and waving their corsetry on sticks, how simple, why has it never happened before…! And standing in the soft rain of burning records from the police house, how clean, how swift…! And then I saw, hurrying from the back door, our men, struggling with cardboard boxes, rescuing the police files from the flames, and it came vaguely to me, this would perhaps be less swift after all…

YOUNG WOMAN: Don't tell me what I never lived through.

OLD WOMAN: I have to tell! Why don't you want to know?

YOUNG WOMAN: In all the books, the same old thing. In all the films, the same old thing.

OLD WOMAN: We have to tell!

YOUNG WOMAN: The heroes and the heroines. The red sashes and the rifles waving in the air.

OLD WOMAN: It was like that!

YOUNG WOMAN: The grinning face of the dirty worker. Grinning and grinning.

OLD WOMAN: And you, with your stockings, tugging at the seams. And your heels, you cannot sit without pointing your heels!

YOUNG WOMAN: I don't ask you to admire my legs. The party executives do that.

OLD WOMAN: You would travel half Europe for your underwear!

YOUNG WOMAN: The party chiefs complain if in the bedroom I am dated by my clothes. They say, don't I deserve the best dressed whores? Am I not a son of the people? You should hear! They talk of fifty years of struggle, and putting their noses to my groin they mutter how my pants redeem all sacrifice… (*Pause.*) Something like that. I am a graduate and I make it witty.

OLD WOMAN: We were happy. Happier than you…

YOUNG WOMAN: No, I am happier because I don't believe.

OLD WOMAN: It is happiness to believe!

YOUNG WOMAN: You must justify your life. Your terrible life.

OLD WOMAN: Mistakes were made –

YOUNG WOMAN: ERRORS.

OLD WOMAN: (*Pause.*) You call them errors, I –

YOUNG WOMAN: THE WORD IS ERRORS. ERRORS IS THE WORD.
(*Pause.*)
I'm sorry.
(*Pause.*)
Shouting at an old woman. Sorry. The young are vile. But I watched the General Secretary on the television and he said, it is a sign of our greatness that we apologize to the people. These are our errors, the people must judge. What errors, too! THE BIGGER THE ERROR THE MORE WE MUST FORGIVE. Excellent. Sometimes I think the spirits of the executed gather round my bed and whisper as I fornicate, how miniature your errors are, your little errors barely leave a stain!
(*Pause.*)
Of course, I am jealous of you also. Jealous of your passions. But I hate you for being alive. You should have perished with the others. By your constant alterations you avoided the bullet. You wallow in error.

OLD WOMAN: History advances, not as I believed at your age, in straight lines, but in –

YOUNG WOMAN: ZIGZAGS LIKE THE SEAM OF A FALLING
STOCKING.

(*Pause.*)

I am dining with a foreign diplomat. I, the daughter of the
revolution, lend my body to the corrupt. He will be half-
inebriated from the casino and may not penetrate. THUS
OUR PURITY MAY YET BE SAVED.

(*Pause.*)

I might have been the director of an enterprise, but I saw
the whores waiting for the foreigners and my pity ran out
to them and I wanted to know their happiness…

OLD WOMAN: Happiness…?

YOUNG WOMAN: It must be happiness! If it is not
happiness, why should the daughters of a free society
submit? It is happiness, or there has been another error.

OLD WOMAN: I don't know…

YOUNG WOMAN: You don't know…

(*She finishes her dressing.*)

How beautiful I am. My teeth. My skin. The revolution has
manufactured perfect girls.

(*She goes out. The OLD WOMAN stares. A YOUNG MAN
enters.*)

YOUNG MAN: Is Magda here? Are you – Is Magda here?
Gone to the brothel? Why do you –

OLD WOMAN: She hurt me…

YOUNG MAN: Yes, she is a bitch, and with a tongue that
– well, she has a tongue to lap a man to ecstasy and lash
a woman into shame! She does. I admire Magda, I love
Magda, but she is a bitch.

OLD WOMAN: I won't be –

YOUNG MAN: No –

OLD WOMAN: Made to –

YOUNG MAN: The young are vile, we are so vile!

OLD WOMAN: APOLOGIZE FOR MY LIFE!

YOUNG MAN: Indeed!

OLD WOMAN: No!

YOUNG MAN: History doesn't advance in straight lines, but –

OLD WOMAN: Who told you that?

YOUNG MAN: Well –

OLD WOMAN: Who told you that?

YOUNG MAN: Everybody knows that –

OLD WOMAN: Everybody?

YOUNG MAN: It's in all the schoolbooks. Have a brandy and –

OLD WOMAN: No!

YOUNG MAN: All right, don't have a brandy, I wasn't stopping anyway.

OLD WOMAN: How can she – how can she choose to –

YOUNG MAN: It's honest work –

OLD WOMAN: Neither work nor honest –

YOUNG MAN: It is work. Service for reward. That's work.

OLD WOMAN: But the body…! How I wanted to say to her, except she frightens me, how I wanted to say – the body!

YOUNG MAN: The labourer also has a body.

OLD WOMAN: YES, BUT THE ACT OF LOVE! (*She stares at him.*) I think I half went to the barricades for love. I think I threw grenades for genuine desire. And once I cut a policeman's throat for it, when he might have known desire more than me…

YOUNG MAN: She knows desire. When she does it with me, then it's desire. You make an icon of her fundament, rather as her clients do. Is this the rationalism of the party?

OLD WOMAN: You have no souls!

YOUNG MAN: I HAVE A SOUL!

OLD WOMAN: You murder love, then!

YOUNG MAN: WE MURDER LOVE? (*Pause.*) You, with your eliminations and your liquidations, your rationalisations and your proscriptions, your prohibitions, your revocations, your knifing of the old and slicing of the mystical, your hacking of the incompatible and choking of the incomprehensible, the slaughter of the unnecessary, the suffocation of prejudice and the notional, the extirpation of the ideal and the fanciful, the terrible scorching of all dissonance, and you say you did it in the name of desire, you talk of souls and love – the mystical of the mystical – TO THE CELLARS WITH THIS ANCIENT BITCH AND ONE SHOT IN THE NECK…!

(*A gulf of silence separates them.*)

Forgive me, you insulted my girl friend. Or it seemed so, anyway.

(*Pause.*)

Forgive me. The young are vile.

(*He hesitates, goes out. The OLD WOMAN is still. She gets up at last, and bending, picks up the discarded garments the YOUNG WOMAN left. She shakes them out, puts them on hangers.*)

Reasons for the Fall of Emperors

CHARACTERS

ALEXANDER

OFFICER

GROOM

•

The Emperor ALEXANDER in his tent at night. A camp bed. An OFFICER in attendance. Terrible sounds distantly at intervals.

ALEXANDER: Listen, the enemy are cutting my soldiers' throats.

OFFICER: It's wolves.

ALEXANDER: No, the enemy are cutting my soldiers' throats.

OFFICER: (*Pause.*) Yes, they are. Go to bed, now.

ALEXANDER: I must listen.

OFFICER: Why?

ALEXANDER: I must.

OFFICER: (*Pause.*) They do that. They will not collect the wounded. They are not like us.

ALEXANDER: I watched the battle. You were with me. Did I tremble?

OFFICER: No, not so very –

ALEXANDER: Not tremble?

OFFICER: You trembled, but not –

ALEXANDER: With fear?

OFFICER: Not with fear, no. Pity, rather, and at one point you seemed to have gone deaf.

ALEXANDER: I heard everything.

OFFICER: At one point you kicked the brandy over, a little wave over the generals' feet, and the brandy glass rolled across the wooden deck of the observation point, splintering as it dropped…go to bed now…tomorrow they will begin a new attack…

ALEXANDER: They die willingly…

OFFICER: Yes, they shout your name.

ALEXANDER: They shout it, and they die. I heard them, shouting and dying I CANNOT STAND THAT SOUND can't we send out patrols?

OFFICER: No, it is too near their lines.

ALEXANDER: It is a terrible sound.

OFFICER: They plead.

ALEXANDER: It is the worst sound in the world.

OFFICER: They plead, but still the enemy cut their throats, such is their hatred for us. I can fetch some wax for your ears.

ALEXANDER: No.

OFFICER: The officers have distributed wax to the sentries. But there is not enough for all the troops. In any case there is some disagreement as to the virtue of this wax. On the one hand it may enrage our soldiers to hear this torture of their comrades, which is good. On the other, it may make their blood run cold and tomorrow they may falter. We have sent to the capital for more wax, but the roads are bad.

ALEXANDER: Leave me now.

OFFICER: As you wish. But if I may advise you, sleep, so you look refreshed and then the troops will think, how confident the emperor is, we must win! Whereas if you seemed tired or full of grief, they will attack despondently.

ALEXANDER: So it is in their interest I do not listen to their cries?

OFFICER: Yes. Are you sure you won't have the wax?

ALEXANDER: Good night.

(*The OFFICER withdraws. The EMPEROR lies down. The sound of a boot brush, incessantly. Suddenly he sits up.*)

Who's there!

(*Pause.*)

Come in, who's there!

(*Pause. A peasant enters, holding the Emperor's boots.*)

GROOM: Excellency?

ALEXANDER: Who are you?

GROOM: I am a groom. I am polishing the Emperor's boots. If the sound of the brushes offends him I will go behind the horse lines, perhaps he will not hear it there, but you can't be sure.

ALEXANDER: You are a peasant?

GROOM: I am. Doing six years' service with the regiment.

ALEXANDER: How does a peasant sleep?

GROOM: He sleeps better than the Emperor.

ALEXANDER: Why, do the sounds of his brothers dying not disturb his rest?

GROOM: They were born in pain. They slit the throats of oxen. They beat and sometimes kill their wives. They die of famine in filthy huts and fall into machinery. The Turk is swift with the knife, though not as swift as the Bulgarian. As for the cry, it's brief. The ox protests as well. Who hears him?

ALEXANDER: I think of this. I think of the grief in distant villages, the orphans who scour the long white lane…

GROOM: They say the Emperor is a sensitive man. Some say they've seen him weep in hospitals.

ALEXANDER: He does.

GROOM: But the war must go on, at least until it stops.

ALEXANDER: (*Pause.*) When I hear you, little brother, I know I must build more schools. Do you read?

GROOM: Read what?

ALEXANDER: The Bible.

GROOM: No, but I listen, and agree with every word of it.

ALEXANDER: Is it not often contradictory?

GROOM: I agree with all the contradictions, too. As for schools, if I could read the gentlemen's books, I should only lose sleep, and then the battle would certainly be lost and the Turks would slit not only our throats but the Emperor's too, and that would surely be the end of the world.

ALEXANDER: Do you love the Emperor?

GROOM: It is impossible not to love him!

ALEXANDER: But he weeps so much!

GROOM: I forgive him for that. I had an aunt who wept continually but could not say why. She just wept.

ALEXANDER: He weeps for you.

GROOM: And we for him! We do! Shall I get on with the boots? He will need them in the morning.

(*He goes to pick them up.*)

ALEXANDER: I THINK THAT'S WRONG.

GROOM: (*Stopping.*) I apologize to His Excellency. I am a boot polisher and unable to follow arguments –

ALEXANDER: LIAR.

GROOM: I am sure we all lie but only by accident –

ALEXANDER: YOU ARE NOT SO WOODEN AS –

GROOM: No, obviously not –

ALEXANDER: AS YOU PRETEND.

(*Pause. They stare at one another.*)

Oh, little brother, I could kiss you on the mouth…

GROOM: My mouth, as all my flesh, is at Your Excellency's service…

(*The EMPEROR sits on the bed and weeps silently. The GROOM watches. Pause.*)

My brother died today. So when I get home I shall have twice as many children. Life…! He was a good father and drank so much he punched their eyes black, one after another! Still, they'll weep! And if I die…!

ALEXANDER: Don't go on…

GROOM: Then it's the orphanage, but the orphanages are chock-a-block after this war, so they'll end up roaming and probably criminals –

ALEXANDER: Don't go on…

GROOM: There's a murderer in all of us, God says so, so a couple will be hanged and a couple flogged, and a stranger hacked to pieces in his drawing room, but then the war has little wars inside it like one of His Excellency's decorated eggs –

ALEXANDER: I SAID I –

GROOM: I only meant – it is not good for an emperor to weep in front of a peasant.

ALEXANDER: On the contrary, what is your love worth if it attaches itself only to a dummy? THAT SOUND!

GROOM: It is a good sound, believe me! It is the sound of sacrifice, you should hear it as another hymn to your house, different in tone but not in quality, from the crowd's gasp at your coronation. The Emperor should know the people will go on dying until the villages are dry sticks and the cattle skeletons. The dead only encourage further sacrifice. Along a road of skulls he might dance if he chose to…!

ALEXANDER: (*Pause.*) I will put an end to slavery. I will abolish feudalism. I will place teachers in every hamlet. I will break the stooping habit and the ingrained servility of serfs. I will run electricity to every hut and create a corps of critics who will yell at every inhumanity!

GROOM: (*Pause.*) I must finish the boots. It will be dawn and they need all hands at the batteries.

ALEXANDER: Undress me.

(*Pause. The GROOM puts down the boots. He goes to the EMPEROR and unbuttons his tunic. He removes it.*)
Your fingers do not tremble…

GROOM: Why should they? If they trembled it could only be because I was disloyal or entertained some thought of treason, or even that I felt my position shameful in some way, which I do not. How much clothing should I remove?

ALEXANDER: The emperor will be naked.

GROOM: He will be cold.

(*A cry in the distance.*)

ALEXANDER: Then it will be him who trembles.

(*The GROOM proceeds.*)
Oh, there is shit in my pants!

GROOM: Yes. Has His Excellency a chill on the bowel?

ALEXANDER: He was seized by terror during the attack…

GROOM: It was a terrible battle. Our soldiers climbed each other to the Turkish trench.

ALEXANDER: I wept, and I shat…

GROOM: (*Folding the clothes.*) The error was the lack of high explosive shell. The trenches were undamaged.

ALEXANDER: And I pleaded, blow the retreat!

GROOM: Yes, I heard the bugle! Which was I think, unfortunate, because the retreating men collided with the second wave and more died in the confusion than if the attack had been pressed –

ALEXANDER: That was me – and only me –

GROOM: It is the Emperor's right to have bugles blown at his whim –

ALEXANDER: They died, and yet more died...

GROOM: Better luck tomorrow. Shall you keep your socks on? The earth is damp.

ALEXANDER: NO SOCKS.

GROOM: The Emperor is goose-fleshed, shall I massage his limb?

ALEXANDER: NO MASSAGE.

(*He stands naked, shivering. A distant cry.*)

You are dressed and I am naked. You are strong and I am weak. You are fine and I am stunted.

GROOM: Yes.

ALEXANDER: Justify your failure to assassinate me, then.

GROOM: Justify...?

ALEXANDER: Yes, justify it.

GROOM: The Emperor takes me for a wolf. I am offended he should think I am a wolf. But let him offend where he wishes. He is the Emperor.

(*A pause. ALEXANDER looks into him. Suddenly he shouts.*)

ALEXANDER: FLOG THIS MAN! HEY! FLOG THIS MAN!

(*The OFFICER enters.*)

GROOM: What for...?

ALEXANDER: FLOG AND FLOG THIS MAN!

GROOM: In Jesus' name, what for... ?

(*The OFFICER takes the man by the shoulder.*)

ALEXANDER: What for? No reason. Flog him for no reason.

(*He is taken out. ALEXANDER sits. A cry in the distance. The OFFICER enters.*)

OFFICER: You want him flogged? You're sure?

ALEXANDER: Yes. And do it now.

(*The OFFICER goes out. Pause. A cry in the distance. He stands. The sound of flogging begins, monotonous. ALEXANDER listens. A cry in the distance.*)

THE BOOTS!

(*The OFFICER enters.*)

No one is buffing the boots.

(*The OFFICER picks up the boots, goes out. To the other sounds, the brushing of boots. ALEXANDER stares into the dark. He is engulfed by sound, the sound fills him.*)

Only Some Can Take the Strain

CHARACTERS

BOOKSELLER

MAN

WOMAN

•

An ageing man appears with a handcart. The handcart is laden with books.

BOOKSELLER: Usual wind on the embankment. Usual unkind wind.

(*Pause.*)

Usual bird shit on the volumes. Usual unkind birds.

(*Pause. He wipes the books.*)

I railed at the birds. I railed at the wind. But I was young, then. Now I say, shit on! Blow on!

(*Pause.*)

Usual fumes from the motor cars. The ever-increasing torrent of motor cars. Our arteries are clogged with anxiety, our lungs are corroded with fumes. WHAT A CONSPIRACY AND NOBODY KNOWS EXCEPT ME. We are out of control, oh, so out of control.

(*He shuffles the books.*)

Yesterday I sold a book. To be precise, I took money and surrendered a book. This was certainly what is commonly known as a sale. Unfortunately, or fortunately, since not every setback appears so on reflection, hardly had the customer left the stall when for some obscure reason I shall never understand, he turned on his heel and replacing the book, asked for his money back. I said, you do this to torture me! But thinking this over during the night, I have concluded that this peculiar action was, in the most general sense, beneficial, since I have the book still in my stock and consequently the knowledge it contains remains in safe

181

hands. I regard it as a bookseller's mission to be cautious regarding who might get his hands on stock.

(*Pause. He fusses.*)

Of course this cannot last. This will not be allowed to last. THEY WILL ACT. Both I and the books will be ELIMINATED. I have lived with this for years. I knew, as if by intuition, that time was short. I knew we would be burned. The books burned, and the booksellers also. You think the stake was something of the Middle Ages? No, they shall be my pyre, and I, their pyre. OH, SOMETHING HAS SHIT ON THE BOOKS!

(*He pulls out a dirty cloth, rubs a volume.*)

Oh, we are out of control, so out of control...!

(*A figure has appeared who stares at the BOOKSELLER. The BOOKSELLER is aware.*)

Police.

(*He rubs on.*)

I act dishevelled. I act the tramp. This way I avoid the attention of both criminals and police. This way the cart appears to be a cart of junk and not, as it is, a pantechnicon of truth which might lever up the world.

MAN: (*Tentatively.*) All right if I –

BOOKSELLER: Browse, yes, do browse.

(*The MAN examines the books.*)

They are closing in on me. They no longer bother to disguise their intentions. I can almost, if I try, I can almost smell the charring of leaves and flesh. But though elimination awaits me with its twisted eye I struggle on.

MAN: (*With a title.*) I have been looking for this everywhere!

BOOKSELLER: Ah.

MAN: Everywhere!

BOOKSELLER: You see, it exists.

MAN: It does, it does indeed.

BOOKSELLER: Oh, yes, it exists.

MAN: How much? It has no price.

BOOKSELLER: It has a price.

MAN: Where?

(*He turns the book round.*)

Is that the price? Is that seriously the price?

BOOKSELLER: The price is perfectly serious, but are you?

MAN: (*Amazed.*) But that is…!

BOOKSELLER: DO YOU WANT EVERYBODY READING IT?

MAN: But –

BOOKSELLER: Its price is merely the reflection of its power.

MAN: That may be so, but –

BOOKSELLER: Anyway, I don't want to let it go.

MAN: You don't want to sell the book?

BOOKSELLER: No.

MAN: But it's on the counter and it's priced –

BOOKSELLER: And you think that's evidence I wish to sell it? It proves nothing. Any day I might regret selling it, and then I should have to track you down. God knows where you might take refuge. In any case, how do I know you will understand it? It may be beyond your comprehension. The book will therefore be wasted. The efforts of the author, the printer and the publisher, all wasted. Criminal. No, I have to be sure.

MAN: I can't find this book anywhere. I must have it, even though the price is –

BOOKSELLER: Not absurd –

MAN: Not absurd, perhaps –

BOOKSELLER: No, in fact, given its scarcity and my reluctance to sell, it is oddly cheap.

MAN: Given that you don't want to sell –

BOOKSELLER: It is dirt cheap AND YOU ARE THE POLICE.

MAN: (*Pause.*) I am the police?

BOOKSELLER: Yes. And that explains your hunger for the title. Only the police show such persistence in the tracking down of literature.

MAN: I assure you I –

BOOKSELLER: Never mind your assurances –

MAN: I wanted the book –

BOOKSELLER: To burn. And then, late in the night, you will return to burn me. I shan't be here, however. I shall be on the road. I shan't say which. And those who want the truth will say, he's not here today, he's on the road. We must tramp the streets of every city. Probably he is in Zurich.

MAN: Listen, I am honourable and want the knowledge I believe this title might contain.

BOOKSELLER: Or Frankfurt. He is in Frankfurt, they will say.

(*The MAN shakes his head, starts to move off.*)

Damn all oppressors!

(*The MAN goes.*)

I hate to swear but I think, to fend off his type, it is permitted occasionally to swear. SHIT! THE PIGEON ALSO HATES MY TRADE!

(*He wipes the counter with a filthy cloth.*)

Understandable. Look how populous and base the pigeon is. The more it shits the more certain I become that I am the last disseminator of knowledge. No doubt the oppressor is returning to his station to collect a squad. This squad will beat me to death here on the embankment, and no one will look. And he pretended, most convincingly, to want the book.

(*He polishes it.*)

I have had this by me twenty years. I have saved it from unscrupulous buyers at least five times. It is a struggle, a terrible struggle not to sell and I am tired. I honestly believe he would have paid THREE TIMES THE PRICE. That is the measure of how unscrupulous he was. How long can I keep this up? This lonely life? In certain states of light I smell my pyre…

(*A WOMAN appears.*)

I am shutting. I have been open long enough today.

(*He starts to pull the canvas over.*)

WOMAN: Are you the bookseller?

BOOKSELLER: No.

WOMAN: Then what's –

BOOKSELLER: Beetroot.

WOMAN: Then why aren't your hands red?

BOOKSELLER: You know everything. Why are you pestering me? I am an old man and they have wanted to eliminate me all these years. God alone knows how I have evaded them.

WOMAN: I will help you.

BOOKSELLER: Help?

WOMAN: Yes:

BOOKSELLER: Help how, exactly? I need no help. You are a murderer. It is a well-known characteristic of murderers to offer help. I have a whistle here which I will blow until the last breath leaves my body. And though they will not stir from their cars but only watch me through the windows still I will whistle.

WOMAN: Your lonely struggle…

BOOKSELLER: I have been married, thank you.

WOMAN: Your imminent death…

BOOKSELLER: What is this? Death is always imminent. It was imminent when I first lay screaming in the scales. Are you a philosopher? Not a very good philosopher and thank you I have been married.

WOMAN: The truth…

BOOKSELLER: What do you know about the truth?

WOMAN: In the cart.

BOOKSELLER: I have to go. I am meeting a man who runs a theatre.

WOMAN: And what have you ever done for the common man?

BOOKSELLER: I have never seen one. Now if you will be so –

WOMAN: I am impounding the books. I am Miss Leishman from the Ministry of Education.

BOOKSELLER: There's no such thing –

WOMAN: Put down the handles of your cart, I am officially sealing your stock.

(*She takes a roll of sticky tape from her bag.*)

BOOKSELLER: I was expecting you! All these years I was expecting you!

WOMAN: This is an Official Seal.

(*She winds it round the cart.*)

BOOKSELLER: MY SPEECH FROM THE PYRE!

WOMAN: Later, someone will give you an inventory.

BOOKSELLER: The cars go by! The truth is sealed and the cars go by!

WOMAN: And the pigeons shit.

BOOKSELLER: They would do, nothing stops their cloacae. I once saw pigeons shit on a tramp as she gave birth, and the fall of the Bastille did not change their habits.

WOMAN: There, sealed up…

BOOKSELLER: NEVER TO SEE THE LIGHT AGAIN.

WOMAN: Policies change. Yesterday's shocker is tomorrow's standard text.

BOOKSELLER: More philosophy, where are you trained?

WOMAN: You are not to break the seals, all right?

BOOKSELLER: I am tired and I ache for the stake…

WOMAN: A van will be along –

BOOKSELLER: Driven by them…

WOMAN: By Brian and Gary, I expect… (*She leaves.*)

BOOKSELLER: They hunted us, and with such human expression. We are out of control when the oppressor has a human face, so out of control…

(*The MAN appears again.*)

MAN: Your rudeness almost dissuaded me. I walked four streets and then I thought, I need the knowledge, why be put off? Knowledge only comes to the one who perseveres. I also called at the bank.

BOOKSELLER: Too late.

MAN: IT'S SOLD?

BOOKSELLER: Not sold, but too late.

MAN: You are maddeningly obscure and I will have the book if I have to fight you for it. Take off your glasses.

BOOKSELLER: The seals of the State are on my stock.

MAN: (*Pause.*) Idiot.

BOOKSELLER: Idiot, yes. All my life I struggled. That is the mark of an idiot.

MAN: Then where is the author?

BOOKSELLER: The author? Dead, or he became a postman. I forget. Anyway, he could tell you nothing.

MAN: Very well. Open the box.

BOOKSELLER: OPEN THE BOX?

MAN: Why ever not?

BOOKSELLER: It's gaol and I am seventy.

MAN: This is gaol and I am twenty.

BOOKSELLER: The van will be here.

MAN: But look, the traffic's heavy, they will be stuck and the engine will overheat. We have hours.

BOOKSELLER: What is this reckless thirst that masters you?

MAN: It is the only copy.

BOOKSELLER. How many did you want?

MAN: I am breaking the seals.

BOOKSELLER: You are going to disseminate it! I knew when I saw you, he is either a policeman or a disseminator! You will copy it on machines and leave the pages in launderettes.

MAN: Yes.

BOOKSELLER: I knew! What do you think knowledge is? Sherbert?

(*The MAN is cutting the seals with a knife.*)

Enticer! What are you trying to do, wreck people's lives?

ONLY SOME CAN TAKE THE STRAIN!

(*The MAN covers the BOOKSELLER's mouth.*)

MAN: Speak and you die.

(*Pause. He frees him, finishes cutting the seals, and removes the book. He conceals it under his coat. The BOOKSELLER is still. The MAN turns to go.*)

BOOKSELLER: Zurich.

(*The MAN stops.*)

Down by the river.

(*The MAN leaves.*)

Under the trees.

The Dumb Woman's Ecstasy

CHARACTERS

TORTURER

WOMAN

YOUTH

•

A widow's house. A man arrives with a bag of tools. The WOMAN is seated.

TORTURER: They said if I came here you would have a
room. Have you a room?
(*She looks at him.*)
You have a room? You have a room but you don't know
if you like me? Understandable. I am not local and the
accent's odd. Perhaps I'm dirty from the road? I'll pay in
advance. Or rather, as I have no money yet, I will give you
the toolbag as a pledge.
(*He puts the bag down.*)
They say they pay on Fridays. What do you say? I am a
foreigner, but though I am in many ways unlike you, in
others I am identical, so we might progress from there.
(*She just looks.*)
I don't know what your silence means. I have come across
many silent people, but in the end, they spoke. Perhaps
that is how it will be with you. I am a skilled man and eat
a light breakfast. Also, I sleep soundly and bring no friends
back to my lodgings. I am not solitary, but neither am I
convivial. What do you say? I won't plead for a room. I
would rather lie in a ditch than plead. I am proud, which is
perhaps my single fault.
(*Pause. He picks up the bag.*)
All right, I haven't satisfied you.
(*He starts to go, then stops.*)

Ah, now I remember. You are deaf and dumb! They told me at the castle, she lets rooms but she is deaf and dumb. Now I have made us both feel foolish!

(*He laughs. Pause.*)

I am the torturer from Poland and I have been offered a post at the castle. The new lord said there could be no more torture it was against his conscience and dismissed the old one, who, like me, set off across the country in search of a new post. But after six months, the necessity for torture made itself apparent, as it always does, and execution also could not be done without for long, so it was my luck to knock at his gate when the vacancy existed and the need was obvious to all. I have references from previous employers, all of whom were sorry to see me go, but I am a wanderer, I love to travel and I know my trade is never low for long, now shall I go up you unpleasant hag I detest the sight of you and one interview in a day is quite enough. Your eye is fixed on mine like a crow on dying vermin and I know your rooms all stink.

(*He picks up the bag, and goes up to his room. A YOUTH creeps in.*)

YOUTH: He's here? He's taken the room? I'll wait.

(*Pause.*)

Listen, he bangs about! He kicks the furniture! And stamping on the boards! Dust falls from the ceiling!

(*Pause.*)

And now he dreams... Bring him some soup! Poles love their dinner!

(*The WOMAN goes out. The TORTURER appears.*)

TORTURER: A stinking crevice of a room.

YOUTH: It is a cheap and dirty hovel for a man like you.

TORTURER: It is a gutter of a room, a sewer of a room which my body shrinks to lie in, and the sheet is steeped in dead men's vomit. However, I am here now.

YOUTH: It is a scandal that a man like you should –

TORTURER: Yes –

YOUTH: Whose skills deserve the highest respect and the appropriate accommodation.

TORTURER: You flatter brilliantly but I do not take
    apprentices. All I do I do myself.

YOUTH: I admire that. The single-minded craftsman who
    leaves behind him only –

TORTURER: Pain –

YOUTH: Or truth? Just as the cabinet maker, with his tools
    on his back, leaves in a string of villages the mended doors
    and little boxes of his craft, so you –

TORTURER: Burst thumbs and leave eye sockets dark as pits.

YOUTH: You are so clear and unambiguous, I do admire you,
    I have no craft –

TORTURER: You flatter brilliantly.

YOUTH: Do I?

TORTURER: Perhaps there is employment for you there.

YOUTH: As a flatterer?

TORTURER: Yes, have you never thought of that?

YOUTH: As a profession? No…

TORTURER: I never thought of pain, either, as a profession,
    yet I have never gone without food, women, or a bed.
    These discoveries are like lightning flashes, they can
    illuminate your life.

YOUTH: I will give it some thought.

    (*The WOMAN enters with a bowl. The TORTURER sits and
    eats.*)

TORTURER: What I despise is bad workmanship.

YOUTH: Oh, yes!

TORTURER: Just as a flatterer flatters best when he half-
    believes his compliments, so a man in my trade must
    concentrate on one thing only – the confession, and not
    indulge in pain for pain's sake. I have sometimes achieved
    my ends not by the infliction of pain, but merely by the
    description. Punishment is another matter. Punishment
    I never thought of as a work for life. But others do,
    obviously. This soup is the very sediment of drains. Why is
    she dumb? Because she's deaf?

YOUTH: She has no tongue. And her eardrums burst.

TORTURER: Is that so?

YOUTH: She is my mother but maternity has limits to its commands, and you're right, she's dirty. I sometimes beat her, and then I think, no, she gave me birth!

TORTURER: So rats do their verminous offspring.

YOUTH: It is a silly sentiment.

TORTURER: Our births result from squalid fornications, we were not thought of then.

YOUTH: I never thought of that! You do go – beyond the obvious.

TORTURER: Your compliments come naturally.

YOUTH: Only out of admiration!

TORTURER: There you go again!

YOUTH: (*Laughing.*) Oh, yes –

TORTURER: You cannot stop yourself!

YOUTH: No, no! But who would employ a flatterer?

TORTURER: A man in power, obviously.

YOUTH: Yes, a man in power.

TORTURER: Or alternatively, a recluse.

YOUTH: A recluse?

TORTURER: Yes, for in renouncing power, he hungers for congratulation.

YOUTH: We all love that…

TORTURER: (*Pause.*) She looks at me like a beaten animal, a mongrel half-drowned, this thing you call a mother.

YOUTH: I don't know why she cannot be content. Her life is not so bad. She was kept in the castle for less than seven years. Some never leave. No, she is lucky but quite without gratitude.

TORTURER: For what offence?

YOUTH: Selfishness.

TORTURER: Is that an offence?

YOUTH: Oh, yes! She claimed to know things others didn't. She spoke in long sentences.
(*Suddenly the TORTURER gets up from the table and going to a corner of the room, he thrusts his finger down his throat and vomits.*)
What? Are you – Is it –

(*The TORTURER makes a sign of impatience, wipes his mouth, returns to his chair.*)

Can I –

TORTURER: It is an odd thing, that sometimes, though only in rare cases, those who have suffered lack the dignity that comes with the experience and seek petty revenge. It is possible the soup was poisoned. I don't assert it, I only say it's possible. And the way the hag looked at me, it's clear she hasn't accommodated to the grandeur of spirit pain can bestow.

YOUTH: (*Pause.*) Amazing man…

TORTURER: It is easy to be amazing, simply by stating the truth. I have so few enemies, yet I have led people down terrible corridors of pain…

YOUTH: For truth.

TORTURER: Truth? I never ask for truth. Only for confession.

YOUTH: I see.

TORTURER: Do you?

YOUTH: I try.

TORTURER: The confession, even if invalid, improves the soul. The victim participates in the act which led to his arrest and in doing so shares, on the one hand, the moral power of the crime, which may have been a crime of freedom, or on the other, the universal evil of mankind, if the crime was only malice. There is no such thing as arbitrary punishment.

YOUTH: You mean we all –

TORTURER: Deserve our pain. I remember this when my victim cries out in despair, 'But I am innocent!' I think, if she were in the throes of illness she would not cry, 'I'm innocent,' would she?

YOUTH: (*Pause.*) So torture's illness?

(*Pause. The TORTURER gets up.*)

TORTURER: Does she sleep at all? She has the hollow eyes of an insomniac.

YOUTH: But you will one day find your own corpse on the rack!

TORTURER: (*Pause, he looks at the YOUTH a long time.*) I expect it daily. Of course I keep my eyes open, no man willingly exposes himself to a disease. And I frequently move on.

YOUTH: You have the right belief for such a craft.

TORTURER: I had the good fortune to be trained by a religious man, and after him, a man who had cursed God out of his life. They shared this view, however, that life and pain are inextricable. Is there an inn here? I drink deeply before bed.

YOUTH: I think you will find the company dull and their stench noxious, you are so fastidious in mind and body –

TORTURER: Remember, when you begin your new career, not to describe yourself as Flatterer, but Truth Teller. Emphasize your cruelty, the harshness of your judgements. Then carry on in your normal way. You will soon be shot of this hovel.

(*He goes out. The WOMAN looks at the YOUTH.*)

YOUTH: Yes. I know. I know and I will. I SAID I WILL. When he returns drunk, or less than drunk, I will. Go up and wait. When you hear it, come down fast, with a swab and a bucket.

(*The WOMAN withdraws. The YOUTH paces uneasily, taking out a pocket knife, which he wipes and clasps again. The TORTURER returns.*)

TORTURER: You're right. It stinks and the quality of life is bestial.

YOUTH: Did you drink much? You were not long.

TORTURER: Much, yes. I find the bestial society brews the best ale.

YOUTH: You drank much? And yet you seem – if anything – more vigorous.

TORTURER: Would you want me otherwise?

YOUTH: Never. Merely that normally our lodgers come back on four legs from there.

TORTURER: Perhaps they have no work to go to in the morning.

YOUTH: None, most of them.

TORTURER: And is the hag asleep?

YOUTH: She's gone up.

TORTURER: Me, too, then, for the pissy blanket.

YOUTH: Good night.

TORTURER: Good night –

> (*Suddenly the TORTURER turns on his heel and seizes the YOUTH in a cruel embrace. He cries out. They struggle.*)
>
> Dance!

YOUTH: What – I –

TORTURER: Dance!

> (*He spins him round in a mocking dance. A chair crashes over.*)

YOUTH: Dance – I –

TORTURER: Dance! Dance with me in this –

YOUTH: Can't – breathe –

TORTURER: – This palace of – hospitality –

YOUTH: Can't –

TORTURER: Love, oh, love…!

YOUTH: Oh…

TORTURER: (*Crushing him.*) Speak, love…!

> (*They spin around the floor.*)
>
> Oh, speak your heart to me!
>
> (*The WOMAN appears with the mop and bucket. The TORTURER stops the dance, holding the YOUTH fixed and half-conscious.*)
>
> She comes, equipped as I do, at the end of a busy day, to swab the stains away… I also love life.
>
> (*Pause. The WOMAN falls on her knees.*)
>
> She pleads…
>
> (*Dumbly, she implores him.*)
>
> Silently… How good it is… her fashion… how eloquent her silence is…
>
> (*The YOUTH struggles.*)
>
> Shh!
>
> (*He tightens his grip.*)
>
> Oh, this is torture…through all her hatred she must plead with me…

YOUTH: She loves me…!

TORTURER: Yes…she offers herself…! Let me…! Let me…! Who has known pain, know more…and all this suffering's for you…it is a second birth…!

(*As the WOMAN acts her agony, the TORTURER throttles the YOUTH, and lets his body slip to the floor. He goes to the table and sits. The WOMAN is still. The TORTURER breathes deep.*) Oh, mother… I confirm you, mother…in your deep fear… I'll be your son, now. I will dig the garden. I'll stay.

She Sees the Argument But

CHARACTERS

OFFICIAL

WOMAN

MAN

•

A woman OFFICIAL, seated behind a desk. A WOMAN enters,
stands before her.

OFFICIAL: We are so glad you could come.
WOMAN: It was –
   (*She makes a gesture of casualness.*)
OFFICIAL: So glad.
   (*Pause.*)
   I can see your ankle.
   (*Pause.*)
   Do you realize that?
   (*Pause.*)
   You do realize, of course.
   (*Pause.*)
   And your eyes are outlined in –
WOMAN: Mascara.
OFFICIAL: Mascara, yes.
   (*Pause.*)
   Very glad you came because we want to understand and I
   think you do, too. Terribly want to understand!
   (*Pause.*)
   You see, all this is, we believe, a positive encouragement to
   criminality. Speak if you want to.
   (*Pause.*)
   We feel you aid the social enemy. You put yourself at risk,
   but also, others. The ankle is – your ankle in particular is
   – immensely stimulating, as I think you know.
WOMAN: I have good ankles.

OFFICIAL: Good? I don't know about good, do you? In what way good? In a sense they are very bad because they stimulate this feeling I am referring to.

WOMAN: I don't like boiler suits.

OFFICIAL: People call them boiler suits! The word boiler suit is meant to – isn't it – prejudice? I don't think we should have called them boiler suits in the first place. In any case we did not succeed with them. For one thing, girls tightened the seats, or undid buttons far below the needs of ventilation. So, indeed, I share your irritation with the boiler suit. But the ankle. What are you trying to do?
(*Pause.*)
You can speak to me, you know. We only want to understand.

WOMAN: (*Pause.*) I wish to – this is a difficult question –

OFFICIAL: Is it? You have drawn attention to your ankle, so presumably you must know why.
(*Pause.*)

WOMAN: Not really, no.

OFFICIAL: You don't know why! How bewildering! You go and buy a length of rather fine wool – many weeks of wages for a typist, I suggest – cut, alter and hem it at this specific point, showing the ankle – without knowing why. Is that honestly the case?
(*Pause.*)
I am so glad you came in.

WOMAN: (*Pause.*) I wanted men to suffer me.

OFFICIAL: (*Pause.*) Suffer?

WOMAN: Torment, yes.

OFFICIAL: (*Pause.*) I think, don't you, society is so riddled with crisis now, so much healing needs to be done? Crisis after crisis? The food crisis, the health crisis, the newspaper crisis, the suicide epidemic, the lunacy epidemic? So much despair and so much healing to be done? And you say, to all this misery I would add a little more despair, a despair of my own making because it is despair, isn't it? The effect of your ankle on the morning tram, despair?

WOMAN: Yes. Longing and despair.

OFFICIAL: Though of course, among the despairing lurks the criminal. And he, tormented as you wish, will not walk home in silence to his wife, and take his children in his arms with a slightly distant look... No, the criminal will own. No city banker has more passion to own. Which is why we stipulated, for a while, the boiler suit. For a long time this damped the criminal statistics. Then they crept up again, thanks to the tightening of the seat and the unnecessary open buttons. You advertise your sexuality.

WOMAN: Yes.

OFFICIAL: I am so glad you came in!

(*Pause.*)

Why don't you marry and show this ankle to your husband?

WOMAN: I am married.

OFFICIAL: You are married! Then why aren't you satisfied to show this ankle in the privacy of your own home?

WOMAN: I don't know.

OFFICIAL: Perhaps you have a secret longing to betray him?

WOMAN: I'm certain of it.

OFFICIAL: You no longer love him?

WOMAN: I love him.

OFFICIAL: You love your husband but you show your ankles to any stranger in the hope of tormenting him, is that correct?

WOMAN: I think so, yes.

OFFICIAL: And where is your responsibility towards the male who cannot contain the lust you stimulate in him?

WOMAN: He should bear his suffering.

OFFICIAL: But you impose it on him!

WOMAN: Yes, and he must bear it. Perhaps I may be seduced. A correct glance or gesture, even a sign of modesty, may do the trick.

OFFICIAL: You are a married woman and you say you may be seduced –

WOMAN: Yes, I am trying to be honest –

OFFICIAL: Bewildering honesty!

WOMAN: Well, do you want me to be honest or not?

(*Pause.*)

I have not yet met this man. But somewhere I have no
doubt he does exist.

OFFICIAL: And you are seeking him?

WOMAN: (*Pause.*) I think so, yes.

OFFICIAL: (*Pause.*) The world goes on, crises occur, we
struggle towards the perfection of democracy, and you, a
married woman, dangles her ankle on the bus.

WOMAN: (*Pause.*) Yes.

OFFICIAL: YOU DESERVE EVERY UNWELCOME ATTENTION
THAT YOU GET.

WOMAN: Ah...

OFFICIAL: And I must say, were some monster brought
before me on a charge of violation I should say half-guilty,
only half!
(*Pause.*)
My feelings. My real feelings have – soaked through...

WOMAN: Good.

OFFICIAL: Don't please, carry your enthusiasm for honesty
to such inordinate and –
(*A MAN has entered and sits at the back.*)

WOMAN: Who's he...?

OFFICIAL: The question is, are you mad?

WOMAN: Who's he?

OFFICIAL: I am married, and I have children also, I am
capable of love, and have a sexual life, but I do not display
myself in public, do I? Perhaps you are mad, have you
considered –

WOMAN: Who is he?

OFFICIAL: You see, you cannot see a man without –

WOMAN: I just wanted to –

OFFICIAL: The very locality of a man sets off in you some –

WOMAN: How can I continue to be honest when there is a –

OFFICIAL: HE IS A HUMAN BEING JUST LIKE US.
(*Pause.*)
Such is the scale of your obsession you refuse to believe
he can observe you simply as a person. You think, my
ankle will prevent him being a PERSON and force him to

be a MAN. You continually subvert his right to be a simple person, you OPPRESS HIM.

(*Pause.*)

But he refuses you. He is free. How peaceful he is. He observes you with a wonderful and objective comradeship. Your ankle is simply an exposed and consequently, somewhat absurd, piece of human flesh. Does he show you his? He also has an ankle.

WOMAN: (*Pause.*) You are trying to wreck our sanity.

OFFICIAL: Oh, listen, if rational argument is going to be construed as an attempt on your sanity, then your sanity has to be doubted. Is it wrecking your sanity if a man does not suffer your sex?

WOMAN: Perhaps.

OFFICIAL: You define yourself by sexuality?

WOMAN: Yes –

OFFICIAL: You admit your slavery to some arbitrary gendering?

WOMAN: Yes –

OFFICIAL: Bewildering!

WOMAN: I think – this man – this person – frightens me more than a violator would –

OFFICIAL: Oh!

WOMAN: I AM TRYING TO BE HONEST.

OFFICIAL: WELL, THAT'S NOT ENOUGH!

(*Pause.*)

That's merely an indulgence. You want us to admire you. But we think you are possibly mad.

WOMAN: (*Pause.*) I have to go.

OFFICIAL: The question is, have we the resources to provide a police force whose time and energy are consumed in searching for the violator of women like you? After all, there is a crisis.

(*Pause. The WOMAN goes to the MAN.*)

WOMAN: You must try to save yourself.

OFFICIAL: Ha!

WOMAN: Yes, you have to try –

OFFICIAL: You look an idiot in those heels –

WOMAN: Look – look at me –

OFFICIAL: He is not moved – he merely suffers the embarrassment any man feels in the presence of a woman who is mad –

WOMAN: Look at me –

(*She slaps him around the face.*)

MAN: She hit me!

(*Pause. The WOMAN goes to the table, leans on it.*)

WOMAN: You want me to be mad, when it is you who is mad.

OFFICIAL: Am I wearing funny heels? Is my clothing so tight I cannot move naturally? Find a mirror…look in it, and ask yourself who's mad. Look in your eyes, which are ringed with soot, and ask yourself who's mad?

WOMAN: (*Pause. The WOMAN is still.*) You make me ashamed…of things I should not be ashamed of…

OFFICIAL: We only want to understand…

(*Pause. The WOMAN leaves the table, goes out. The sound of her heels descending stone stairs.*)

The Unforeseen Consequences
of a Patriotic Act

CHARACTERS

JUDITH

SERVANT

WOMAN

•

*JUDITH, a year after the slaying of Holofernes, has returned to the
country.*

JUDITH: The Israelites could not overcome their enemy,
whose resourcefulness was greater than their power. So
they sent me to seduce him, being the most beautiful
woman of the time, and simple. I went with a servant to his
camp, and seduced him. And while he slept, I cut off his
head.

SERVANT: We put the head in a bag. We carried it past the
sentries. What's in the bag, they said. The future of Israel,
we replied. A week later Judith lost the power of speech.

JUDITH: For eight months I was dumb.

SERVANT: What a blow this was! Because she was the
heroine of Israel and looked so sick. What use is a sick
hero? So they sent her to the country, and there she gave
birth. And with the child, came speech.

(A WOMAN from the city enters.)

WOMAN: How happy you seem here…!

SERVANT: She is!

WOMAN: How happy, but no one can place their happiness
above all things. Sadly. No one.

SERVANT: Why not?

WOMAN: Judith, what an example you have set to women
everywhere. And on every front our armies drive the
enemy beyond the frontier! New frontiers now!

SERVANT: And new enemies.

WOMAN: None of this was possible but for you. Come back to the city.

JUDITH: I love the quiet.

WOMAN: Yes, but just as you owed service to your people, so your people must be allowed to express its gratitude to you!

SERVANT: Too bad.

WOMAN: It does seem churlish, this exile, this lingering. It curdles the pride they feel in victory. And bring the child! We can accommodate the child. Through the child we show we might be reconciled even with Holofernes's tribes.

SERVANT: We haven't packed the olives.

WOMAN: Judith, I appeal to you in the name of the people!

SERVANT: Oh, don't do that –

WOMAN: MUST THIS PERSON BE ALLOWED TO SPEAK!

(*Pause.*)

I'm sorry. I spit. I froth. Forgive me.

JUDITH: I have done enough for the people.

WOMAN: Can anyone?

JUDITH: Yes, I have. I have done too much.

WOMAN: You made a sacrifice, perhaps the greatest sacrifice a woman can –

JUDITH: I think so, too –

WOMAN: To sleep with a man against your will, and you are ashamed –

JUDITH: Oh, no –

WOMAN: You feel humiliated and –

JUDITH. No. I often slept with men I did not love, often, I assure you, and never felt ashamed.

WOMAN: (*Pause.*) That is as maybe.

JUDITH: And acts of violence, I have done them, too. His head admittedly, I had to saw, and hack, it was an ugly act, the sound of it will live with me until I die, but no, that's nothing.

(*Pause. The WOMAN looks at her.*)

WOMAN: Then I don't see why –

JUDITH: It was a crime.

WOMAN: (*Pause.*) A crime? And the war Holofernes made against our infant state? Was that not a crime also? And the extermination of our people which he swore to do, the scattering of our tribe, was that not also, crime? Small crime you did, creeping insect of a crime. Microbe of a crime. Come to Jerusalem and be worshipped for such a crime. I owe you the lives of all my grandchildren. I kiss you, criminal.
(*She kisses her.*)

JUDITH: I spoke desire to him. She heard. Did I not utter such desire that –

SERVANT: Even I was –

JUDITH: She was thrilled, and he, too –

SERVANT: He looked at her and stood away – when she was naked – stood away –

WOMAN: Do I need to know this…!

SERVANT: They sat naked, and apart. Intolerable, and wonderful! They looked, they drank and ate the sight of one another naked, the air was solid with their stares –

WOMAN: I think, enough, don't you?

JUDITH: You see, I did desire him.

WOMAN: The ironies! So it was not entirely acting, nor entirely sacrifice…

JUDITH: By no means, no.

WOMAN: We are human. Or maybe, animal.

JUDITH: And the Israelites, I quite forgot the Israelites.

WOMAN: I can imagine…

SERVANT: No, you can't.

JUDITH: I thrived on him. I was in such heat.

WOMAN: They say he was a handsome man.

JUDITH: Not in the least.

WOMAN: No?

JUDITH: Even his breath I longed to breathe. And take him in me, head and shoulders also, if I could.

WOMAN: (*Pause.*) It seems very satisfactory to have found, on a mission for the state, such private pleasure –

JUDITH: OH, I HATE THIS PLEASURE!

WOMAN: Listen, I come here not to be regaled with –

SERVANT: Shut up, she is telling you –

WOMAN: (*Turning on her.*) AND YOU.

JUDITH: (*Pause.*) I could not have cared if he dripped with my father's blood, or had my babies' brains around his boot, or waded through all Israel.

WOMAN: You were obsessed. And in my opinion this makes your triumph greater, an epic of will and the supremely patriotic act. Even tragedy. Come to the city and tell this, I'll be by you.

(*She smiles.*)

Judith...

(*She extends a hand.*)

My dear...

(*Swiftly, JUDITH draws a sword and slices off the preferred hand. A scream.*)

SERVANT: Oh, now you've done it!

WOMAN: AAAAAAHHHHHH!

SERVANT: Oh, now you've really done it!

WOMAN: AAAAAHHHHHHH!

JUDITH: I cut the loving gesture! I hack the trusted gesture! I betray! I betray!

WOMAN: Get me to – some hand man – quick!

(*The SERVANT staggers out with the WOMAN.*)

Hand...

(*The SERVANT rushes back, picks up the hand and puts it in a cloth. She hurries away.*)

The Philosophical Lieutenant and the Three Village Women

CHARACTERS

OFFICER

FIRST WOMAN

SECOND WOMAN

THIRD WOMAN

CORPORAL

•

A hot day. An OFFICER seated in a canvas chair, his eyes closed. Three WOMEN enter in peasant costume of the region. They abase themselves.

OFFICER: (*His eyes unopened.*) I see you. You have gone down on your knees, and your white foreheads touch the dirty ground. You think nothing of your costume, which is grey with dust. This morning, you took the garments from your wardrobe, washed and ironed them, and picked fresh flowers from the mountain side. Not since your wedding day have you been so pristine and immaculate.
(*He opens his eyes.*)
Is this the national dress? I am not acquainted with the peasant costume of this region. Do rise, I am the lieutenant of the battery and not a god, though secretly perhaps I think I am a god, for reasons you need not concern yourself with.
(*They rise.*)
I have every intention of demolishing the village and all the virgins in the continent and all the petticoats however perfectly embroidered would not stop me but –
(*He gestures with his hand.*)
Plead. I am not so arrogant as to ban your pleading, notwithstanding it could not move me, not a jot.

FIRST WOMAN: My first child was born blind for God knows what sin. In the village he has found work among the cattle who love his voice. The animals pity him and yield more milk to his fingers than any others. If the village is destroyed, he will wander, fall into ditches, and die.

OFFICER: On the contrary, the destruction of the village will be the making of him. You describe a rare gift which any farmer would be glad to hire. He is losing precious opportunities in such a small place, where he remains only to satisfy your charity. You oppress him by your kindness, have you never considered that? No, when the battery fires, it will liberate the blind herdsman. If, as you say, he has such power over animals, they will help him out of any ditch.

SECOND WOMAN: It's obvious you can't be moved by pity, so I won't list the cripples or the hours I spent tying in the thatch. I won't tell you of the thousand hours we put into the sinking of the well, digging the drain to stop the main street flooding, the labour the women went to embroidering the church, or the carving the men did on the altar, no, nor even the trouble we went to building the little gaol, no, this recitation could not touch you so I only add, if you believe yourself to be a god, and at this moment, we accept you as god, however ugly your face and dirty your uniform, shouldn't gods perfect their souls, polish their consciences and be altogether better than the common infantry whose raping we, whose blinding we, must get accustomed to since our troops are gone?

OFFICER: I am afraid you have a narrow view of deity, which I assert is not to do with virtue but only with truth. I think when I feel myself most superhuman, it is in this way, that I discharge myself of all pity and responsibility and recognize the only laws are those of history, or, to put it very simply, I have a house in the capital and we must win this war or my ability to think in comfort and in peace will be terribly impaired. It was clever of you, and subtle, to seek to persuade me by appealing to my love of my own soul, but gods are by definition, above conscience. It is you mortals who must grapple with that one.

THIRD WOMAN: You can fuck me if you want.
(*Pause. The OFFICER gets up and walks around, contemplatively.*)

OFFICER: I think you are only offering me what, on the one hand, I can simply take. And on the other, something my philosophic nature has subdued.

THIRD WOMAN: You can't take my acquiescence, on the one hand, and on the other, I can see from your trembling lip, you haven't subdued anything.

OFFICER: What kind of bargain would it be, between a god and a mortal? I admit your willing submission would make our union qualitatively different from one achieved by force, and I admit too, your observation that even the most stringent mind cannot suppress the cry of future generations who already send my blood pounding, DON'T LIFT YOUR SKIRT, but I have to say I should enjoy you and still wreck the village, what's my bond worth? A god doesn't respect bargains of that sort.
(*Her skirt falls.*)
So now, by my honesty, I have deprived myself of three satisfactions any normal man would leap at – the satisfaction of showing pity to the weak, the satisfaction of festooning my soul, and the satisfaction of having a child by a woman I shan't see again. You see, I am not corrupted by power! I must be a god! And if you've finished, I will tell the corporal to begin moving the people out.
(*Pause. The WOMEN take knives from their skirts.*)
Ah, now that is desperation itself! And scarcely an argument.

FIRST WOMAN: You have more words than us, you will win all the arguments. We have to save the village and logic's a bastard or we would not be in this war. When we have cut your throat we will go to the corporal and cut his. And having cut his…etcetera…down to the regimental spaniel. And having buried you and thrown the guns off the cliffs, we'll watch the crops grow thicker round your pit.

OFFICER: May I expose the fallacy in this?

SECOND WOMAN: You are talking for your life and we are deaf.

OFFICER: I have no option. It is the purpose of my life to think, and to express truth, for example, the truth that soldiers are like wasps round jam, in putting one under the knife you only draw others, and instead of losing the village, you also forfeit life.

THIRD WOMAN: We are the village, and the village is us.

FIRST WOMAN: What you say is true, but we still do it.

OFFICER: You possess a truth, and refuse to act on it? This bewilders me.

THIRD WOMAN: For a man like you, to die bewildered can't be a bad thing, and we might have both enjoyed that fuck...

(*They crowd round him, and murder him.*)

CORPORAL: Hey... !

(*They flee. THE CORPORAL runs in with a gun.*)

Hey...!

(*He runs after them. The sound of three shots.*)

Not Him

CHARACTERS

WOMAN

SECOND WOMAN

MAN

•

A WOMAN waits for a man. A SECOND WOMAN waits with her.

SECOND WOMAN: Shh!

WOMAN: Not him.

SECOND WOMAN: Could be.

WOMAN: Not him.

SECOND WOMAN: His horse.

WOMAN: But he is not the rider.

SECOND WOMAN: Unless he's changed.

WOMAN: Or I have.

SECOND WOMAN: His step!

WOMAN: He limps…

SECOND WOMAN: A wound?

WOMAN: He would not wound…

SECOND WOMAN: His knock!

WOMAN: Some other imitates it.

SECOND WOMAN: Oh, this is love! This is hunger! You
    dare not think, you dare not imagine! All these years
    and you refused anticipation. Proof itself arouses your
    suspicion!
    (*A further knock.*)

WOMAN: Don't go.

SECOND WOMAN: Why?

WOMAN: Something isn't right.

SECOND WOMAN: What?

WOMAN: Either it is not him, or he isn't himself.

SECOND WOMAN: It is his house!

WOMAN: It was, and I was his woman.

SECOND WOMAN: You are so much in love you dread the slightest difference. You have both changed, but only like two skiffs in a river, swung parallel in the current.
(*She goes to answer the knock.*)

WOMAN: You will say it's him, but all you will be saying is, it looks like him.

SECOND WOMAN: It has been a long war. Do welcome him.
(*She goes. The WOMAN covers her face with a veil. The SECOND WOMAN returns.*)
I think it's him…
(*The MAN enters with a heavy sack. He puts down the sack.*)

MAN: It was a long war, so the sack is heavy.

SECOND WOMAN: You killed many?

MAN: (*Looking at the WOMAN.*) Killed and killed. Sometimes they were brave, sometimes they were reckless, and sometimes they fled! It was never certain. So we sometimes advanced expecting them to flee, and they assaulted us. And other times, in dread of their reputation, we shuddered before the attack, and then they melted away in the darkness, weeping. This was all apparently without reason. But whether they had been stubborn or turned their backs, we still caught them and beheaded them. So in the bag are the heads of heroes and of cowards, which from which is now impossible to distinguish. And now, a chair for me, if I might sit in my own house.
(*The SECOND WOMAN peers in the bag.*)

SECOND WOMAN: It's true! These are all heads!

MAN: What did you think, I'd cheat you with cabbages?
(*SECOND WOMAN goes to fetch a chair.*)
You do not raise your veil, quite rightly. You keep your distance, and quite rightly. I have been patient, so what's the delay of a few hours?
(*SECOND WOMAN returns. He sits.*)
The house is clean. The smell of baking tells me all's well.

WOMAN: And what of their women?

MAN: We raped, of course. And some we murdered, but not often. Their skins were oddly white. As for their villages,

211

they won't forget our visits. Do I babble? I am full of
stories and gloat. Say if I bore you, or if I am too loud. Ask
her to leave now, I am desperate to talk intimately.

(*SECOND WOMAN gets up.*)

WOMAN: Don't go.

MAN: Don't go, she says…!

(*He smiles.*)

You are as cruel as ever.

WOMAN: What became of him?

MAN: Of who?

WOMAN: I am also desperate to make love, but first, what
became of him?

MAN: (*To SECOND WOMAN.*) There have been no men here?

SECOND WOMAN: No one near! Anyway, who was there?

MAN: Troops passed through, I saw their wheeltracks.

SECOND WOMAN: Some did.

MAN: Some dusty officers, with rose red epaulettes. Some
manly troopers in collapsed boots.

SECOND WOMAN: She hid.

MAN: A woman must.

SECOND WOMAN: Even from her allies.

MAN: Well hid! And now she aches for a man.

WOMAN: I do ache. And soon I'll show you how, but what
became of my husband?

MAN: I am your husband, and if you raise your veil I'll
believe you are my wife. Though I could love you now,
veil or not, here on the tiles.

WOMAN: The more you talk the more I clamour for your
body, but I still ask –

MAN: WHAT IS THIS QUESTION?

SECOND WOMAN: She wonders if –

MAN: Is the sack not full enough? The dead not dead
enough?

(*He goes to the sack, tips it. Heads spill out.*)

I'll hammer bullet cases through the eyes if she requires
it, tell her. I did not maim so many, look, these still have
ears, would she prefer I pruned them? I come back, not
only having saved the village, not only having defended
the frontier but crossed it, over mountain ranges where

the shepherds have strange eyes, and punished the enemy
in their green valleys, burned their churches and their
schools, and now the emperor moves the frontier by a
dozen miles, what more can a husband do? Lie down,
and I will give you children, fill your belly as I tore open
others, give you laughing infants as I skewered others,
make you a mother here as I ended maternity elsewhere.
(*Pause. The WOMAN raises her veil and kisses his mouth.*)

SECOND WOMAN: She desires him, as she did not her first
husband.

WOMAN: For a long time I did not recognize you. Your voice
has changed, and even your shape. And now you speak
long sentences when once you grunted.

SECOND WOMAN: Well, if it's him, I'll leave you.

WOMAN: It's him, though his hair is different and his eyes
are brown, not grey. And look, his fingers are so slender!

SECOND WOMAN: I'll leave you.

(*She goes out. The MAN goes to reach for the WOMAN.*)

WOMAN: Put the heads away! I don't want their eyes to see
me naked.

(*He thrusts them back in the sack, then goes to undress her.*)
No! Their gore is on your fingers!

(*He grabs a cloth and wipes himself, thrusts it aside and goes to
her again.*)
Wait… Wait, you smell of death. Quick, to the bath and
return as perfect as I am.

MAN: Did any man require such reservoirs of patience?

WOMAN: Anticipation of this moment kept me whole
through seven years. If we rush through our feelings it
will be all over in a second and I shall have no memory to
cherish in my widowhood.

MAN: Widowhood?

WOMAN: To lick and roll around my mind on stagnant
evenings –

MAN: WIDOWHOOD?

WOMAN: Shh! My neighbour will run in –

MAN: No, explain this widowhood –

WOMAN: Shan't you die? Are you immortal?

MAN: One day.

WOMAN: (*Pause.*) Then I'll be your widow. That's all.

MAN: (*Pause, he smiles.*) I made widows.

WOMAN: Yes.

MAN: I made them weep so much in places I shall never even see…

WOMAN: Good. Let them suffer. Let them weep the sight out of their eyes. Go now, the bath's full.

(*The MAN turns.*)

How beautiful you are. Your hip, and your tense thigh. Nothing is imperfect in you. Nothing offends me, in manner or in speech.

(*Pause, the MAN goes out. The SECOND WOMAN enters.*)

SECOND WOMAN: Is it – has he –

WOMAN: Oh, God, I am sick with desire!

SECOND WOMAN: Oh, wonderful…! And is he – has he –

WOMAN: I sent him to wash –

SECOND WOMAN: I'll go…!

WOMAN: No, no, wait with me. I am shaking with wanting him, look at my fingers – and his nakedness!

SECOND WOMAN: I daren't imagine!

WOMAN: His voice –

SECOND WOMAN: Wonderful voice –

WOMAN: His words, his hunger –

SECOND WOMAN: Wonderful words –

(*Pause.*)

But is it him?

(*Pause.*)

It isn't, is it? Not him?

(*Pause.*)

Shh! He's coming! His unbearable haste!

(*She goes out. The MAN comes in.*)

WOMAN: You were swift.

MAN: I didn't linger –

WOMAN: Swifter than –

MAN: I didn't lie –

WOMAN: Your skin is –

MAN: Damp still – I didn't –

WOMAN: Damp as earth –

MAN: Touch the towel –

WOMAN: Shh!

MAN: (*Pause.*) What now?

WOMAN: (*Pause.*) Listen, the heads…

MAN: The heads?

WOMAN: Mutter.

MAN: Mutter?

WOMAN: Howl!

MAN: I will remove the heads –

WOMAN: No. It's we who must go.

MAN: Go? But –

WOMAN: I know a place –

MAN: BUT THIS IS OUR –

WOMAN: Not here, though.

> (*Pause.*)

> I will take you in another place.

MAN: What other place? There is no other. We are peasants
not landlords, what place…!

WOMAN: I know one. Where I would rather take you.

MAN: (*Pause.*) No. Here and now.

WOMAN: No. There and soon.

MAN: WHAT IS THIS…!

> (*She looks at him. Pause.*)

> Very well. The meadow if you want. The barn if you want.
The stable by all means.

> (*They leave. Pause. The SECOND WOMAN enters. She sits. She
waits. The WOMAN returns.*)

WOMAN: I am pregnant.

SECOND WOMAN: (*Happily.*) Yes, I believe you are!

WOMAN: Oh, yes. His desire reached so far, and his splash
was such a wave. I have a child or nothing is true.

SECOND WOMAN: And did he yell?

WOMAN: He cried out with the awful cry of disbelief that all
men make, and his eyes were searching for their focus…

SECOND WOMAN: (*Pause.*) You have killed your husband…

WOMAN: Shh…

SECOND WOMAN: You have –

WOMAN: Shh… (*Pause. She sits.*) He thrilled me. Oh, his
     words of violence, how he thrilled me! And his murders,
     how they flooded me with desire…
SECOND WOMAN: It was him…
WOMAN: It was him. Did he think I was fooled?

SCENES FROM AN EXECUTION

Characters

GALACTIA, a Painter

CARPETA, a Painter

URGENTINO, the Doge of Venice

SUFFICI, an Admiral

RIVERA, a Critic

OSTENSIBILE, a Cardinal

PRODO, a Veteran

THE SKETCHBOOK

SUPPORTA, Daughter of Galactia

DEMENTIA, Daughter of Galactia

SORDO, a Painter

PASTACCIO, a Prosecutor

OFFICIAL

MAN IN THE NEXT CELL

GAOLER

LASAGNA, a Painter

FIRST SAILOR

SECOND SAILOR

THIRD SAILOR

WORKMEN

MOURNER

SCENE ONE

A studio in Venice. A naked man sketched.

SKETCHBOOK: The sketchbook of the Venetian painter
Galactia lying on her parted knees speaks of her art, speaks
of her misery, between studies of sailcloth in red chalk the
persistent interruption of one man's anatomy... On every
margin where she has studied naval history his limbs or
look intrude the obsession alongside the commission...

GALACTIA: Dead men float with their arses in the air.
Hating the living, they turn their buttocks up. I have this
on authority. Their faces meanwhile peer into the seabed
where their bones will lie. After the battle, the waves were
clotted with men's bums, reproachful bums bobbing the
breakers, shoals of matted buttocks, silent pathos in little
bays at dawn. The thing we sit on has a character. Yours
says to me KINDNESS WITHOUT INTEGRITY. I don't think
you will ever leave your wife.

CARPETA: I shall leave my wife, I have every intention of
leaving my –

GALACTIA: No, you never will. I believed you would until I
started this drawing, and now I see, your bum is eloquent
on the subject, it is a bum that does not care to move...

CARPETA: I resent that, Galactia –

GALACTIA: You resent it –

CARPETA: I resent it and I –

GALACTIA: Resentment is such a miserable emotion. In fact
it's not an emotion at all, it's a little twitch of self-esteem.
Why resent when you can hate? DON'T MOVE!

CARPETA: You are the most unsympathetic, selfish woman
I have ever had the misfortune to become entangled with.
You are arrogant and vain and you are not even very good
looking, in fact the contrary is the case and yet –

GALACTIA: You are moving –

CARPETA: I couldn't care if I am moving, I have my –

GALACTIA: You are spoiling the drawing –

CARPETA: I have my pride as well as you, and I will not
　　lie here and be attacked like this, you have robbed me of
　　all my resources, I am exhausted by you and my work is
　　going to the –

GALACTIA: What work?

CARPETA: I HAVE DONE NO WORK!

GALACTIA: Carpeta, you know perfectly well you only stand
　　to benefit from the loss of concentration you have suffered
　　through loving me. You have painted Christ among the
　　flocks eight times now, you must allow the public some
　　relief –

CARPETA: YOU DESPISE ME!

GALACTIA: Yes, I think I do. But kiss me, you have such a
　　wonderful mouth.

CARPETA: I won't kiss you.

GALACTIA: Please, I have a passion for your lips.

CARPETA: No, I will not. How can you love someone you
　　despise?

GALACTIA: I don't know, it's peculiar.

CARPETA: Where are my trousers?

GALACTIA: I adore you, Carpeta…

CARPETA: I AM A BETTER PAINTER THAN YOU.

GALACTIA: Yes –

CARPETA: FACT.

GALACTIA: I said yes, didn't I?

CARPETA: And I have painted Christ among the flocks eight
　　times not because I cannot think of anything else to paint
　　but because I have a passion for perfection, I long to be
　　the finest Christ painter in Italy, I have a longing for it,
　　and that is something an opportunist like you could never
　　understand –

GALACTIA: No –

CARPETA: You are ambitious and ruthless –

GALACTIA: Yes –

CARPETA: And you will never make a decent job of anything
　　because you are a sensualist, you are a woman and a
　　sensualist and you only get these staggering commissions
　　from the State because you –

GALACTIA: What?

CARPETA: You –

GALACTIA: What?

CARPETA: Thrust yourself!

GALACTIA: I what?

CARPETA: Oh, let's not insult each other.

GALACTIA: Thrust myself?

CARPETA: Descend to low abuse –

GALACTIA: IT'S YOU WHO –

CARPETA: I am tired and I refuse to argue with you –

GALACTIA: Get out of my studio, then, go on, get out –

CARPETA: Here we go, the old Galactia –

GALACTIA: You are such a hypocrite, such an exhausting, dispiriting hypocrite, just get out –

CARPETA: As soon as I've got my trousers –

GALACTIA: NO, JUST GET OUT.

PRODO: (*Entering.*) Signora Galactia?

CARPETA: I want my –

GALACTIA: No! Ask your wife for some trousers, she'll make you some trousers, down on her knees, eye to the crutch, sew, sew, sew, little white teeth nipping the thread –

CARPETA: We can't go on like this, can we? We can't go on like this –

GALACTIA: Snip, snip, snip, lick, lick, lick –

PRODO: Signora Galactia?

GALACTIA: I HATE YOU, YOU ARE RUINING MY LIFE.
(*Pause, then the door slams.*)
I am losing my mind. My mind is breaking up and drifting in all directions, like an ice field in some warm current, hear the crack, drifting blocks of consciousness that took me forty years to put together, I look ten years older and I already looked old for my age, I cannot let myself be splintered like this, can I? I cannot! Who are you? What do you want?

PRODO: I'm Prodo, the Man with the Crossbow Bolt In His Head.

GALACTIA: Oh, yes.

PRODO: Come at two o'clock, you said.

GALACTIA: Yes…

PRODO: It is two o'clock.

GALACTIA: Yes...

PRODO: I am prompt because I am in demand. Where there is no demand, there is no haste. I would appreciate it if we got on, I am required by a Scotch anatomist at half past three.

GALACTIA: Yes.

PRODO: The fee is seven dollars but no touching. I also have an open wound through which the movement of the bowel may be observed, and my hand is cleft to the wrist, if you're interested. I suggest two dollars for the bowel, and the hand you can look at with my compliments. It is a miracle I am alive, I am a walking manifestation of organic solidarity and the resilience of the Christian state. Shall I proceed?

GALACTIA: Please.

PRODO: I will take off my hat. Are you ready?

GALACTIA: Ready.

(*Pause.*)

PRODO: *Voilà*. The tip is buried in the centre of my brain and yet I suffer no loss of faculties. Pain, yes, and alcohol may occasion blackouts. The shaft may be observed to twitch perceptibly at times of mental exertion. If you would care to set me a simple arithmetical sum I may be able to exhibit this phenomenon.

GALACTIA: Incredible...

PRODO: Go on, ask me.

GALACTIA: Twelve plus five.

PRODO: No, simple, simple.

GALACTIA: Seven times eleven.

PRODO: Seven times eleven...is....

GALACTIA: It's moving...!

PRODO: Is seventy-seven! There is no other recorded evidence of a man sustaining traumatic damage to the brain of this order and retaining consciousness. Would you care to examine the bowel?

GALACTIA: Why not, while we're at it?

PRODO: I do not normally reveal this to a woman.

GALACTIA: Try not to think of me as a woman. Think of me as a painter.

PRODO: I will think of you as a painter. Are you braced for the exposure? I will lower my belt.

GALACTIA: Good God...

PRODO: Please do not faint.

GALACTIA: I am not going to faint...

PRODO: The passage of undigested material along the alimentary canal by the process known as peristalsis can be clearly observed. The retention of the bowel within the pelvic cavity is sometimes problematic given the absence of a significant area of muscularity.

GALACTIA: Spilling your guts...

PRODO: As you wish. That is nine dollars, please.

GALACTIA: Are you bitter, Prodo?

PRODO: Bitter?

GALACTIA: For being left a specimen?

PRODO: God gave me life. God led me to the battle. God steered the bolt, and in his mercy turned my maiming to my benefit. That is nine dollars, please.

GALACTIA: Unbuttoning yourself in rich men's rooms...

PRODO: Thank you.

GALACTIA: Grotesque celebrity. Shudder maker. Clinging like a louse to dirty curiosity...

PRODO: Do you require a receipt?

GALACTIA: What about the battle, Prodo?

PRODO: I do not talk about the battle. Thank you. One dollar change.

GALACTIA: Oh, come on, I love your wounds, but tell me how you got them.

PRODO: A treatise on my condition is to be published in the Surgical Gazette. I am also featured on a box of matches, one of which I leave you as a souvenir. I hope you have enjoyed the trivial interest of my misfortune –

GALACTIA: Paint your pain for you.

PRODO: Oh, bloody hell, it's raining –

GALACTIA: Your butchery.

PRODO: Is there a short cut to the Rialto?

GALACTIA: Paint your anger. Paint your grief.

PRODO: I'll see myself out, thank you –

GALACTIA: IDIOT.

(*Pause.*)

PRODO: What?

GALACTIA: Holding your bowel in. With an arrow sticking
out the middle of your head. IDIOT.

(*Pause.*)

PRODO: If you'll excuse me, I –

GALACTIA: I am painting the battle, Prodo. Me. The battle
which changed you from a man into a monkey. One
thousand square feet of canvas. Great empty ground to fill.
With noise. Your noise. The noise of men minced. Got to
find a new red for all that blood. A red that smells. Don't
go, Prodo, holding your bowel in –

PRODO: What sort of woman are you?

GALACTIA: A midwife for your labour. Help you bring the
truth to birth. Up there, twice life-size, your half-murder,
your half-death. Come on, don't be manly, there's no truth
where men are being manly –

PRODO: Don't trust you, got a mad eye –

GALACTIA: Shuffling away there, stop, will you?

PRODO: Afraid of you.

GALACTIA: Afraid of me? Me? Why?

PRODO: Hurt me –

GALACTIA: Never –

PRODO: Ruin it –

GALACTIA: What?

(*Pause.*)

What?

PRODO: MY PEACE WITH LIFE.

GALACTIA: Listen. Listen, look at me, look at me, what
sort of a face do I have? Look at it, is it a good face? Is it
generous?

PRODO: It's all right –

GALACTIA: No, it's more than all right, it's a good face, it's
an honest face, broad and generous –

PRODO: Yes –

GALACTIA: Of course it is, I know it is and so do you, I
   know my face, I paint it, over and over again, I am not
   beautiful and I wouldn't be beautiful if I could be –
PRODO: (*Sarcastically.*) No, you wouldn't be –
GALACTIA: I tell you I would not, I do not trust beauty, it is
   an invention and a lie, trust my face, I am a woman who
   has lived a little, nothing much, I have not been split up
   the middle like you have, but I have picked up a thing or
   two and I tell you I have never been at peace with life,
   I would not be at peace with life, there is no such thing
   and those who claim they have it have drugged their
   consciences or numbed their pain with futile repetitions of
   old catechisms, catechisms like your patter, oh, look at you.
   WHO DID IT TO YOU, PRODO, AND WHAT FOR? I will paint
   your violence for all the passing crowds who mock your
   daft appearance…
   (*PRODO sobs.*)
   There, there…we must be brave…
PRODO: Nightmares…
GALACTIA: Yes…yes…
PRODO: Down the bottom of the sheets all arms and legs…
GALACTIA: Go on…
PRODO: Bones going…air full of cracking bones…oars
   going…bones going…
GALACTIA: Yes…
PRODO: Flesh falling down…flesh raining down…bits
   going…everywhere bits going…rain of bits and THIS
   TUMULT IN MY BED…!
GALACTIA: Oh, my poor ridiculous man, I shall paint the
   why of all your terrors, shall I?
PRODO: Give me back my little peace…
GALACTIA: Why was the battle fought, Prodo?
PRODO: My little ease, you –
GALACTIA: Why?
   (*Pause.*)
PRODO: Freedom, of course.
GALACTIA: Freedom…
PRODO: Glory, of course.
GALACTIA: Glory…

PRODO: The Honour of the Great Republic and the
    Humiliation of the Pagan Turk!
GALACTIA: Oh, look, the arrow's twitching! Round and
    round it goes…
PRODO: DOESN'T!
GALACTIA: Twirling, feathered thing, oh, look!
PRODO: DOESN'T!
GALACTIA: Wonderful man, grappling with dim truths!
PRODO: WHAT ARE YOU TRYING TO DO TO ME, SIGNORA!
    (*Pause.*)
GALACTIA: Truth, that's all, just truth. See yourself out, will
    you?
PRODO: You are an unkind woman, you…
GALACTIA: Thank you for coming.
PRODO: Digging out my –
GALACTIA: Sketchbook! Sketchbook! Where have I –
PRODO: Horror of my –
GALACTIA: Laid it down and –
PRODO: STUPID LIFE.
GALACTIA: Good bye.
SKETCHBOOK: The upper left hand corner shows a parting
    in the angry sky; the clouds have opened and sun bursts
    through the aperture, flooding the canvas and highlighting
    all the subjects that lie under the slanting beams, a
    dramatic diagonal that draws the eye, pulls the eye down
    jerky surfaces of battle and through passing horizontals to –

SCENE TWO

A palace in Venice. The Doge examines a drawing.

URGENTINO: I can't see my brother.
    (*Pause.*)
GALACTIA: You can't see your –
URGENTINO: Well, of course I can see him, don't be obtuse.
    Obviously I can see him, I mean I cannot see *enough* of my
    brother. I like my brother and I want to see more of him.
    He is the Admiral and he is not big enough.
GALACTIA: He is – fourteen feet high.
    (*Pause.*)

URGENTINO: Listen, I do hope we are going to become friends.

GALACTIA: Me too.

URGENTINO: I like to be friends with everybody. It is a weakness of mine. But if we are to be friends I think we have to understand one another. I know you are an artist and I am a politician, and we both have all sorts of little mannerisms, turns of speech, beliefs and so on, which neither of us will be happy to renounce, but for the sake of easy communication may I suggest we stop the little dance of personal regard and concentrate on facts? Simple, incontrovertible facts? My brother is Admiral of the Fleet and he does not occupy a prominent enough position in this drawing. There! Do you like my jacket? It's damascene.

GALACTIA: It's very fine.

URGENTINO: It is fine. I take clothes very seriously.

GALACTIA: I admire that in a man.

URGENTINO: Do you! We are going to get on! I pride myself on my good taste, and my good taste extends to artists too. You know Carpeta almost got this job? The cardinals on the fine art committee were hot for him.

GALACTIA: Is that so?

URGENTINO: I fought them bitterly. I said he is spent. He is spent, isn't he? Utterly.

GALACTIA: He is only thirty-five.

URGENTINO: What does it matter if he's seventeen? He's spent. Listen, I know artists pretend to be kind to one another, but be honest, you all hate one another's –

GALACTIA: That isn't actually the case –

URGENTINO: No, no, of course not, but when it comes down to it you –

GALACTIA: No. Actually. No.

URGENTINO: You won't admit it. I like that. All right, you won't admit it! Signora, I have taken a chance with you, do you know why? Because you sweat. Your paintings sweat. Muscle. Knuckle. Shin. No one drapes in your pictures. They clash. Kissing even, is muscular. You see, I have eyes,

I look, but also I smell, I smell your canvas and the smell is
sweat. Do you find me offensive? I am a devotee.

GALACTIA: I rejoice in your appreciation.

URGENTINO: Good! But listen, this is a State commission,
an investment, an investment by us, the Republic of
Venice, in you, Galactia. Empire and artist. Greatness
beckons, and greatness imposes disciplines. Do you like
these grapes? They come from Crete. We left two thousand
soldiers dead there, but we have the grapes. Little bit of
sand. Little bit of history.

GALACTIA: What are you trying to say to me?

URGENTINO: I am saying you have not been asked to paint
the back wall of the vicarage. I am saying that a canvas
which is one hundred feet long is not a painting, it is a
public event.

GALACTIA: I know that. It's why I'm here.

URGENTINO: Good! You are ambitious, and ambition is
a fine thing, but it involves changes of perspective. My
brother is quite big enough, but is he in the right place?
That is what I meant when I said I could not see my
brother. I have a sense of humour, you see!

GALACTIA: Yes, yes –

URGENTINO: You see!

GALACTIA: I also have a sense of humour –

URGENTINO: Signora, obviously you have a sense of
humour, only an artist with a sense of humour would place
the Admiral of the Fleet in such an obscure position! For
all his size, he does not dominate the drawing. Now, that
is very witty of you, but you see, I am witty, too, so let's be
serious, shall we?

GALACTIA: Are you faulting me for composition?

URGENTINO: Signora Galactia! Would I do such a thing?
You are the artist! I only remind you of certain priorities. A
great artist must first of all be responsible, or all his brush
strokes, and all his colouring, however brilliant, will not lift
him out of the second rank.

GALACTIA: I am painting the Battle of Lepanto. I am
painting it in such a way that anyone who looks at it will

feel he is there, and wince in case an arrow should fly out of the canvas and catch him in the eye –

URGENTINO: Excellent!

GALACTIA: So that children will tremble at the noise and cling to their parents as the ships collide –

URGENTINO: Excellent!

GALACTIA: Such a noisy painting that people will stare at it holding their ears, and when they have dragged themselves away, look at their clothes to see if they have been spattered with blood or brain –

URGENTINO: Marvellous! You see, you are passionate, you are magnificent!

GALACTIA: Make them breathless, make them pale!

URGENTINO: Yes! Yes! But also make them PROUD.

GALACTIA: Proud?

URGENTINO: Great art will always celebrate! Celebrate! Celebrate! Do you love Venice, Signora Galactia?

GALACTIA: I am a Venetian.

URGENTINO: So you are, but –

GALACTIA: I have said, I am a Venetian.

URGENTINO: Then praise Venice. I think I need say no more than that. Bring me another drawing soon.

SCENE THREE

A disused barracks in the Arsenal.

SUPPORTA: It's cold in here!

GALACTIA: Paint in gloves.

SUPPORTA: Paint in gloves?

GALACTIA: If you concentrate hard enough you'll forget the temperature. Anyway, it won't always be winter.

DEMENTIA: It stinks.

GALACTIA: Of what?

DEMENTIA: Men. There is a proper male stink in here.

GALACTIA: Of course. It used to be a barracks.

DEMENTIA: Vile.

GALACTIA: It is absolutely the right smell for the subject. If you are painting soldiers, you should live among soldiers.

DEMENTIA: It is disgusting coming here. If you wear a
    coloured scarf they take you for a prostitute.
GALACTIA: Wear black.
DEMENTIA: Why should I wear black? I'm not a widow.
GALACTIA: Listen, I asked to come here. When I asked
    for a place big enough to paint in I was offered all sorts
    of things, even a museum. But who wants to paint in a
    museum? Live among what you are painting, among who
    you are painting. Look at their faces, the way they move.
    You will never be anything but drapery painters if you
    do not want to look. I have tried to make you look since
    you were children. The habit of looking. Come here, look
    through the window.
SUPPORTA: I don't want to climb up on –
GALACTIA: No, look! The way they walk, the soldiers. It is
    not a walk, is it? It is a hip thrust, a pelvic deformation.
    Hip and thigh, the stiff buttock and the contorted face. The
    soldier when he is not dying…
    (*Pause.*)
    Enjoy looking and stop thinking everyone wants to fuck
    you.
DEMENTIA: They do not pester you, you are an old woman!
GALACTIA: All right, nothing's proper, nothing's right! But
    it's a free room and you can get a hundred feet of canvas
    in it!
DEMENTIA: Male groin. Male swagger.
GALACTIA: I don't know why it frightens you. I never
    brought you up like it.
DEMENTIA: Doesn't *frighten* me.
GALACTIA: I was kissing at seven and gave birth at twelve.
SUPPORTA: Here we go –
GALACTIA: I had twelve lovers by my fifteenth birthday –
DEMENTIA: Oh, God, mother –
GALACTIA: For all that I knew nothing until I met Carpeta,
    nothing! At forty-six I find – I knew nothing. And Carpeta
    is spineless. Pity.
WORKMAN: (*Calling off.*) Signora!
SUPPORTA: The scaffolders have finished.

DEMENTIA: There really isn't enough light in here.

GALACTIA: It's the afternoon.

DEMENTIA: There's still not enough light –

GALACTIA: Painters make too much of light. I can work by a candle.

DEMENTIA: There's no light, it stinks and I –

GALACTIA: Dementia, if you do not wish to be involved in this run away and look after your children –

DEMENTIA: Now, don't be silly. I am only saying –

GALACTIA: Go on, run away and –

DEMENTIA: Why do you have to be so –

WORKMAN: (*Approaching.*) Finished it, Signora –

GALACTIA: Children's piss and husband's dinner, clean underwear and dinner party stuff, go on!

DEMENTIA: Why is she –

GALACTIA: So many people wanting – what – what is it?

WORKMAN: Finished the scaffolding.

(*Pause.*)

GALACTIA: Let me see.

(*Pause.*)

No. you didn't listen to me.

WORKMAN: Three tiers you said –

GALACTIA: I said three tiers –

WORKMAN: An' that's what you –

GALACTIA: What do you think I am? Do you think I am a monkey? How am I supposed to crawl along –

WORKMAN: 'ho said you were a monkey? I never said you were a –

GALACTIA: Got to stand up there for six or seven hours, do you –

WORKMAN: Remind you what you said, you –

SKETCHBOOK: The sketchbook of the fifth daughter of the painter Galactia, known as Supporta, also an artist and scenery painter, in red chalk, shows her mother sitting with her legs apart, mouth hanging open like a rag, remonstrating with workmen in a vast room empty but for stools and scaffolding…

SCENE FOUR

GALACTIA's studio.

GALACTIA: Do you like my flesh, Carpeta? Tell me you
do, although it's coarse and the pores are dark as pepper.
Aren't I all colours? White eyelids, mottled on my
shoulders, blue veined in my thigh and red veined on my
cheeks? Are you fascinated by me? I have a sagging basket
of flesh where my children have swung, and my navel
protrudes like a rude tongue. But my tongue! You love that,
don't you, restless tongue! Do I exhaust you? Oh, God, I
exhaust him, he has a weary look…
(*Pause.*)
I want to show the effect of cutlasses on flesh, the way they
slice out pieces, like a melon, flinging the scrap into the
air. It is not something I shall ever see, but I imagine it. It
is not important to witness things. I believe in observation,
but to observation you must lend imagination. The Doge
says I am to submit to him another drawing in which the
Admiral is given greater prominence. Well, I shall do. I
shall show him not only prominent but RESPONSIBLE. And
a face which is not exulting but INDIFFERENT. No, let go
of me, you always start to touch me when I think, what are
you afraid of, don't you like me to think? You see, you feel
my breasts as if – I INSIST ON THINKING even though you
have your finger – WHAT IS IT YOU OBJECT TO?
(*Pause.*)
What?
(*Pause.*)
Oh, come on, you –
CARPETA: I have been displaced.
GALACTIA: By what?
CARPETA: The battle.
GALACTIA: Rubbish.
CARPETA: I have been. I am not on your mind.
GALACTIA: Of course you are on my mind –
CARPETA: Not all the time!
GALACTIA: No, not all the time, how can I –

CARPETA: You see! Not all the time!

GALACTIA: Oh, God… Oh, God, Carpeta…

(*He sobs.*)

CARPETA: You make me – utterly childish…

GALACTIA: Yes…

CARPETA: Clinging…rag…

GALACTIA: I wish I were not sensual. I wish I had not got from my mother, or my father was it, this need to grasp and be grasped, because it drives me into the arms of idiots who want to crush me. Wonderful, idiotic crushing in the night. Can't you just crush me in the night? I am very happy to be crushed in bed but I am a painter and you can't have that off me. Oh, don't sulk, please don't sulk, there really isn't time for all this mending and accommodating to your sensitivity, which in any case isn't really sensitivity, it's brutality, but never mind that –

CARPETA: It is not brutality, it is possession –

GALACTIA: All right, you say it's –

CARPETA: IT IS NOT BRUTALITY.

GALACTIA: No…all right…

CARPETA: I am humiliated by my feelings for you. Humiliated.

(*Pause.*)

GALACTIA: Carpeta, how do you paint pity? You've always painted pity, and I never have. Tell me how to do it.

CARPETA: I don't think you could paint pity, Galactia.

GALACTIA: Why?

CARPETA: I don't think you have pity, so you can't paint it.

GALACTIA: Ah. Now you're being spiteful.

CARPETA: No. You are violent, so you can paint violence. You are furious, so you can paint fury. And contempt, you can paint that. Oh, yes, you can paint contempt. But you aren't great enough for pity.

GALACTIA: Great enough'?

CARPETA: It's hard luck on you, because if you could paint pity, the Church would stand up for you, and if you could paint glory, you would have the State. But you will please nobody.

GALACTIA: You know what I think? I think you are marvellous at honouring yourself. Marvellous. But pity's got nothing to do with greatness. It's surrender, the surrender of passion, or the passion of surrender. It is capitulating to what is. Rather than pity the dead man I would say – there – there is the man who did it, blame him, identify, locate responsibility. Or else the world is just a pool, a great pool of dirty tears through which vile men in boots run splashing. You paint pity very well, but you endure everything, and in the end you find Christ's wounds – enticing. You find suffering – erotic. Your crucifixions – there is something wrong with them. They love them in the Church, the bishops wet themselves with appreciation, but really they are rather dirty pictures, Carpeta. And if you were normal, you would love a younger woman.

SCENE FIVE

The barracks.

SKETCHBOOK: Painting the Turk.

GALACTIA: I scoured Venice for a Turk. I could not find a Turk, but I discovered an Albanian.

DEMENTIA: The Albanian is staring at me. Will you ask him not to stare at me.

GALACTIA: He sells pineapples on San Marco. Look at his eyes!

DEMENTIA: I do not wish to see his eyes.

GALACTIA: Perfect head. Rotund, male head…

DEMENTIA: He is rubbing himself and staring at me. DO KEEP STILL!

GALACTIA: At first I thought, paint him dead. With arms flung out and backwards, falling headlong from the Muslim deck, and then I thought, what a waste of a head, because who will look at a head which is upside down? DO STOP WHATEVER IT IS YOU ARE DOING, YOU WILL MAKE MY DAUGHTER ANGRY. So instead I did a suppliance. I did a figure begging for his life, and I put him at the feet of the great Admiral, with his palms extended, and I thought

I would put into his expression the certain knowledge
he would be murdered on the deck. So with one figure I
transformed the enemy from beast to victim, and made
victory unclean. And I suspect, even as I draw it, they will
hate this...!

SUPPORTA: Can I say something?

GALACTIA: Mmm...

SUPPORTA: I am your daughter and I love you.

GALACTIA: Yes...

SUPPORTA: But I am also a painter, and old enough not to
flatter you.

GALACTIA: Yes...

SUPPORTA: And I know, as you do, that you are the best
painter in Venice.

GALACTIA: (*Stops sketching.*) Have you noticed this, I wonder,
that when someone is about to pay you a crippling and
devastating compliment, they always preface it by saying
they are not going to flatter you. What do you want?

SUPPORTA: You always spoil things.

GALACTIA: Do I?

SUPPORTA: Have to prove something. Superior insight,
incisive wit. Whatever. I want to talk to you.

GALACTIA: I'm sorry. Yes.

SUPPORTA: It doesn't matter how they patronize you, or
attack you for your promiscuity, you are still the best
painter in Venice, and if you were not promiscuous, but
severe, prudish and had no appetites at all, they would use
that against you, they will always have to find something
because you are brilliant and a woman.

GALACTIA: What are you trying to say, Supporta? The
preamble is very comforting but what exactly –

SUPPORTA: You have this vast commission in front of you,
which will prove beyond all argument what you are, and I
am frightened you will waste it.
(*Pause.*)

GALACTIA: Waste it.

SUPPORTA: Yes. You will offend, and when people are
offended, they cannot see the brilliance, only the offence.

DEMENTIA: I feel I am being burned here. Burned by eyes.
I am going out to mix some paint. Look at it, sticks to you,
sticky little Albanian thing!
(*She goes out.*)

GALACTIA: Go on.

SUPPORTA: Give the people what they want, and they will
love you. They will exclaim over you. And after that, no
woman painter here will have to struggle against prejudice,
because you will have proved us. You see, I think you have
a responsibility – not to the State, but to Venetian women.
Paint your feelings, by all means, that is your power, but
let the public in, share with them. The drawing of the Turk
insults them.

GALACTIA: You want me to paint like a man.

SUPPORTA: No –

GALACTIA: Yes, you want me to paint a man's painting.

SUPPORTA: I do not. What man can paint like you in any
case? The vigour, the effort, the agony? No man.

GALACTIA: And no man honestly hates murder, either. You
ask me to be responsible, when what you really mean is,
'celebrate the battle!'

SUPPORTA: I am thinking of you.

GALACTIA: Oh?

SUPPORTA: I am thinking how mean life is, how it gives you
one bite only. Think how they'll attack you, they'll say this
woman scorns us, mocks our sacrifice. You scour your own
mind, you hunt down your own truth, but perhaps you're
vain, too, not to compromise. Maybe you're arrogant, have
you thought of that?

GALACTIA: Arrogant, me?

SUPPORTA: You joke, but –

GALACTIA: Supporta, listen to me. The act of painting is an
act of arrogance. It is arrogant to describe the world and
then to shove the thing into the world's face. It is arrogant
to compete with nature in painting a flower, or to challenge
God by improving views. To paint is to boast, and if you
don't like boasting you ought not to paint. Now, let me
concentrate. I will negotiate with power because I have

to. I will lick the Doge's crevices if need be, because he has power. I am not wholly an idiot and I like to eat and drink as well as you. MUSTAFA I MAY BE TALKING BUT I AM WATCHING YOU. Look at him, he can't sit still if Dementia is out of the room, fidgets like a ferret in the trousers –

SUPPORTA: You will not listen to advice, will you?

GALACTIA: (*To the Albanian.*) It's all right, she's coming back! Do look at him!

SUPPORTA: You are adamantly self-opinionated and –

GALACTIA: Here she comes, look at her waist, her lovely waist –

DEMENTIA: Will you not encourage him!

GALACTIA: His eyes, look! Look at his eyes, isn't he amazing?

SUPPORTA: INTOLERABLE.

(*Pause.*)

GALACTIA: The Turk thinks he will die. How does he know he will die? Because the Admiral's expression is bereft of mercy, is a mask of –

SCENE SIX

The Admiralty.

SKETCHBOOK: Painting the Admiral.

(*A clock ticks in the room.*)

The preliminary sketch.

(*Pause.*)

SUFFICI: Do you like my face?

GALACTIA: Well, that's a bold question.

SUFFICI: I like bold questions.

GALACTIA: Normally they ask it in a different way. They say, 'Is my face difficult to draw?'

(*Pause.*)

It is difficult to draw.

SUFFICI: I have always been painted – cravenly.

GALACTIA: How do you mean, cravenly?

SUFFICI: The real me not attempted.

GALACTIA: What is the Real You?

(*Pause.*)

Come on, what's the Real You?

SKETCHBOOK: The Admiral of the Atlantic, the Admiral of the Two Seas, the General of the Home and Distant Waters, is shown leaning on a desk with one fist underneath the chin, staring with a melancholy gaze into the middle distance, in red ink, the victor of Lepanto in civilian dress, patrician forehead weary from high office, he is –

SUFFICI: A homosexual gardener.

GALACTIA: You're teasing me.

SUFFICI: Garacci guessed it, and painted my fingers on the muzzles of my dogs in such a way that all the armour in the world could not conceal my nature…

GALACTIA: Garacci is superficial.

SUFFICI: I felt, for all the steel in which I was encased, naked. He is wonderful with hands, don't you think?

GALACTIA: I cannot stomach Garacci.

SUFFICI: My hands said The Warrior Prefers the Living Flesh. In no uncertain manner. But who looks at hands?

GALACTIA: They will look where they are told to look, where the composition compels their attention. I do hands better than Garacci, you'll see. Everyone will see the hands, it will be a hand painting, the hands of the killed, the hands of the killers, hands red to the wrists, hands without owners. Can you think of anything more pitiful than a severed hand? Or eloquent? I think it is the ultimate in pity. My lover says I have no pity, but you don't have to have Christ hanging off a tree trunk to show pity, do you? Hands are the points of contact between man and man, man and woman, the instruments of friendship, symbols of love and trust. And in battles they drop from the sky, and men shake stumps in anger, don't they? Raw things prodding. I must say I am furious to find you like this, so gentle and so subtle, I am drawing badly. I am drawing rubbish –

SUFFICI: Don't I keep still enough?

GALACTIA: Yes, terribly still, terribly dignified. 1 did not see you in the victory parade, I do not go to victory parades, I

have only seen Garacci's portrait, and I thought it slavish
and flattering, but I come here with my book and pencils,
and blow me down, you have to hand it to him, he's
done you right, you have the most compassionate face
I've ever seen. Silly me, I should know the world is full of
contradiction, but it's thrown me. See first, and look after. I
saw you, and then I looked, and the two don't tally. Never
mind, it must be that I'm not looking deep enough.
    (*A page is ripped from the sketchbook.*)
    Start again.
SUFFICI: From this window you can see the Fleet.
GALACTIA: Yes.
SUFFICI: Riding at anchor. Do you care for ships?
GALACTIA: I have spent a fortnight drawing them.
SUFFICI: Do you like them?
GALACTIA: The trader, in a good wind, bringing things, yes.
SUFFICI: And the warships?
GALACTIA: No.
SUFFICI: Why did the committee choose you, Signora, to
    paint the Battle of Lepanto?
GALACTIA: Because I do what no one else can. I paint
    realistically. Either that or the papers got mixed up.
SUFFICI: I feel sure they made the wise choice.
GALACTIA: Oh, now, don't be generous, sitting so still there
    with your grey eyes resting on your empire…
    (*Pause.*)
SUFFICI: I think you are rather angry with me…
GALACTIA: Grey eyes with no chink for doubt to enter,
    only the little veiling of the lazy lid, the droop of bedroom
    miseries…
    (*Pause.*)
SUFFICI: Go on…
    (*Pause.*)
    My drooping eyelid?
    (*Pause.*)
    Go on, I am not offended…
GALACTIA: (*Refusing.*) Sometimes you have to admit they
    get things right, the bureaucrats; for all their corrupt

deliberations, they pick an artist who might just TELL THE
TRUTH. And then God help us, it's blood and mayhem
down the cold museums.

SUFFICI: My eyelid.

GALACTIA: I don't know whether Venice is a good republic
or a bad one, I am not political –

SUFFICI: Me neither, what about my –

GALACTIA: The moment you go in for politics, you cavil,
you split up the truth –

SUFFICI: Please –
(*Pause.*)

GALACTIA: I go from my belly. Yes or no. And when I show
meat sliced, it is meat sliced, it is not a pretext for elegance.
Meat sliced. How do you slice meat?
(*Pause.*)

SUFFICI: I think you are, for an artist, rather coarse.

GALACTIA: Coarse for an artist? It's an artist's job to be
coarse. Preserving coarseness, that's the problem.

SUFFICI: And simple. By which I do not mean unintelligent.
I mean there are things you choose not to know.

GALACTIA: Such as that Admirals like to run naked among
flowers? I do know that.

SUFFICI: I mean, the Necessary War, and the Unnecessary
War.

GALACTIA: (*Sarcastic.*) Ah, now you are stretching me…

SUFFICI: You see, you mock so! So replete with your own
belief, you bustle and assail me, you lend no space to
opposition, or risk yielding me some credibility. You see
the eyelid droops, but you are afraid of it, afraid to be
sucked down into the well of a different truth. You have
seen me, but you are not looking. They told me you were a
better painter.

GALACTIA: Your sensitivity. Your great, swaggering
sensitivity. Do not look at the armour, look at the fingers.
Do not look at the sword, look at the eyelids. Ignore the
blood, think of the buttocks in the garden.
(*Pause.*)
Sorry, no.

URGENTINO: (*Entering.*) I interrupt! Philistine bore invades the sitting!

SUFFICI: We were not progressing…

URGENTINO: I was passing Ponte Dore on my way to the Treasury and who do I meet, I meet Gina Rivera, distinguished critic, poet and sensualist, and I say at once, damn economics, didn't I, damn economics, let us creep into the Admiralty and see how artists work!

RIVERA: Yes.

URGENTINO: Look, her sketchbook on the floor, all hot with smudges and corrections, Gina, look! Touch it! Can she touch it?

GALACTIA: Why not?

URGENTINO: A critic should watch a painter. How many critics witness the moment of production? None! They let fly at the finished canvas and know nothing of its history! By the way, Signora, the latest sketches are superb, they are perfect, I wish you to proceed at once to the painting. My brother is big enough.

GALACTIA: Good.

URGENTINO: Gina, finger the book, finger it, the smell of it! I am a fetishist for art, forgive my infantile enthusiasm!

RIVERA: The composition for the battle is most original, Signora.

GALACTIA: Yes, I try to be original.

RIVERA: You cannot try to be original. Either you are or you are not, surely?

GALACTIA: No, originality is as much an effort as anything else. It is sweated for, unfortunately.

RIVERA: It's inspiration, surely? You cannot labour for brilliance –

URGENTINO: Suffici, listen! Two of the most remarkable women in Venice, divorced, promiscuous and combative!

RIVERA: I am not divorced. It's you that is divorced.

URGENTINO: It is absurd that the critic and the artist are not better related, absurd! You are utterly dependent on one another and yet you squirm with mutual suspicion!

RIVERA: The critic is afraid of the artist and envies her power. She is ashamed of what she secretly believes to be an inferior gift, that of exposition. So instead of serving the artist, she humiliates her.

URGENTINO: There, that is a bad critic. There are good ones, too.

RIVERA: Of course.

SUFFICI: Signora Galactia has had a trying morning, coping with my face.

URGENTINO: What is wrong with his face? He has a lovely face!

GALACTIA: Yes.

URGENTINO: What I should like for my brother is this – clemency in victory, modesty in triumph, virtue in –

SUFFICI: Do shut up.

URGENTINO: All right, I leave him to your imagination! But show him for what he is – a tactical genius.

RIVERA: How does she do that? Show him holding a compass?

URGENTINO: Yes.

RIVERA: In the middle of a battle?

URGENTINO: Why not?

RIVERA: Because she is a realist.

URGENTINO: All right, she is a realist! I don't understand these terms.

RIVERA: It means she paints what happened.

SUFFICI: There is no such thing as what happened, surely? Only views of what happened. Just as there is no such thing as a man. Only images of him.
(*Pause.*)

URGENTINO: Excellent! Signora, I shall forever be dropping in your studio. It is the nature of a good patron that he shows his curiosity.

GALACTIA: I do not welcome visitors as a rule.

URGENTINO: I am not a visitor, as a rule. But this is not a private commission. It is the gold and silver of the Venetian people on your paintbrush, is it not? We must be off, we have had our treat.
(*Pause.*)

Listen, listen! The murmur of the fleet, the whack of the wind in the canvas, that is a beautiful sound, the sound Odysseus heard as he kipped on his deck with dirty sailors... I spent three years in the Navy, didn't I? Didn't I? Cesare?

SUFFICI: Yes...

URGENTINO: Yes, he says. Eloquent yes. I was the Great Naval Disaster. But Cesare is a Great Man, a great, Great Man. We had different mothers, unfortunately. Come on, Gina, let's get out from under the genius's feet.

RIVERA: How do you paint a Great Man, Signora?

GALACTIA: I'm not sure, Signora. I know the conventions, of course.

RIVERA: The conventions, yes, of course...

(*They depart. Pause.*)

GALACTIA: Carry on, shall I?

(*Pause.*)

No?

(*Pause.*)

Oh, now don't say you're not going to speak...!

(*Pause.*)

All right, don't speak...

SCENE SEVEN

Inside a church. A priest intones a funeral oration.

CARPETA: I don't think you should stand next to me.

GALACTIA: Not stand next to you?

CARPETA: In public.

GALACTIA: What?

CARPETA: Shh.

GALACTIA: I don't understand. If I sleep with you I don't see –

CARPETA: Shh.

GALACTIA: EVERYBODY KNOWS WE –

CARPETA: Please, this is a colleague's funeral!

(*Pause.*)

GALACTIA: He wouldn't have objected. He was never in his wife's bed, either.

CARPETA: I should be very grateful if you'd –

GALACTIA: It's funny but a funeral is calculated to make me
    want to fuck –

CARPETA: Please –

GALACTIA: Not fuck, exactly – mate.

CARPETA: I shall move away from you.

GALACTIA: You know, heat to heat, the procreative,
    mindless dog and bitch thing down the –

CARPETA: I am standing over there –

GALACTIA: Don't dare move.

CARPETA: You are hurting my –

GALACTIA: I haven't finished yet –

CARPETA: My wrist, you –

GALACTIA: All right, go!

    (*Congregational responses.*)

CARPETA: Please, why are you following me?

GALACTIA: Do you know what I hate?

CARPETA: No, and I don't –

GALACTIA: I hate the way you act in public. It disgusts me.
    Is it because you are a religious painter?

CARPETA: (*To a bystander.*) Excuse me –

GALACTIA: Who do you think you are fooling? The way
    you stick your nose up in the air, and your eyes go all –

CARPETA: Excuse me, excuse me –

GALACTIA: I know you have to please your patrons, but
    really! Farini hated all this, and so do I.

CARPETA: His wife wanted it. She wanted a proper funeral.

GALACTIA: She would have done. She hated him.

CARPETA: Nonsense.

GALACTIA: She could not dispose of him in life so she –

CARPETA: Shh!

GALACTIA: Catch Farini with a crucifix – hey, Sordo –

MOURNER: Shh!

GALACTIA: Sordo, imagine the old man watching this! We
    do terrible dishonour to dead men. And he was an atheist!

MOURNER: Be quiet!

GALACTIA: Fact! He was investigated by the Inquisition –

MOURNER: Rubbish.

GALACTIA: In 15 –

MOURNER: Rubbish.

GALACTIA: Oh, do stop saying rubbish, he was a great
painter and he couldn't stick God, I should know, he
taught me.

SORDO: That isn't true.

GALACTIA: No?

SORDO: It isn't true, Galactia, that he –

GALACTIA: All right, correction, he wasn't a great painter,
he was a moderate painter and he hated God. Is that
better? I was being generous because he's dead.

SORDO: Galactia, you are drunk.

GALACTIA: Oh, God…!

SORDO: You are drunk and everyone –

GALACTIA: Why is it you cannot speak the truth without
someone saying you must be drunk? That or barmy? They
put Farini in the madhouse for saying the Pope could not
tie his own shoelaces –

(*Protests.*)

They did – FACT! He recanted.

(*More groans and complaints.*)

I must get some fresh air. All this death worship is getting
up my nostrils, where's my lover? Oh, look at him, he has
the face of – now I see it, Carpeta's Christ paintings are
self-portraits! And half an hour ago he had his mouth –

(*Shouts of protest.*)

All right, I'm going!

(*The door closes. Sounds of the street.*)

A dead painter, claimed. The dissenting voice, drowned in
compliments. Never happier than when lying in the gutter
with a bricklayer, drunk out of mind. Human, warm, and
round. And yet a frightful liar. Couldn't put a brush to
paper without lying – the happy poor, the laughing rags
of tramps and scabby dogs pawing the dirt. Guilty old
fornicator…

CARPETA: I wish you wouldn't do that.

GALACTIA: What?

CARPETA: Exhibit yourself.

GALACTIA: Is that what I do?

CARPETA: Yes.

GALACTIA: I thought I was keeping death at bay.

CARPETA: No, why do you –

GALACTIA: They worship death because, listen –

CARPETA: WHY DO YOU? WHY?

(*Pause.*)

GALACTIA: I don't know…I don't know…I am not happy, Carpeta, which is why I laugh so much.

(*Pause.*)

I must work now.

CARPETA: Come home with me, my wife –

GALACTIA: I left Dementia finishing the oarsman's cuff, I want to see she –

CARPETA: My wife's at the –

GALACTIA: Your wife…

(*She laughs a little.*)

CARPETA: Come home with me –

GALACTIA: GET OFF.

(*Pause.*)

CARPETA: It is all right for you to finger me in public, murmuring things in churches, naughtiness and desecration, but when I –

GALACTIA: Yes –

CARPETA: When I ask for what I –

GALACTIA: Absolutely –

CARPETA: What I –

GALACTIA: EGOTISTICAL AND MONSTROUS WOMAN.

(*Pause.*)

Yes.

SCENE EIGHT

The barracks. A door slams.

SKETCHBOOK: Painting the Dying. The dead and dying occupy one third of the entire canvas, which is no less than six hundred and sixty-six square feet, an area not strictly in accordance with the sketch submitted to the authorities. They lie sprawled, heaped and doubled against gunwales and draped over oars, with expressions of intolerable pain,

and by a method of foreshortening, their limbs, attached
and unattached, project uncomfortably towards the
viewer...

GALACTIA: Who's there? Oh, come on, who's – Look, I
only have to call and –

RIVERA: Working late, Signora?

GALACTIA: People choose the most extraordinary times to
visit you.

RIVERA: Candles...the incense of the pigment...rather a
religious atmosphere...

GALACTIA: Is it.

RIVERA: A woman alone in a barracks.

GALACTIA: Not really alone. There are several hundred
marines within shouting distance.

RIVERA: You squat up there like – skirts pulled up like
– perched on your scaffolding – a full and undone breast
– these nights are hot, I couldn't hold a brush for sweating,
do you sweat, Signora? And the oil which trickles down.
You have got smudges of burnt umber on your cheek.

GALACTIA: It's not umber, it's sienna.

RIVERA: I have just come from church. Do you like
churches? The whispering of women! 'Lord, make me
pregnant!' 'Lord, stop me being pregnant!' Women
pleading, women dragging their pain up to the altar, and
I thought, I must see Galactia, and there you are, sleeves
rolled up like a plasterer...superb. The Doge is terribly
unhappy. I thought I'd tell you.

GALACTIA: Yes.

RIVERA: You know.

GALACTIA: Yes. He visits me, and he feels sick. He is
frightened I will paint some awful truth. So he walks up
and down, and looks. And feels sick.
(*Pause.*)
No fun being a doge.

RIVERA: Are you interested in politics?

GALACTIA: No.

RIVERA: May I tell you a little about politics, or would it
spoil your concentration?

GALACTIA: Yes.

RIVERA: I'd like to anyway.

(*Pause.*)

The Doge is actually a highly responsible patron of the arts. Dilettante, of course, and slightly vulgar. But then, to someone of your sensibilities, all patrons are vulgar, I expect. He loves artists, and the harder he loves them, the more vulgar he becomes, it's all rather pitiful, really, but –

GALACTIA: Bang goes the concentration.

(*Pause.*)

RIVERA: Sorry. The point is this. The Doge is insecure. It would not take a great deal to have him removed from office.

GALACTIA: Doges come, and doges go…

RIVERA: It isn't as simple as that, unfortunately.

GALACTIA: Isn't it?

RIVERA: There is a climate very favourable to painting here. To poetry, to sculpture. It is a climate that permitted the appointment of a controversial painter like yourself to represent the greatest triumph of Venetian history –

GALACTIA: Represent what?

RIVERA: The greatest triumph of Venetian –

GALACTIA: I think you've come to the wrong studio. On my contract it says – I can't find the contract at the moment but it says – I'm sure it says – 'The Battle of Lepanto'. Nothing about triumphs of – triumphs of what?

RIVERA: The Doge has taken an extraordinary risk in commissioning you. If you humiliate him, you aid his enemies and invite his fall. And if he falls, there will be a new incumbent, and I assure you, as someone who is interested in politics, none of the other candidates cares one iota for –

GALACTIA: You're a critic, aren't you?

RIVERA: Yes, but I must have something to criticize.

(*Pause.*)

GALACTIA: Excuse me, this figure of a man dying of wounds sustained during the greatest triumph of Venetian –

RIVERA: IT ISN'T THAT SIMPLE.

(*Pause.*)

I make no attempt to influence you on points of style, I
only –

GALACTIA: The muscle hanging off the bone is rather
difficult to do with you –

RIVERA: DIRTY MESS OF TRUTHS, SIGNORA, CLINGING TO
THE MOUTH.

(*Pause.*)

It is really beautiful in here, and the candles catch your
eyes. I am not ashamed of what I tell you, bringing world
of muck against your doors. Absolutely not ashamed.
How beautiful my clothes are, and my whiteness, most
impeccable woman, drifting through galleries. But it is very
violent, criticism. A very bloody, knocking eyeballs thing.
Knives out for slashing reputations, grasping the windpipe
of expression. I try to look nice, though it's murder I do for
my cause. Good night.

(*She withdraws.*)

GALACTIA: Sitting through the dark, thirty feet aloft on
creaking boards, with moths gone barmy round the
candles, someone's got to speak for dead men, not pain
and pity, but abhorrence, fundamental and unqualified,
blood down the paintbrush, madness in the gums –

VOICES OF THE CANVAS: The Dying – The Dying –

GALACTIA: The Admiral is a hypocrite. Humility my arse.

VOICES OF THE CANVAS: The Dying – The Dying –

GALACTIA: Algebraic. Clinical. Shrivelled testes and a sour
groin.

VOICES OF THE CANVAS: The Dying – The Dying –

GALACTIA: The soldier does not smell his own lie but
repeats the catechism of the State, bawling pack of
squaddies yelling male love –

VOICES OF THE CANVAS: THE DYING! THE DYING!

GALACTIA: The painter who paints for the government
recruits the half-wit and stabs the baby in its mess –

VOICES OF THE CANVAS: THE DYING! THE DYING!

FIRST SAILOR: OI!

(*Silence. Three drunk SAILORS have come in.*)

Woman up a ladder…

SECOND SAILOR: Anybody seen my bed?

GALACTIA: This is out bounds to naval personnel, will you –

FIRST SAILOR: Oi!

(*Pause.*)

Woman up a ladder…

GALACTIA: You will kick the paint jars over –

SECOND SAILOR: Seen my bed!

GALACTIA: You have kicked them over, stupid!

SECOND SAILOR: Beg pardon, looking for my –

THIRD SAILOR: 'ho are you callin' stupid?

SECOND SAILOR: Not a bed…

GALACTIA: Who is your commanding officer?

SECOND SAILOR: Table, not a bed…

THIRD SAILOR: 'ho is she callin' stupid?

GALACTIA: You have come to the wrong door, this is not a barracks, it's a –

FIRST SAILOR: Oi!

GALACTIA: Studio and I –

FIRST SAILOR: Oi!

(*Pause.*)

SECOND SAILOR: Wha'?

(*Pause.*)

Christ…!

SKETCHBOOK: The sketchbook shows three seamen variously disposed about a massive canvas, mouths open, hands hanging at their sides. One of them holds a bottle loosely in his hand, as if, out of sheer amazement, he has forgotten to be drunk…

(*The bottle splinters.*)

THIRD SAILOR: MUR-DER!

FIRST SAILOR: Daggers! Rifles! Arms!

SECOND SAILOR: ATT-ACK! ATT-ACK!

FIRST SAILOR: Christ and the Republic, Ho!

GALACTIA: DO NOT STAB THE CANVAS!

SECOND SAILOR: Fire! Fire!

FIRST SAILOR: Look out, be'ind yer!

THIRD SAILOR: HELP! HELP!

FIRST SAILOR: Guard yer backs!

(*The SAILORS rampage.*)

SECOND SAILOR: Cut-lass!

GALACTIA: Mind that tray of –

 (*A pile of bottles is scattered.*)

FIRST SAILOR: Slash the bugger!

THIRD SAILOR: MUR-DER! MUR-DER!

GALACTIA: MIND MY PALETTES, YOU –

 (*A collapsing table and items.*)

SECOND SAILOR: Blood!

FIRST SAILOR: GOT-CHA!

THIRD SAILOR: AAAGGHHH!

GALACTIA: GET OUT! GET OUT OF HERE, YOU –

FIRST SAILOR: Ow! She 'it me!

GALACTIA: OUT! OUT!

 (*With whoops, two of the SAILORS run out. Pause.*)

 And you.

SECOND SAILOR: I think – I think –

GALACTIA: Look at this mess…! How am I to work when
 you – when people like you – look at it!

SECOND SAILOR: I think I –

GALACTIA: Do you have any idea of the cost of these things?
 Have you?

SECOND SAILOR: Think I –

GALACTIA: Twenty dollars for an ounce of that, you –

SECOND SAILOR: Go and –

GALACTIA: Lunatics, I'll –

SECOND SAILOR: Be sick…

 (*Pause.*)

GALACTIA: Sit still.

SECOND SAILOR: Be sick, Mrs…

 (*Pause.*)

GALACTIA: Why do you drink so much? Is it because
 – everybody is half cut round here, is it because –

SECOND SAILOR: Not the drink…

 (*Pause.*)

 The picture.

 (*Pause.*)

 Is death like that? In battle, is it?

 (*Pause.*)

GALACTIA: Yes. I have never seen it, but I think so.

SECOND SAILOR: I think so, too.
> (*Pause.*)

GALACTIA: Sit there, and I'll draw you…

SKETCHBOOK: The Young Sailor Struck.
> (*Pause.*)
>
> The Young Sailor Struck does not exist in any of the preliminary sketches for The Battle of Lepanto, and a close examination of the paint reveals him to be an addition to the composition painted at a later stage. He is shown huddled against an abandoned cannon, staring with an expression of disbelief at the violence raging about him. It is the only face in the entire canvas of over two hundred faces which is in repose, and painted in a liquid, translucent colour in an almost religious manner, acts as a barometer of human incomprehension, in contrast to the fixed and callous stare of the Admiral Suffici against whom he is placed in diametrical opposition. The two figures are separated by a shoal of dying figures sliding out the canvas to the left, while to the right, in the third point of a triangular configuration, in utter desolation against the mayhem, The Man With The Crossbow Bolt In His Head covers his ears, rocking to and fro at his oar, fathoming the shock of what's befallen him and inviting us to share his passionate desire to be somewhere else…

SCENE NINE

A passageway in the palace.

OFFICIAL: Signor Carpeta?

CARPETA: Yes.

OFFICIAL: Take a seat, please. Have you brought your folder?

CARPETA: Yes.

OFFICIAL: What a big folder!

CARPETA: Yes, I do a lot of art.

OFFICIAL: Wait here, please.

SORDO: (*Emerging.*) Carpeta! You here, too!

CARPETA: Naturally.

SORDO: Same old faces. Same old hacks!

CARPETA: I don't think you should call yourself a hack, or
    you will start to believe it.
SORDO: I do believe it! I am a hack. And so are you.
CARPETA: I have no wish to be included in your –
SORDO: You may not wish it, old son, but –
CARPETA: I resent that, Sordo. No, more than that. It makes
    me angry. If you do not wish to paint seriously, you should
    not paint at all.
SORDO: Excellent. What have you brought along, Christ
    Among The Flocks, is it? Oh, don't be angry, it's as much a
    performance as my self-denigration and twice as difficult to
    keep up. They are looking for movement.
CARPETA: Movement?
SORDO: Yes, it's a secular subject.
CARPETA: What?
SORDO: Ah, well, you wait and –
OFFICIAL: Signor Carpeta!
SORDO: We must get together, have a talk some time –
CARPETA: Yes –
SORDO: They call us a school of painters but we never meet,
    except at funerals. Funny school!
OFFICIAL: Signor Carpeta!

SCENE TEN

A room in the palace. The door closes.

OSTENSIBILE: Thank you for your folder.
CARPETA: Oh, I –
OSTENSIBILE: It's too big.
CARPETA: I'm sorry.
URGENTINO: Really, we scarcely need educating in the
    nature of your talent, Signor Carpeta.
CARPETA: Thank you.
URGENTINO: Or perhaps you thought the Head of State
    has not the time to keep abreast of current movements in
    the field of painting? Christ Among the Flocks! There, you
    see!
CARPETA: I am delighted you –

URGENTINO: This is Cardinal Ostensibile. He knows Christ Among the Flocks.

OSTENSIBILE: I have one.

URGENTINO: He has one! You see, you are among admirers here!

CARPETA: I also have a number of secular drawings which you may –

URGENTINO: The Cardinale, as you know, is Secretary of State for Public Education, which is to say he is very worried about Signora Galactia and so am I. Sit down, will you? Let me tell you straight away that any time I spend on the subject of art is not wasted. Art is opinion, and opinion is the source of all authority. We have just spoken to Sordo. He is spent, don't you think? Quite spent?

CARPETA: He is only thirty-seven...

URGENTINO: What does it matter if he's seventeen? He's spent.

CARPETA: Perhaps.

OSTENSIBILE: They pretend to be kind to one another, but they are each other's cruellest critics. How well do you know Galactia?

CARPETA: I know her.

OSTENSIBILE: I didn't ask that, I said how well. Very well? Or hardly well?

CARPETA: Pretty well.

URGENTINO: They say you go to bed with her. Pretty often.

CARPETA: Do they?

OSTENSIBILE: Of course they may be wrong. And in any case to go to bed with someone is not to know them, I suspect. Were they to be known to one another, to go to bed would for most people, be something of a problem, I dare say. And, conversely, you might sleep with someone every night and after ten years turn around and say, in honesty, you knew them only 'pretty well'. I speculate.

CARPETA: I have had a relationship with Signora Galactia of a – of a rather casual nature which – which is rather casual...

OSTENSIBILE: Yes... Yes...

(*Pause.*)

URGENTINO: You see, I have the most profound respect for Signora Galactia, as a painter, as a woman.

CARPETA: Me, too. I think she –

URGENTINO: Don't interrupt –

CARPETA: I'm sorry –

URGENTINO: A profound respect. She is not spent. Most certainly she is not spent; she moves, she travels, a meteor cleaving her way through dark spaces, undisturbed by gravities, I mean the gravities of greater stars, she is under no influence but her own will, she has by her perseverance – and possibly, perversity – achieved a following, she has a school of sorts, and she is brilliant. And the Cardinale and I thought, decided between ourselves, we could not let Venice fail to celebrate her genius, because for an art establishment like us, a cynical clique of bureaucrats like us, who like to pride ourselves on taste, to let a great fish through the net of our sponsorship would be a lapse. I tease you, but we hate to miss anyone.

OSTENSIBILE: We hate to miss you.

URGENTINO: We hate to miss you, too. And so we adopted her. Talent is rare and precious, and of course, explosive too. What is the matter with her, is she mad?
(*Pause.*)

CARPETA: Mad? Is she mad? She – yes, she may be a little mad, she – keeps asking me to leave my wife. And – so on. It is a sort of madness.

URGENTINO: Is it? I should have thought that rather depended on your wife. Or perhaps she loves you.

CARPETA: Loves me, well, she –

URGENTINO: Loves you. More than you are worth. I have seen the painting called The Battle Of Lepanto in various stages and it is not getting any better, it is getting worse, not from the technical point of view but from the moral one. And I ask you very frankly, is she a moral woman?

CARPETA: Moral? No, I don't think you could – not moral, no.
(*Pause.*)

257

OSTENSIBILE: How quickly can you paint a canvas of three
thousand square feet, Signor Carpeta?
(*Pause.*)
CARPETA: A month.
URGENTINO: Now, that's silly –
CARPETA: No, I'm saying –
URGENTINO: I have heard of ambition, but that's –
OSTENSIBILE: Let him finish.
CARPETA: I'm saying I could, I could paint a canvas of that
size in a month, only it wouldn't be –
URGENTINO: It damned well wouldn't, would it?
CARPETA: Be very – very good –
URGENTINO: Quite. You are not a rash man, Signor
Carpeta. I am glad to see.
CARPETA: For a decent composition and – with the right
assistants, I think – seven weeks.
OSTENSIBILE: You see, Signora Galactia has not been
altogether fair with us.
CARPETA: No, no, she hasn't been –
OSTENSIBILE: She has –
CARPETA: Gone her own way –
OSTENSIBILE: Gone her own way, yes! Which is all very
well in certain circumstances, but in a public matter such
as this –
CARPETA: You have to think of –
(*Pause.*)
OSTENSIBILE: What?
(*Pause.*)
What do you have to think of?
CARPETA: What – the circumstances – require.
(*Pause.*)
URGENTINO: Well, that's it, then, isn't it? Can you start
today?
CARPETA: Yes.
OSTENSIBILE: The way you do Christ – the nobility of
Christ – transmit that feeling to the officers.
CARPETA: Yes…

OSTENSIBILE: The battle is not – unwholesome – it is, rather, the highest moment of self-sacrifice. It is as divine – in essence – as the crucifixion –

CARPETA: Yes...

OSTENSIBILE: And the soldiers are – not victims of a sacrifice but – a fraternity on Christian crusade, do you follow?

URGENTINO: Yes. But you must paint it for yourself! It is your painting!

OSTENSIBILE: It is his painting, yes!

URGENTINO: Congratulations! You are – from this moment, promoted to the pantheon of Venetian masters, yes, you are!

CARPETA: Thank you, it will be my finest opportunity to –

URGENTINO: Sordid financial matters can be arranged by others at a later date!

CARPETA: Of course, I long to satisfy both my own requirements as a painter and –

URGENTINO: Good bye! Good bye!

CARPETA: Thank you for –

URGENTINO: Do leave your folder. Yes, leave it.

(*Pause. A door is closed.*)

Why is it, I wonder, the base instinct is so often the spur to fine achievement? I suspect Signor Carpeta will, in seven weeks, do his greatest for us, though it will be modest enough as greatness goes... Do you want any of his drawings?

(*Turned cartridge paper.*)

There, that's quite good...and look! I swear that's Galactia naked...!

OSTENSIBILE: What about Galactia?

URGENTINO: She loves him...the great woman...dotes on...the little man...

OSTENSIBILE: Please.

URGENTINO: What about her?

OSTENSIBILE: We cannot overlook the provocation. We cannot, can we, on delivery of this calculated and obscene affront to History, lie down, can we? Say many thanks and put it in the basement? It is all meat and chopped up genitalia, it is not a battle and she knows it. We cannot simply overlook.

URGENTINO: No.

OSTENSIBILE: And she wouldn't want us to.

URGENTINO: She would hate it.

OSTENSIBILE: We have to make an appropriate response.

(*Pause.*)

URGENTINO: Prison.

OSTENSIBILE: You think prison?

URGENTINO: I think prison is – a little prison, not too much – is what this desperate woman wants…

OSTENSIBILE: Yes.

URGENTINO: Confirmation. Of our baseness. Is what she wants.

SCENE ELEVEN

The barracks.

GALACTIA: It's done.

(*Pause.*)

CARPETA: Yes.

(*Pause.*)

GALACTIA: IT'S DONE. And you will be the first to see it. Do you know I have never shown a finished canvas to a man before, a man first, except my father, and he taught me? Do you know you are the first?

CARPETA: Yes.

GALACTIA: I do it because I love you. I love you, Carpeta.

CARPETA: Yes.

(*Aside.*) I believe there is nothing so exquisite, so refined in its cruelty, as to be the object of a passion which you no longer reciprocate…

GALACTIA: Kiss me…!

CARPETA: (*Aside.*) It is humiliating, not of the one who loves you, but of you yourself. Splashed with adoration, it burns your skin…

GALACTIA: Kiss me…

CARPETA: (*Aside.*) And your lips moan. Sin in it, ache in the eyes...
(*To her.*) Is it really finished? I don't feel worthy of –

GALACTIA: Don't be silly!

CARPETA: Actually don't feel I deserve –

GALACTIA: Don't be so – what's the matter with you? Don't deserve – what are you –

CARPETA: Just – the honour –

GALACTIA: Be quiet, you'll spoil it for me! Stand there. There. Now, I will open all the shutters, and you – keep your eyes shut. Wait! Don't move!
(*The shutters are flung open along the length of the room.*)
Don't turn round! I feel utterly childish about this. I – I have never made a cult of this, of first showings but – flood in, daylight! Look, clear, liquid light and –
(*The last one clatters open.*)
Now, wait.
(*Pause.*)
Open your eyes.
(*Pause.*)
What?
(*Pause.*)
Carpeta?
(*Pause.*)
What, are you – are you crying? You are crying! Oh, my dear, you're crying! Because it's good, is it?
(*His sobs become audible.*)
Is it that good? Tell me! Oh, God, is it so good you have to –
(*He wails.*)
Oh, wonderful, great lover, shh!
(*Sound of hammering wood.*)

SCENE TWELVE

Some hours later. The studio is dismantled.

SUPPORTA: It is a great waterfall of flesh. It is the best thing you have ever done. But I don't think, forgive me, I want to be associated with you any more. Professionally, that is.

GALACTIA: I competely understand –
SUPPORTA: No, let me finish, mother, please –
GALACTIA: Absolutely get what you –
SUPPORTA: YOU NEVER LET ME FINISH.
(*Pause.*)
Because whilst it is your best work, I don't feel sympathy
with what you –
GALACTIA: Quite! I am not in the least wounded by your
rejection of me which –
SUPPORTA: Why do you –
GALACTIA: Which I thoroughly anticipated and therefore –
SUPPORTA: WHY WON'T YOU BE HURT! Always, you pretend
to be prepared! I am giving up a professional relationship
of twenty years, why don't you be hurt for just a minute?
(*Pause.*)
GALACTIA: Because it was obvious you would desert me, it
was as clear as daylight to me I could not count on you any
more.
SUPPORTA: I think you enjoy seeing people fail.
GALACTIA: Yes, I think I do. I expect it. I drive for it. And
when it happens, all right, I'm gratified. I have shattered
tolerance. You are a drapery painter, Supporta, you could
not understand where I was headed and now you want
– absolutely comprehensible! – to save yourself. Change
your name or something. I don't care for your method
anyway. Everything shines. Not all fabric shines, you paint
too many highlights –
SUPPORTA: I think you are – I hate to say this – you are a
little mad.
GALACTIA: Well, yes of course, you would reiterate the
popular opinion. I must help them they are taking it off the
stretcher, I have to supervise them or they –
SUPPORTA: I am not deserting you, I am saying –
GALACTIA: (*To WORKMEN.*) WAIT FOR ME, THERE! Listen,
I am not injured. Set up a little studio, paint wedding
pictures –
SUPPORTA: You always have to ridicule –
GALACTIA: Yes, dash it down! I haven't time to listen to
your motives, and who cares about them anyway? If we

all had to understand one another's motives! Christ! I will write you a cheque for your services –

(*To WORKMEN.*) DON'T DO THAT, THERE, IT'S NOT A CARPET!

(*To SUPPORTA.*) They are putting it on a barge, and the barge will sail up the canal, like some great bomb smuggled under tarpaulins, and they will unload it and carry it into the palaces of power, and it will tear their minds apart and explode the wind in their deep cavities, and I shall be punished for screaming truth where truth is not allowed. IT MADE CARPETA WEEP WITH ITS POWER!

SCENE THIRTEEN

A room in the palace.

URGENTINO: It is hanging. It is not framed, but it is hanging. In the gallery.

SUFFICI: Let me see it.

URGENTINO: No hurry! No hurry! Finish your drink.

(*Pause.*)

Finish your drink.

(*Pause.*)

There comes a point – with painting – at which no amount of intervention can significantly alter the outcome of the project.

SUFFICI: It is not what you –

URGENTINO: It is not what Venice –

(*Pause.*)

SUFFICI: Ah.

(*Pause.*)

URGENTINO: Because of what I can only describe as a – mental disorder – which prevents the artist satisfying the aspirations of her customer.

(*Pause.*)

SUFFICI: It's –

URGENTINO: It's a bit – it's not like anything I've seen before. Or want to see again for that matter.

SUFFICI: I see. And I – I am –

URGENTINO: In it. Yes. You are. You figure very
    prominently, but –
SUFFICI: I want to see.
URGENTINO: No hurry –
SUFFICI: I want to see.
    (*Pause.*)
URGENTINO: Very well. It is an area of human activity in
    which control comes from within, in which the artist either
    exercises discretion, and wills discretion, or – I have got
    someone else doing one so it doesn't really matter what
    kind of mess she's made of – there. Feel free to be sick.
    (*Pause.*)
    Spew up if you –
SUFFICI: SHUT UP.
    (*Pause.*)
    The hands – the hands are utterly vile. They are not my
    hands.
URGENTINO: Nope.
SUFFICI: Look, look at my hands, look at them –
URGENTINO: Yes –
SUFFICI: LOOK AT THEM!
URGENTINO: I AM LOOKING AT THEM!
SUFFICI: That is not a likeness of my hands, is it?
URGENTINO: Of course it isn't –
SUFFICI: My hands which are beautiful in fact, despite my
    age, are beautiful and not claws as she has painted!
URGENTINO: Cesare –
SUFFICI: Not claws, are they!
URGENTINO: Cesare, you will have the servants running in –
SUFFICI: What is the point of making me attend three sittings
    if she goes away and copies some talons out of –
URGENTINO: Cesare –
SUFFICI: Some ornithological atlas!
URGENTINO: I have never seen you so animated –
SUFFICI: I am animated, I am animated!
URGENTINO: Quite rightly, but –
SUFFICI: Not because I am vain, I am the least vain of men,
    but because it is simply untrue –
URGENTINO: Untrue, yes –

SUFFICI: And consequently it is a lie, and I –

URGENTINO: Abhor a lie, I know you do –

SUFFICI: And the face –

URGENTINO: The face is worse –

SUFFICI: Whilst it looks like me –

URGENTINO: Vague resemblance – very vague resemblance –

SUFFICI: Is painted with contempt –

URGENTINO: Well, we don't know –

SUFFICI: It is contempt and you only have to see Garacci's portrait of me in the flower garden to see –

URGENTINO: This is a different genre, but yes –

SUFFICI: I am saying Garacci understood me and this is – I am sorry to be so angry but –

URGENTINO: No, no –

SUFFICI: I am not normally angry but she simply cannot paint, she cannot be allowed to do this thing which is – in effect – a calculated offence to me and to the sailors who so heroically laid down their – what is this, what are all these bodies doing – it is all bodies, everywhere with gaping – I do not pretend to be an artist but it was not like that!

SCENE FOURTEEN

A room.

URGENTINO: How are you feeling?

(*Pause.*)

Are you feeling uncomfortable?

GALACTIA: Yes.

(*Pause.*)

And good at the same time.

URGENTINO: How's that?

GALACTIA: Virtuous. And scared.

URGENTINO: Delicious combination.

(*Pause.*)

GALACTIA: Firstly, I am –

URGENTINO: Shut up –

GALACTIA: I am prepared to repay every penny of the fee I –

265

URGENTINO: Shut up! I have seen a drawing of your breasts.

GALACTIA: What has that got to –

URGENTINO: Shut up.

GALACTIA: I don't see what that –

URGENTINO: SHUT UP.

(*Pause.*)

This is my palace. This is my cushion. You have your empire, I have mine. I said I have seen a drawing of your breasts. It is on my desk, look. WHAT AM I GOING TO DO WITH THAT PAINTING?

(*Pause.*)

You should not think, because we are not artists, we are stupid. Because we are governors, or bureaucrats, stupid. Terrible error. Terrible vanity. Leads to the noose, the wall, the death chamber –

GALACTIA: I take full responsibility for –

URGENTINO: I DON'T CARE IF YOU TAKE RESPONSIBILITY OR NOT.

(*Pause.*)

What do you think that means? 'I take full responsibility – ?' Arrogant! Sit there, on my cushion, on the armorial of Venice, in your steam of cleverness, unafraid long jutting woman's jaw, HATE THAT! Really, humility would do you good. Please don't stare at me, look at the floor or something, what did you think you were doing, because the Committee is assembling and they are insulted, the Republic is insulted, don't you like the Republic? If you do not like it it is treason, don't tell me you didn't think of that?

GALACTIA: Not terribly.

URGENTINO: Not terribly, didn't terribly think of it, what are you –

GALACTIA: CRY OF THE BLOOD.

(*Pause.*)

URGENTINO: There is a bridge over there. On one side of the bridge there is a carpet. And on the other side of the bridge there is bare stone. And on this side of the bridge there are cushions, and on the other side there is straw.

And on this side there are windows, but on the other side it is dark. On this side we laugh, and on that side they cry. Do you know the bridge?

(*Murmurs of approaching voices.*)

GALACTIA: The Bridge of Sighs.

URGENTINO: I cannot tell you how it excites me to think of your bare breasts against the wall, and my buttocks on this brocade…

(*The committee enters the room.*)

GALACTIA: I am great. I am great because I conceded nothing, but utterly was myself. And all these artists hanging on the walls, were not themselves, but other people…

OFFICIAL: Sit down, please.

GALACTIA: I am prepared to refund to the State of Venice all monies I received for –

OFFICIAL: Silence, please, and sit down.

GALACTIA: I want to make this statement –

OSTENSIBILE: We do not want your statement –

GALACTIA: Why can't I make a statement?

OFFICIAL: Are you Anna Galactia, of Via –

GALACTIA: You know bloody well I am Galactia, everybody knows I'm Galactia, why else would I be here –

OFFICIAL: And are you the executor of the subject painting 'The Battle of Lepanto' which is hanging on the wall opposite the window there –

GALACTIA: Really, this is – what is the point of –

OSTENSIBILE: I think, ditch all that. Thank you.

(*Pause.*)

Signora, we do not understand your painting.

GALACTIA: It is a painting of a battle at sea.

OSTENSIBILE: It is a slaughter at sea.

GALACTIA: A battle is a slaughter.

OSTENSIBILE: No, it is the furtherance of political ends by violent means.

GALACTIA: I showed the violence.

OSTENSIBILE: But not the ends. So it is untruthful. The ends were the freedom of the seas, the affirmation of the

Christian faith, the upholding of a principle. Why did you
not paint those?

GALACTIA: How do you paint the upholding of a principle?

OSTENSIBILE: You show it by the nobility of the
participants.

PASTACCIO: Do you believe in the principle, Signora?
(*Pause.*)

GALACTIA: I am a painter, I'm not –

OSTENSIBILE: Oh, now, you cannot hide behind your
sensuality, your instinct –

GALACTIA: Why not?

OSTENSIBILE: That is dishonest, that is trying to slam the
gate on our debate, isn't it?

GALACTIA: I painted death because all I saw was death.

PASTACCIO: So you admit to being partial? You admit to
attending to one aspect of the truth?

GALACTIA: Yes. And I don't admit it, I embrace it.

PASTACCIO: You admit to attending to one aspect of the
truth to the exclusion of the other?

GALACTIA: What other?

PASTACCIO: The nobility of the struggle.

GALACTIA: I deny its nobility.

OSTENSIBILE: You deny the virtue of the actions of the
State of Venice?

GALACTIA: I – I suppose if you –

OSTENSIBILE: You obviously deny it. And the evidence is
in the portrait of the Admiral, who is presented with an
expression of the utmost callousness –

GALACTIA: Callousness?

OSTENSIBILE: Well, what else is it?

GALACTIA: I hadn't put a name to it.

OSTENSIBILE: I will do it for you. It is callousness.

PASTACCIO: You see, we have to get behind the picture,
and you want us to look at the surface. You say, look at the
surface, the brush strokes, the colour, the anatomy! Yes, all
very good, that is your strength, who can quarrel with you
on that territory? You are supreme. But behind the painting
we are all equals. What are you saying? It seems to us you

are saying you revile the State of Venice. Do you want to
argue with that?

OSTENSIBILE: Argue if you want.

(*Pause.*)

GALACTIA: What are you going to do with me?

PASTACCIO: Please, argue the point.

GALACTIA: No.

PASTACCIO: Why not?

GALACTIA: Because you will only win the argument.

PASTACCIO: How do we know until you have offered your
defence?

GALACTIA: No. I am not going to give you the satisfaction
of proving me wrong. If the surface of the painting is my
territory, the back of it is yours. You are specialists in
arguments. I hate arguments. What are you going to do
with me?

OSTENSIBILE: I have never heard of an artist who did not
want to engage with his opponents, there is nothing they
love more than expostulating about their genius, what is
the matter with you? Defend yourself or we shall become
irritated.

GALACTIA: You see, you must win.

OSTENSIBILE: It is not a question of –

GALACTIA: WIN. WIN.

OSTENSIBILE: (*Bitterly.*) NOT A QUESTION OF WINNING BUT
OF –

GALACTIA: Hang the painting. Take it in the street, and
hang it.

OSTENSIBILE: Never.

GALACTIA: Why?

OSTENSIBILE: Because there is the little matter of public
morals, miss!

PASTACCIO: Hang it in the street…!

OSTENSIBILE: The artist's cry! The whine of the corrupter!

GALACTIA: Ah, real thing now, the real strangler!

OSTENSIBILE: The irresponsibility of your manner is of
course, only a mask, the posture of artistic freedom, look
at the way you dress, you have not washed that garment in
God knows how many –

GALACTIA: (*Disbelief.*) How do you know when –

OSTENSIBILE: And your breasts quite clearly unsupported –

GALACTIA: How does he –

OSTENSIBILE: All calculated to make us think ARTISTIC IRRESPONSIBILITY, WELL, NO, WE ARE NOT FOOLED! (*Pause.*)

You are an enemy of the Republic. You wish to destroy its unity and its power for an end you will no doubt admit in time but the great thing is WE ARE NOT FOOLED. (*Pause.*)

I really do despise artists and that is why I am so perfectly qualified to sit on this committee. I despise artists as much as I love art, and I can look at that plane before me, glistening with colour and say it is an evil surface. There!

GALACTIA: I shall have to be punished, shan't I? You can't let someone say – on the back of the canvas – all your principle is actually dirt, and stench, and matted buttocks floating in the sea. I shall have to be broken in some way. (*Pause.*)

Well, won't I?

(*A door slams in a prison.*)

SCENE FIFTEEN

The prison.

GALACTIA: There's no light in here! Give us a candle!

GAOLER: (*Receding.*) No candles.

GALACTIA: No candles, no, of course not! A candle? What? Give you a bit of light, give a painter colour? Don't be charitable.

MAN IN THE NEXT CELL: Shut up.

GALACTIA: Shut up, he says. Voice from the depths. Shut up. IT STINKS IN HERE. I do think you might change the straw, the previous occupant had crabs – no I haven't seen them, I speculate –

MAN IN THE NEXT CELL: SHUT UP.

GALACTIA: Shut up yourself! Get another room if you don't like it! It's not as dark in here as you might think. Now, that is interesting. It's like black, the colour black. People think there is only one black, but there is black and black, there is black the absence of light and black – are we under the canal here? UGH, I TOUCHED SOMETHING!

(*She gasps with horror.*)

I touched some-thing, Oh, God, I…

MAN IN THE NEXT CELL: You have only been in there two minutes.

GALACTIA: Shut up, voice from the depths.

MAN IN THE NEXT CELL: TWO MINUTES.

GALACTIA: Well, of course it's difficult, I expected it to be difficult. I am not surprised there is something disgusting on the floor, there would be and I – Ugh –

(*MAN IN THE NEXT CELL laughs.*)

Listen, my friend, you have the advantage of experience, you mustn't take such delight in –

(*He laughs on.*)

All right, laugh on, laugh on, I never expected to get an intellectual as a neighbour –

MAN IN THE NEXT CELL: WHO SAYS I'M NOT AN INTELLECTUAL? WHO SAYS I'M NOT?

GALACTIA: Look at my squalor, look at my filth, this is what happens to the one who loves the truth, I fully expected this, I was prepared for it, no one visits me and when they do they tell me lies, NO WONDER. How long have I been here, you cannot count in the dark, the only proof that you have told the truth in this life is that you are punished for it! Am I to be tortured? I must be tortured, obviously, it would be inconsistent if I weren't tortured, driven mad and murdered in some corner. They hate the truth, don't they, they yank the teeth out of its mouth and kick the lips to blubber UNDERSTANDABLY IT'S A DANGEROUS THING. I shall say to the one who tortures me I FULLY UNDERSTAND YOUR MOTIVES, IT HURTS YOU, DOESN'T IT? I shall say that, which of course, only provokes more punishment, if you scream here can the Doge hear you? What sort of face have you got? You sound like you have a big nose.

MAN IN THE NEXT CELL: I have a big nose.

GALACTIA: Fancy that!

MAN IN THE NEXT CELL: I haven't seen my face for seven years.

GALACTIA: Well, we don't get mirrors, do we, we might grow vain, threading filthy straw through plaited hair and using shit for powder, mind you I was an untidy bitch to start with, paint up my fingernails and so on, though sometimes I liked to show off a bit, clean skirts and blouses, rather fragrant, but then I always forgot something, hair washing or turned up with dirty feet, I miss my lover, you lose your lover, don't you, lose your children, CALCULATED FACTOR IN THE PUNISHMENT, have an awful need of something physical and gross and old, banal thing up against the – WILL SOMEONE PUT A LIGHT ON...!

(*Pause. Breathless.*)

MAN IN THE NEXT CELL: Be still, because you have such a long time to endure. Be still, and preserve yourself.

(*Pause.*)

GALACTIA: Yes...

MAN IN THE NEXT CELL: Because if you scream and struggle you will wear down what you have, which is little enough in this bitterness. Be an animal in the straw. Be the toad.

GALACTIA: Yes...

MAN IN THE NEXT CELL: And slow your heart beat down.

GALACTIA: Yes...

MAN IN THE NEXT CELL: Lie, waiting. Hibernate the long winter of your offence.

GALACTIA: Thank you, yes...

MAN IN THE NEXT CELL: Anger, hang it up now. Prisons are such loud places. But only the quiet ones live. The noisy ones, they've carried passed my door...

SCENES FROM AN EXECUTION

SCENE SIXTEEN

A studio in Venice.

URGENTINO: Ostensibile wants to charge her with being
an agent of the Sultanate. He likes to win an argument
and she refused to argue with him, so now he's furious
and says she is a Muslim. She is not a Muslim, is she?
The exaggerated sense of mission is something I cannot
stomach in clergymen. Since she is quite obviously not
an agent of anyone except herself it will involve torturing
her to a confession. I do think that is vile. Torturing and
bribing witnesses. It is all extremely ghastly and has a lot to
do with the fact of celibacy. Torture! Really, what are you
to do with them? I would like more red there, where the
sun is setting...yes...there...perhaps orange, you say.

CARPETA: Orange.

URGENTINO: All right, orange. And she is in any case mad,
I abhor a cliché, but you know it better than anyone. That
figure is not very celebratory, I think –

CARPETA: This one –

URGENTINO: Holding the banner, yes, is not elated, is he?

CARPETA: He has got an arrow in his –

URGENTINO: Yes, but he is the standard bearer, isn't he,
and standard bearers have to be elated because – that is
why they are standard bearers, surely? There is altogether,
and I'm sorry if I sound irritable, a certain lack of
celebration in your work –

CARPETA: I have done everything you –

URGENTINO: Everything, I know, you have, you have –

CARPETA: Painting so quickly that –

URGENTINO: You have been wonderful, you have, and of
course it is hurried in some respects – the horn blowers
look a little – do you know Raphael?

CARPETA: Of course I know Raphael –

URGENTINO: Yes, well, he would have –

CARPETA: I'm sorry, I can't go on with this.

URGENTINO: More energy and – WHAT!

   (*Pause.*)

CARPETA: I can't go on with this.
  (*Pause.*)
URGENTINO: You're being silly.
CARPETA: I –
URGENTINO: Yes, you are, now, listen –
CARPETA: Endless interruption and –
URGENTINO: Shh, shh!
CARPETA: CAN'T GO ON WITH IT.
  (*Pause.*)
URGENTINO: You are overwrought. The responsibility of
  accepting a commission of this scale is obviously –
CARPETA: It's not that –
URGENTINO: Yes, it is that and –
CARPETA: I WANT TO SEE GALACTIA.
  (*Pause.*)
URGENTINO: Galactia? Why?
CARPETA: Because I love her and –
URGENTINO: You –
CARPETA: HAVE TO SEE HER.
  (*Pause.*)
URGENTINO: I have taken a great risk in commissioning
  you to do this work –
CARPETA: I know and I –
URGENTINO: I took a great risk in commissioning her and I
  took a great risk in commissioning you and I –
CARPETA: I am sorry I –
URGENTINO: I AM SICK OF BEING MESSED ABOUT BY
  ARTISTS.
  (*Pause.*)
  You did not say you were in love with her, you said –
CARPETA: I know, I –
URGENTINO: Said it was a little –
CARPETA: I know I did –
URGENTINO: A sordid little sexual transaction.
CARPETA: I wanted to –
URGENTINO: WELL, NO YOU CAN'T, NOT UNTIL YOU'VE
  FINISHED IT, you –
  (*He gropes blindly.*)

It's not in my hands, it's the Committee of Public
Education you should make petition to, not me –

CARPETA: You're the Doge –

URGENTINO: I am the Doge, but –

CARPETA: So you can –

URGENTINO: THIS IS A DEMOCRATIC COUNTRY!

RIVERA: (*Entering.*) Hello?

URGENTINO: I HATE YOU ALL.

RIVERA: What are you –

URGENTINO: I wish I had never seen a painting in my life!
I blame you for this!

RIVERA: Me?

URGENTINO: Yes, you! You encouraged me, Rivera! I
have been – through my own sensitivity – been drawn
into needless conflicts with people who, crazed by self-
indulgence, will not, and perhaps, God help them, cannot,
sympathize with the problems of governing a modern
state! Whereas I am forever having to sympathize with
them, they are in love, they have a mission, they have a
headache, they are menstruating, IT IS A MOST UNEQUAL
RELATIONSHIP. (*Pause.*) I sometimes wish I was a brute.

RIVERA: No, no…

URGENTINO: Yes, a brute with brute senses. Sending
regiments to toss pianos out of windows. Really. You
cannot imagine how I long to send pianos flying out
of windows! But I don't, do I? I don't, and I am made
miserable.

(*He turns on CARPETA.*)

If you do not finish the painting, I will put you in a cell
with her, there! And you can deliver babies on the filthy
straw!

(*He turns to RIVERA.*)

Gina, Gina, come here, come here!

(*They walk away.*)

I am so upset, I cannot tell you. I am reduced to making
threats against my favourite people, artists! Help me, tell
me they are vaguely human, I am beginning to doubt my
own perceptions…

275

(*Whispers.*)

What is this painting like? The thing he's...tell me, is it –

RIVERA: Yes.

URGENTINO: What?

RIVERA: Shit.

URGENTINO: Is it? It is, isn't it! It is! I knew it was! Oh, God!

RIVERA: Sit down.

URGENTINO: Take me out of here – take me out – the smell of paint – I used to love a studio and now I could bring up my breakfast – he is a banal and gutless hack –

RIVERA: That is not fair –

URGENTINO: He is, he will not listen when I –

RIVERA: He has listened, he has listened too much –

URGENTINO: He has no imagination of his own, what do you expect me to do?

RIVERA: He is a very sound painter of religious subjects, he is not an epic painter –

URGENTINO: Why did he turn up, then? Imposter!

RIVERA: It is an offence against art to flatter minor artists with projects they are not equipped to handle –

URGENTINO: What am I to do, then!

RIVERA: Will you be quiet for a moment?

URGENTINO: I can't be quiet, I'm furious!

(*Pause.*)

All right, what?

RIVERA: I have seen Galactia's painting.

URGENTINO: Ostensibile wants it burned!

RIVERA: Yes, but he won't. He will put it in a cellar. Now, listen to me, and I will tell you what I know, as a critic, and a loyal supporter of your party and your cause. In art nothing is what it seems to be, but everything can be claimed. The painting is not independent, even if the artist is. The picture is retrievable, even when the painter is lost...

SCENE SEVENTEEN

The prison. A door crashes back on its hinges. Pause.

CARPETA: Galactia…Galactia?

    (*Sound of scraping on stone.*)

    IS THERE A LIGHT IN HERE?

    (*Movement.*)

    Are you there? It's me, are you there or –

GALACTIA: Have you ever painted blind?

    (*She stops scraping.*)

    Actually it isn't dark. We make so much of light, but light's relative. I now think daylight is terribly CRUDE.

CARPETA: Where are you, I –

GALACTIA: Clumsy thing you are, blundering in this little space. You can always find me by my smell.

CARPETA: I – I –

GALACTIA: It is a little fruity, isn't it? Like the badger's den and me the female badger, don't be frightened, look, I have drawn a man, in granite, with granite. It's you. In monochrome, but in this light who wants polychrome, or poly anything? Nothing's poly in a prison, it's all mono, mono dinner, mono supper, mono stench. This wall is covered with remarks, I could not read them for the first three months but –

CARPETA: Three months? You have not been here three –

GALACTIA: Then you find them, treasures! Whole biographies, and sexual miseries, and me the first to make a picture! An artist always will, won't she, get decorating the cruel old wall of torture –

CARPETA: Listen, the Doge –

GALACTIA: The Doge? Kind Doge!

CARPETA: Has given me the letter of –

GALACTIA: Sweet, fat Doge! Listen –

CARPETA: No, you listen –

GALACTIA: YOU LISTEN TO ME. (*She whispers, urgently.*) I find I am still fertile. I find, in this damp den, fertility back at my age! Lovely shock! Have you two minutes?

CARPETA: You aren't listening to me –

GALACTIA: I want a child, they are not allowed to execute the pregnant, I bleed again, you see, in this dark stillness, here, come here –

CARPETA: Look, I –

GALACTIA: Come, quick before they –

CARPETA: It isn't – I don't –

GALACTIA: (*Sarcastic.*) Oh, wonderful! Oh, reluctant Carpeta who was all over me once!

CARPETA: I can't actually see you and anyway –

GALACTIA: What does that matter? I want to lie in the straw like a badger, littering, quick do your stuff –

GALACTIA: NO.

GALACTIA: Why are you here? Don't smile, why are you here? Have they burned the Battle?

CARPETA: No.

GALACTIA: LIAR! Of course they have burned it and you have brought the ashes –

CARPETA: It is not burned –

GALACTIA: Of course it is burned, how could they tolerate it, it is too powerful for them, and I am too powerful for them, I am Galactia who told the truth and all you do is lie to me!

GAOLER: (*Entering.*) On yer way.

GALACTIA: Why do they lie to me? I tell you this, you with the bent back and the club fist, I like you best, you are no liar!

GAOLER: On yer way, I said.

(*Pause.*)

GALACTIA: What?

(*Pause.*)

What is this?

GAOLER: Out.

(*Pause.*)

GALACTIA: Out? I live here.

GAOLER: Two minutes to get yer things –

GALACTIA: WHAT IS THIS? ALL THE TRUTH TELLERS LIVE HERE.

CARPETA: You're free. This is the order, look –

GALACTIA: (*Snatches it.*) Show me –

CARPETA: Signed by the –

GALACTIA: CAN'T SEE – IN THIS LIGHT, CAN'T –

(*She screws it up.*)

I CANNOT BE RELEASED! HOW CAN THEY RELEASE ME I AM TOO DANGEROUS!

MAN IN THE NEXT CELL: Would you show a little sliver of consideration to the –

GALACTIA: THEY ARE RELEASING ME...!

MAN IN THE NEXT CELL: Forgive me, I cannot work up any happiness for you, I have been here seven years, and it hurts me when someone goes out, it hurts me terribly, so please enjoy your freedom quietly.

GALACTIA: (*Quietly.*) What did you do, strange dark thing in the straw?

MAN IN THE NEXT CELL: Nothing. I did nothing. And that is why I shall never be released.

(*Pause.*)

GALACTIA: I'll paint you! I'll paint you and I will show your innocence!

MAN IN THE NEXT CELL: Please, you –

GALACTIA: TRUTH OF THE IMPERIAL JURISDICTION!

MAN IN THE NEXT CELL: Please –

GALACTIA: EXPOSE THE TRUTH AND BACK I'LL COME!

GAOLER: Come on, you daft bitch –

GALACTIA: Don't clean it out, I'm coming back!

(*Suddenly she sobs, falters.*)

Hold me, hold me oh, daylight...!

SCENE EIGHTEEN

A public place. Subdued murmurs of a crowd passing in line before a National Treasure.

URGENTINO: To have lost such a canvas would have been an offence against the artistic primacy of Venice. To have said this work could not be absorbed by the spirit of the Republic would be to belittle the Republic, and our barbarian neighbours would have jeered at us. So

we absorb all, and in absorbing it we show our greater
majesty. It offends today, but we look harder and we know,
it will not offend tomorrow. We force the canvas and the
stretcher down the gagging throat, and coughing a little,
and spluttering a little, we find, on digestion, it nourishes
us! There will be no art outside. Only art inside.

OSTENSIBILE: THE MESSAGE. What about the MESSAGE.

URGENTINO: Cardinal, your single-mindedness is a credit
to your Jesuit professors, but you must stop hacking. The
blunt, dull hack of Christian persecution, the urge to the
bonfire. Hate it. With all respect, hate it...

(*Murmurs of crowd.*)

PRODO: Thank you, thank you! That's me, I am the figure,
thank you, same bolt, same head! Note the bolt which I
endured for my nation, this is me here, a very reasonable
likeness, I think you will agree, thank you, you see I
shudder in an ecstasy of patriotic fervour...!

SORDO: It is a success.

LASAGNA: You mean it is popular. Yes, it is popular...

SORDO: I mean, people like it.

LASAGNA: Yes.

SORDO: They have nicknamed it The Slag's Revenge.
Galactia has never kept a man. Several of the corpses look
like Carpeta.

LASAGNA: And that's you, surely? With the javelin in the
throat...

SORDO: And Bertocci, falling out of the rigging, yes!

LASAGNA: If it had been painted by a man it would have
been an indictment of the war, but as it is, painted by the
most promiscuous female within a hundred miles of the
Lagoon, I think we are entitled to a different speculation.

SORDO: It is very aggressive. You and I, we wouldn't have
been so aggressive. A woman painter has a particularly
– female – aggressiveness, which is not, I think, the same as
vigour. Do you agree with that distinction?

LASAGNA: Yes. It is coarse.

SORDO: Coarse, yes. Because she is so desperate to prove
she is not feminine, a flower-painter, an embroiderer, she
goes to the extremes and becomes, not virile, but shrill.

LASAGNA: It is shrill. It defeats its purpose by being shrill.

SORDO: She can paint, of course –

LASAGNA: She can paint, but it's excessive. And so is she.

SORDO: (*Pained.*) And yet they seem to like it…

LASAGNA: Carpeta! Giulio and I have been speculating as to whether that object there – that figure with the head slewed off – is actually you. The Slag's Revenge, you see. It has your teeth.

CARPETA: I don't think it matters what –

SORDO: Humour, Carpeta –

CARPETA: What you or any other –

SORDO: Oh, come on –

CARPETA: It is a public picture and you can't dishonour it!
(*Pause.*)
Sorry. Just – the little nausea, you know, the little belch of loathing at the fellow artists gnawing at each other's bones. Passing disgust at sound of tooth on bone. Gone now. Gone now!
(*Popular noise, then silence.*)

SCENE NINETEEN

GALACTIA's studio.

RIVERA: May I come in?
(*Pause.*)
May I, there is no light so I –
(*She kicks something.*)
Ow!

GALACTIA: I don't have lights.

RIVERA: Could I just draw –

GALACTIA: Don't draw the curtains.

RIVERA: Well, where are you –

GALACTIA: In my black hole. In my gaol.
(*Pause.*)

RIVERA: I'm sorry if –

GALACTIA: Sorry? You PANDERED. You LIED. Got me out by LICKING AND LAPPING. One hundred feet of pain and you LICKED IT SMOOTH.

RIVERA: They had no intention of leaving you in gaol, it was a gesture and –

GALACTIA: SMOTHERED MY DANGER. SHAMELESS CONCILIATOR.

(*Pause.*)

There are some words, in this mendacious time, this age of mendacity, which still bear filth and evil and the worst of those is CONCILIATOR! Unclean word!

RIVERA: I promise you a week was all they intended to –

GALACTIA: CONCILIATOR!

(*Pause.*)

RIVERA: Yes…

(*Pause.*)

You are terribly difficult to deal with. I thought – I honestly believed – you wanted the picture to be seen. I'm sorry. I really do not understand you –

GALACTIA: I am not meant to be understood. Don't you see? Oh, you miserable, well-meaning, always-on-the-right-side, desperate little intellect! Death to be understood. Awful death…

RIVERA: They are flocking to the exhibition. The hanging in San Marco. Doors are jammed and –

GALACTIA: Any soldiers trampled on their tunics? Much mutiny down the docks?

RIVERA: What?

GALACTIA: I can't hear rioting, but the curtains are thick…

RIVERA: In my catalogue I talk about the anatomy, which is – some people say they can touch the flesh, such is the realism of it, they –

(*Pause.*)

Listen, it is art I am interested in. I have saved your art. Get up.

GALACTIA: Carpeta came. Holding a little bag. My lover, left his wife –

RIVERA: Get up, will you!

GALACTIA: Little bag in the doorway, and I thought, 1 do not need you, it is so terrible to know I do not need you any more…

SCENE TWENTY

The exhibition.

PRODO: The figure on the right is me. Same bolt, same head, thank you, who got this disability in service of my nation, sweeping the atheistic power from the sea –

GALACTIA: Doing all right, Prodo?

PRODO: Signora Galac –

GALACTIA: Shh!

PRODO: (*Quietly.*) Signora, it has been a godsend, what with winter coming on –

GALACTIA: Nothing's in vain! Nothing is wasted! If one beggar is kept from starving, no effort is too extreme! What do they say, you know more than any critic, what do they say? Trash, do they say?

PRODO: Unfortunately I am obliged by the custodian to perch here at the right end of the picture, so they pass me as they enter and they have no opinion. It is the other end, the exit, you should listen. One hundred feet later, a man might change his mind about many things. Some have catalogues, but most can't read. The ones who can't read gasp, the ones with catalogues go 'mmm'. So it's either gasp or mmm, take yer pick. Excuse me, I must get on. (*He declaims.*)
This is me, my portrait at the moment of my agony, in service of my nation…
(*GALACTIA passes along the murmuring crowd.*)

GALACTIA: What do you think?

MAN: Me?

GALACTIA: Yes, what do you think of this?
(*Pause.*)
Incredible or –
(*Pause.*)
Or not?
(*Pause.*)
Have you come far to –

MAN: The Piave –

GALACTIA: The Piave! You know I've never seen the Piave!
To see a picture – that is rather a long way to see – I'm not
trying to accost you, don't look for the custodian – I AM
NOT ACCOSTING YOU – He thinks I – I just –
(*Pause.*)
I painted it. It's mine. All right? I did the –
(*Pause.*)
No, I'm not mad. Please don't look at me as if I'm mad – I
STRENUOUSLY DENY THAT I AM MAD I JUST –
(*Pause.*)
He's holding my hands…he's holding my hands…!
URGENTINO: (*Wading in.*) Galactia comes, not to admire her
work – she is not so vain – but to admire the admirers! The
queue is fifty metres long and the man there has returned
eight times, ask him, it is a fact, he kneels there and he
weeps. Look, you have drawn tears from him, wrung water
from his coarse imagination! Do you feel powerful? I have
such power, but no such power. I can make men weep, but
only by torturing them, while you – don't resent me. In a
hundred years no one will weep for your painting, only
respect it. Cold, dull respect. Enjoy your peculiar authority!
It is a great nation, is it not, that shows its victories not as
parades of virility, but as terrible cost? My brother accepts
he is a calculating man, but admirals must be! You have
winkled out his truth, he is full of admiration for you,
hands notwithstanding! Will you dine with us? I hate to
miss a celebrity from my table.
(*Pause.*)
GALACTIA: Yes.

HOWARD BARKER
PLAYS TWO
THE CASTLE • GERTRUDE – THE CRY
ANIMALS IN PARADISE • 13 OBJECTS

The plays in this volume examine collisions of culture, gender and creed at moments of turmoil, developing the tragic form Barker defines as Theatre of Catastrophe.

The Castle is set at the end of the Crusades and describes the clashes that occur when returning soldiers bring home with them as a prisoner an Arab architect. Barker's abiding interest in interrogating the great classics for their 'silences' is shown in his re-writing of the Hamlet story in *Gertrude – the Cry*. Scarcely examined in Shakespeare, the passion of Gertrude for Claudius is made the centre of this harrowing tragedy, casting new light on the personality of Hamlet himself. *Animals in Paradise* was commissioned by the Swedish and Danish governments to celebrate their connection by bridge, a symbolic finish to centuries of antagonism. Barker's unpredictible treatment of the theme provoked unrest on its first showing. *13 Objects* movingly reveals the investment we make in inanimate things, their power to unsettle us, and how their talismanic qualities license new ways of seeing the world.

ISBN 1 84002 648 0 • £14.99

www.oberonbooks.com

For information on these and other plays and books
published by Oberon, or for a free catalogue,
listing all titles and cast breakdowns, visit our website

www.oberonbooks.com

info@oberonbooks.com • 020 7607 3637